A STUDENT'S GUIDE TO EASEMENTS, REAL COVENANTS, AND EQUITABLE SERVITUDES

Stephen A. Siegel
Professor of Law
De Paul University College of Law

STUDENT GUIDE SERIES

SECOND EDITION
1999

MATTHEW◆BENDER

MATTHEW◆BENDER

MATTHEW BENDER & CO., INC.
EDITORIAL OFFICES
2 PARK AVENUE, NEW YORK, NY 10016-5675 (212) 448-2000
201 MISSION ST., SAN FRANCISCO, CA 94105-1831 (415) 908-3200

TABLE OF CONTENTS

CHAPTER 2 — REAL COVENANTS AND EQUITABLE SERVITUDES

DEDICATION

To my parents

ACKNOWLEDGEMENTS

The author acknowledges DePaul University's support and encouragement of the composition of the second edition of this <u>Student Guide</u> through a grant from the University Research Leave Program.

GENERAL INTRODUCTION

Easements, real covenants, and equitable servitudes are distinct property interests; yet they are so intimately related that they have a collective designation. As a group, easements, real covenants and equitable servitudes are known as servitudes. For convenience, the term "servitude" will be used when saying something that applies to all three interests.

What distinguishes servitudes from other property interests is that they give their owner the right to use, or to prevent the use of, property that she neither owns nor possesses.* Classic examples are a right to cross a neighbor's land, or to prevent her from altering its natural state.

Because servitudes involve rights to use property that one neither owns nor possesses, legal theorists consider them present but nonpossessory property interests. In this regard, they stand in contrast to the fee simple and leasehold estates which are considered both present and possessory.

It may seem strange to say that servitudes are nonpossessory property interests. Pipeline companies and railroad companies frequently establish their routes by acquiring easements. Yet, it may be difficult to explain to someone who has just tripped over an oil pipeline or railroad track that the pipeline or railroad company does not possess the ground its pipeline or track occupies. And in any event, what distinction is there between the right of possession and the right of use? Possession, after all, is a use of property.

But the legal concept of possession is not a physical fact; it is an abstract, subtle legal concept. Possession certainly involves the right to make present use of the property. But possession involves more than just any right of use. Possession involves the right to make an extended number of uses of property. The right to make a specific or a limited number of uses of property <u>does not</u> possession make.

Thus, the distinction between possessory and nonpossessory interests focuses on the generality or specificity of the uses which the interest authorizes its holder to make. Fee simple and leasehold estates are possessory property interests because they carry the right to make general—not necessarily unlimited— use of property. Servitudes are nonpossessory interests because they carry the right to make only a specific or a limited number of uses of property.

The function and importance of servitudes in a system of private property arises from the interdependence of land-use. Land-use involves what economists call "externalities." The use of one parcel of land affects other parcels, either beneficially or harmfully. Servitudes are the preeminent means by which individuals adjust these externalities. Public law, through such bodies of law as nuisance and zoning, has tools by which land externalities are adjusted. But servitudes are the main private law mechanism by which individuals anticipate, alter or fine-tune the provisions of public law to their particular desires.

Servitudes are not the only private law means for adjusting the interdependence of land-use. Frequently, however, they are the most efficient. Consider the position of a landowner who needs a path across neighboring land in order to provide her land with more convenient access to main thoroughfares. Or consider the position of a landowner who needs assurance that neighboring land will not be developed commercially before she will develop her land residentially. The landowner could acquire the desired path or assurance by acquiring a fee estate, a long-term leasehold, or a servitude in the neighboring land. Any of these interests would give the concerned landowner the path or assurance she needs.

A fee estate or leasehold would give the concerned landowner the general right to control the neighboring land. A servitude would give her only the specific right to use the neighboring land that she needs. And therein lies the significant difference.

---

* For convenience, throughout the remainder of this <u>Student Guide</u> the phrase "right to use" should be understood as meaning "right to use, or to prevent the use of."

By giving the concerned landowner the general right to control the neighboring land, the fee estate and leasehold give her more rights than she really wants and wishes to use. And their cost is commensurately higher. Servitudes, by providing for the acquisition of narrow, specific rights to use land that is owned by another allows for the acquisition of the narrow, specific rights that frequently are all that are necessary to adjust the externalities that result from land-use interdependence. In sum, the function and importance of servitudes is that they allow landowners to acquire rather specific rights to control land-use. By so doing, servitudes allow a landowner efficiently to acquire specific rights of control over neighboring land and, thereby, secure beneficial, or prevent harmful, interactions.

Land-use has always been interdependent. Accordingly, a law of servitudes has always been a part of the common law. Nonetheless, the law of servitudes has undergone vast development and transformation in the past two centuries. This is because the past two centuries have witnessed a quantum jump in the frequency and severity of land interdependence.

Over the past two centuries, our society has evolved from one predicated upon a rural and agricultural economic base to one predicated upon an urban and industrial economic base. Land-use in a rural-agricultural economy involves less complex and dense development than land-use in an urban-industrial economy. Consequently, land-use in a rural-agricultural economy is far more self-sufficient, and less interdependent, than land-use in an urban-industrial economy. Accordingly, a rural-agricultural society may be well served by a law of servitudes that is less elaborate, and perhaps even different, than the law of servitudes required by an urban-industrial society.

In fact, that the early common law had a law of servitudes has proven more of a bane than a boon to the modern law. The roots of the modern law may be traced to the early common law. But with the increase in land interdependence stemming from the nineteenth century urban-industrial revolution, the traditional law of servitudes proved inadequate. It was refashioned. Part of the mold in which the existing law was set was carried forward. But other parts of the inherited mold were transformed, indeed broken, and fundamentally new law was developed under the guise of continuity. New principles reworked old doctrines; and old principles created new doctrines. The legal aphorism of pouring new wine into old bottles, or of new corn springing from old fields, fairly accurately describes the judiciary's development of the modern law of servitudes during the nineteenth and early twentieth centuries.

Particulars of the industrial revolution's transformation of servitude law will be taken up in §§ 3.02 and 3.04, below. Postponement is necessary until a context has been developed through a completed exploration of easement law. Suffice it to say, at this point, that the development of real covenants and equitable servitudes was due to limitations in the existing law of easements which until the industrial revolution was the most important form of common law servitude. Real covenants and equitable servitudes developed as a means of circumventing the limitations of the law of easements.

All that needs be grasped at this time is that (a) easements, real covenants, and equitable servitudes are related in that they all give their owners the right to make fairly specific use of land owned by another; and (b) the primary function of all these interests is the efficient adjustment of land-use externalities. Historical accident, more than policy rationale, is responsible for many features of the modern common law of servitudes; including its division into three distinct but related doctrines.

Indeed, one central issue of the current law of servitudes is whether the three part division should be continued. Some legal scholars suggest combining real covenants and equitable servitudes into one doctrine; others suggest reducing easements as well as real covenants and equitable servitudes to one doctrine; still others oppose any unification of these property interests. Law review articles, even a symposium, propounding diverse perspectives and answers have been devoted to this issue.

The American Law Institute's recently completed Restatement (Third) of the Law of Property: Servitudes project decision to integrate easement, real covenant and equitable servitude law into a unified body of doctrine is certain to fuel reform of servitude law. For years to come, the usually staid field of servitudes law will be in ferment as the <u>Restatement (Third)</u>'s suggested reforms are tested in the courts.

But whatever the future holds, the three part division of the common law of servitudes has existed for the past two centuries. It exists at present. Law students must come to terms with the law as currently laid down and as it might evolve. Aiding you in this work is the goal of the following <u>Student Guide</u>, which discusses both current law and the <u>Restatement (Third)</u>'s integrated approach.

ABBREVIATIONS

The following abbreviations are used in this <u>Student Guide</u>:

ALP	<u>American Law of Property</u> (A. Casner ed. 1952)
CSW	R. Cunningham, W. Stoebuck, & D. Whitman, <u>The Law of Property</u> (2d ed. 1993)
Powell	R. Powell, <u>The Law of Real Property</u> (1997-)
Restatement (First)	American Law Institute, <u>Restatement of the Law of Property</u> (1944)
Restatement (Third)	American Law Institute, <u>Restatement (Third) of the Law of Property: Servitudes</u> (Tentative Drafts No. 1-7 (1989-98)

CHAPTER

ONE

EASEMENTS

§ 1.01 INTRODUCTION

Easements are the oldest common law servitude. Even the word "easement" bespeaks their ancient lineage. In medieval English, easement was a nonlegal term. It referred to something that assisted in the enjoyment of something else. An easement was a convenience to the use of something else. Medieval lawyers borrowed the term to describe nonpossessory rights in land because the nonpossessory rights typically aided in, and added to, the enjoyment of other land. Easements in land were conveniences to the use of other land. As mentioned in the General Introduction, the other common law servitudes are an outgrowth of the easement concept; they all retain the notion of being conveniences to the use of other land.

The study of easements requires the introduction of a new vocabulary, a vocabulary that—with minor modification—will be of use in the study of all the other servitudes. This basic vocabulary consists of three sets of terms: easement appurtenant and easement in gross; affirmative easement and negative easement; dominant estate and servient estate.

1. EASEMENT APPURTENANT and EASEMENT IN GROSS: All easement owners have the privilege of making certain specific use of land that they do not own. Easements appurtenant give that right to whoever is the present owner of a particular parcel of land; easements in gross give that right to a particular person regardless of her ownership of another parcel of land. Easements appurtenant are thought of as annexed to some parcel of land; easements in gross are easements that are the personal right of some individual. Individuals enjoy easements appurtenant in their status as landowner; individuals enjoy easements in gross in their own right. For these reasons, easements in gross are also known as personal easements.

Q1: O grants A an easement in gross that allows her to hunt and fish on O's land. Is A's easement personal in the sense of

a. not being alienable to B?

    A: No. As will be discussed in § 1.05, below, the alienability of easements in gross is a complex subject. Some easements in gross are alienable, others are inalienable. Because some easements in gross are alienable, saying that easements in gross are personal means only that they are owned by the easement holder in her status as a person, not in her status as owner of any particular parcel of land. Saying that easements in gross are personal means that they are not "real," i.e., they are not annexed to any parcel of real property. Accordingly, saying that A's easement in gross is personal does not mean that it may be enjoyed by A and only A, and therefore, never transferred by A through conveyance or devise.

b. not allowing A to bring B with her as a guest?

    A: No. As stated in the answer to part (a), saying that A's easement in gross is personal does not mean that it may be enjoyed by A and only A. An easements in gross are a species of property, generally entitling its owner to exercise rights normally associated with ownership. The right of use normally includes licensing guests to enjoy the property with oneself.

2. <u>AFFIRMATIVE EASEMENT</u> and <u>NEGATIVE EASEMENT</u>: An affirmative easement is an easement that allows its owner to do something on the land that is subject to the easement; a negative easement is an easement that allows its owner to prevent the owner of the land that is subject to the easement from doing some particular thing on her land. A right of way is an illustration of an affirmative easement; a right to compel the owner of a parcel of land to preserve it in its natural state is an example of a negative easement.

Q2:   Are the following easements affirmative or negative?

a.   An easement that allows A to cross B's land.

   A: This is an affirmative easement because it allows A, the easement holder, to make an active use of the land subject to the easement.

b.   An easement that allows A to mine all sand and gravel from B's land.

   A: Same as part (a).

c.   An easement that allows A to hunt and fish on B's land.

   A: Same as part (a).

d.   An easement that prevents A from using her land in any way that interferes with the flow of an irrigation ditch that runs through A's and B's adjacent land.

   A: This is a negative easement because it does not allow B, the easement holder, to make an active use of the land subject to the easement. It merely restricts the use that the owner of the land subject to the easement may make of her land.

e.   An easement that prevents A from using her land in any way that interferes with the lateral support it gives to B's adjacent land.

   A: Same as part (d).

3. <u>SERVIENT ESTATE</u> and <u>DOMINANT ESTATE</u>: A servient estate is the land that is subject to an easement. A dominant estate is the land to which an easement appurtenant is annexed. A dominant estate is land the ownership of which gives an individual ownership of an easement. Whenever there is an easement appurtenant there is both a dominant and a servient estate; that is, there is some land the ownership of which gives the right to use another parcel of land. Whenever there is an easement in gross there is only a servient estate.

Q3:   In the following easements, who owns the dominant estate and who owns the servient estate?

a.   A, owning two adjacent parcels of land, grants one of them to B along with the right to cross A's retained land.

   A: Assuming that the easement is appurtenant to the land granted to B, B owns the dominant estate and A owns the servient estate. This is because B's land has the benefit of the easement annexed to it, and A's land has the burden of the easement, i.e., is subject to the easement.

   If the easement were personal to B, then there would be no dominant estate because there is no land to which the benefit of the easement is annexed. Nonetheless, A would still own a servient estate because her land would still be subject to an easement.

b.   A, owning two adjacent parcels of land, grants one of them to B, but reserves to herself the right to cross the lot she conveyed to B.

   A: Same as part (a) only A owns the dominant parcel and B owns the servient parcel.

c.   A and B are adjacent landowners. A grants B an easement by which A agrees not to use her land in any way that interferes with the flow of an irrigation ditch that runs through A's and B's adjacent land.

A: Same as part (a). The only novelty in this Question is that the easement is negative rather than affirmative. Dominant and servient estates are determined the same way whether the easement is affirmative or negative.

d. A, owning a three story building, leases the third story to B, along with an easement of access over the building's staircase.

A: Same as part (a). The only novelty in this Question is that the easement is annexed to a leasehold estate rather than a fee simple estate.

e. A, owning a parcel of land, grants to B, who owns no land, the right to mine all the sand and gravel on A's land.

A: There is no dominant estate because the easement is an easement in gross. Consequently, there is no land to which the benefit of the easement is annexed. However, A's land is a servient estate because it is subject to an easement.

§ 1.02 EXPRESS EASEMENTS

[A] Definitions

EXPRESS EASEMENT: An express easement is an easement created by documents satisfying the Statute of Frauds and all other requirements for the transfer of real property interests. Because formal documents are required for the creation of express easements, express easements are also known as formal easements.

GRANT: In the traditional common law, deeds that transferred nonpossessory property rights were known as grants. When a landowner transfers a nonpossessory property right—an easement, for example—she is said to "grant" that right.

CONVEYANCE: In modern usage, deeds that transfer any property interest may be called conveyances. In the traditional common law, only deeds that transferred possessory, freehold estates were known as conveyances. Only when a landowner transferred a possessory, freehold estate—a fee simple, for example— was she said to "convey" that right.

RESERVATION: In the traditional common law, a reservation clause was the part of a deed in which the grantor stated her intention to retain some property right in the land that she was conveying. Whenever a grantor retains some property right in land she is conveying, she is said to "reserve" that right.

EASEMENT APPURTENANT: See § 1.01, above.

EASEMENT IN GROSS: See § 1.01, above.

SERVIENT ESTATE: See § 1.01, above.

DOMINANT ESTATE: See § 1.01, above.

[B] Discussion and Questions

Easements may be created by express act, by implication, and by prescription. Prescriptive easements, which are related to the concept of adverse possession, will not be considered in this text. This section considers the creation of easements by express act. The following section considers the creation of easements by implication.

Easements are real property rights. Any dispositive instrument that is sufficient to create a property interest may create an express easement. Most frequently, express easements are created by deed; but they also may be created by will or contract enforceable in equity.

Ambiguities in the creation of express easements arise in the same way ambiguities arise in the creation of other property interests: through the use of ambiguous words and phrases, conflicts among documentary clauses, and inattention to conveyancing rules. Ambiguities concerning the creation of express easements are resolved in the same way ambiguities concerning property rights generally are resolved.

As may have been mentioned in your study of present estates and future interests, resolution of ambiguity in deeds and wills focuses on determining the intent of the parties. Usually, the parties' intent is garnered from a consideration of the words used in the document, the circumstances surrounding the transaction, and the judiciary's constructional preferences and precedents. There is, as always, some interplay between a rule bound and a more free-form search for the parties' meaning.

In sum, the principles concerning the drafting and construction of deeds and other dispositive documents that create present estates and future interests carry over into the drafting and construction of deeds creating easements. They set the general context within which the particular issues of easement draftsmanship and interpretation arise.

Of course, dispositive instruments creating easements need not use ambiguous words or phrases, or contain conflicting clauses, or fail to observe applicable conveyancing rules. Yet, all too frequently, they do. Easements seem to evoke careless drafting, not only in regard to their creation, but in regard to all of their incidents. See § 1.04[B], below (discussing Scope).

For introductory purposes, issues and problems in the creation of express easements center on three major areas. The first involves determining whether the interest transferred is an easement or a fee simple estate. The second involves determining whether the easement transferred—assuming it is an easement—is an easement appurtenant or an easement in gross. The third involves the continued vitality of an ancient conveyancing rule that prohibits conveying a property interest to "a stranger to the deed." Determining whether the interest transferred is an easement or a fee simple estate is the most frequent issue, and the most difficult to resolve. For that reason, it will be considered first.

(Another area rife with difficult construction problems involves distinguishing among the various servitudes—easements, real covenants, and equitable servitudes. Because the other servitudes have not been discussed yet, constructional problems involving distinguishing among them are postponed. See §§ 3.02 and 3.04, below.)

[1] Determining whether the document transfers an easement or a fee simple estate

Disputes frequently arise over whether a particular document transfers an easement or a fee simple estate. Given the vast difference between a fee simple estate and an easement, it may seem difficult to understand how the two may be confused. The difference between fee simple estates and easements, however, relates to the operation of the two interests. It only highlights the importance of the outcome of a dispute over which interest was transferred. Small differences in the wording of a document are all that it takes to transfer a fee simple rather than an easement.

As different as they are in operation, fee simple estates and easements are similar in that they both may be transferred in perpetuity; or they both may be transferred subject to a special limitation or condition subsequent. Potential longevity is unavailing as a means to distinguish between fee simple estates and easements. Something other than an interest's potential duration is necessary to differentiate a fee simple from an easement.

Unfortunately, draftsmen are used to distinguishing between common law property interests based upon potential longevity, i.e., the estate concept you studied as part of your treatment of present estates and future interests. All too frequently, draftsmen neglect to add something to their documents to indicate whether the interest of potentially infinite duration that they are creating is one of the fee simple estates or an easement.

Consider, for example, a grant to a railroad of "a strip of land for a railroad right-of-way." Assuming that the interest transferred is to last in perpetuity, is it a fee simple absolute or an easement? Assuming that the interest transferred lasts only so long as the strip is used for railroad purposes, is it a fee simple determinable or a determinable easement? The answers to these questions are ambiguous.

Important outcomes turn upon the answers to these questions—outcomes such as whether the railroad owns the minerals under the surface of the strip of land, or the air rights over it; or whether, when the railroad abandons the track, the railroad or the grantor of the interest (or her successors) can sell the strip to a fast-food restaurant; or whether statutes are applicable that destroy possibilities of reverter after a period of time, and thereby turn the railroad's right into an indefeasible interest. That important outcomes turn upon resolving the ambiguity concerning whether a fee simple or easement was transferred only underscores the importance of resolving the ambiguity.

Resolving conflicts over whether a dispositive instrument transfers a fee simple estate or an easement turns upon an appreciation of the fundamental conceptual difference between these two property interests. Both fee simple estates and easements may have a potentially infinite duration. But fee simple estates convey extensive rights to use property and to exclude others from its use; easements convey only limited rights to use property and to exclude others from its use. The right to make limited use of property one neither owns nor possesses was stated in the General Introduction as the hallmark of a servitude. That hallmark is what distinguishes easements—as well as all the other servitudes—from fee simple estates.

In other words, although fee estates and easements are alike in their potential longevity, they are different in the quantum of uses that they authorize their owner to make during that time period. Dispositive instruments that transfer the general right to use property for most purposes transfer fee simple estates; dispositive instruments that transfer specific rights to use property for particular purposes transfer easements.

Of course, the difference in quantum of use authorized by the transfer of a fee simple estate or an easement is a matter of degree. Fee simple estates are not necessarily unlimited in the uses they authorize; easements are not necessarily narrowly limited in the uses they authorize. Focusing on this basic issue, therefore, is not necessarily determinative. Courts have articulated a number of factors the consideration of which aids their determination of whether an ambiguous instrument transfers the right to make a general or specific use of the property.

Among these factors, which may be drawn from the dispositive instrument or the transaction's surrounding circumstances, are:

(1) The precedented connotation of certain words—the words "convey," and "bargain and sell" are traditionally used in the transfer of fee simple estates; "grant" is traditionally used in the transfer of easements. Also, "right of way" has a double signification: it can mean a tract of ground as well as the right to pass over a tract of ground.

(2) The specificity with which the document describes the property affected by it—the less precise the description, the more likely the interest is an easement.

(3) The specificity of the use which may be made of the interest—the more limited and specific the interest's use, the more likely the interest is an easement.

(4) The amount of consideration—the less the consideration reflects the full market value of the property affected, the more likely the interest is an easement.

(5) How the parties to the conveyance and their successors-in-interest have treated the property—the acts of the parties are probative evidence of their understanding.

(6) To whom the property was assessed—payment of taxes is an indication of an expectation of more complete ownership.

(7) The type of interest that best serves the purpose of the parties.

In addition, certain constructional preferences frequently are relevant to disputes involving documents purportedly creating easements. Some of them, such as the presumption that all transfers are in fee simple, are useful in the construction of all dispositive property documents. But others are unique to this area. Chief among them is the preference, under certain circumstances, for construing an interest as an easement rather than a possessory estate—this policy is based upon the view that when rights of way are involved, dividing land into narrow strips that are not in conformity with surrounding ownership patterns inhibits land-use and marketability.

(Matthew Bender & Co., Inc.)

Q4: A grants to B "land, twenty feet wide, for the purpose of allowing B to cross A's land." C makes the same grant to D. Which grant is more likely to convey an easement, and which grant is more likely to convey a fee simple estate, if

    a.   The A-B grant nowhere describes where the land is physically located; the C-D grant specifically describes where the land is physically located.

        A: The A-B grant is more likely to be an easement than the C-D grant. One factor in determining whether a grant creates an easement or a fee simple estate is whether the land involved is specifically described. Courts require that fee simple conveyances describe the land involved with specificity because one of the essential terms of a deed is description of the <u>res</u>. However, courts relax this rule with regard to easements and allow the subsequent behavior of the parties to determine the land subject to the easement. Easements that require subsequent behavior of the parties to locate them are known as "undefined" easements.

    b.   The consideration for the A-B grant is nominal; the consideration for the C-D grant is $10,000.

        A: The A-B grant is more likely to be an easement than the C-D grant. Another factor in determining whether a grant creates an easement or a fee simple estate is the amount of consideration. Fee simple estates give greater rights of use; thus courts presume that they cost more than easements which give limited rights of use. Nonetheless, adequacy of consideration is a tricky factor to use because the adequacy of consideration depends on many factors. It is conceivable that—given the value of the land involved—the $10,000 consideration for the C-D grant was nominal.

    c.   A continues to use the land involved for all purposes that do not interfere with B's use; C never uses the land involved in the grant for any purpose.

        A: The A-B grant is more likely to be an easement than the C-D grant. Another factor in determining whether a grant creates an easement or a fee simple estate is the subsequent behavior of the parties. A's and B's behavior is consistent with the grant of an easement and inconsistent with the grant of a fee simple. C's and D's behavior is just the opposite. (Note that C may point to other circumstances that explain her behavior. Her non-use of the land involved in the grant is not determinative; it is just a factor to be weighed in the overall determination.)

    d.   The taxes on the land involved in the A-B grant continue to be assessed to A; the taxes on the land involved in the C-D grant are reassessed to D.

        A: Once again, the A-B grant is more likely to be an easement than the C-D grant. Taxes are usually assessed against the fee owner. Thus A's payment of taxes on property indicates her understanding that she is the fee owner. The same is true of D's payment of taxes. But once again, this is a tricky factor. A may be able to rebut the force of this factor by explaining that she was unaware that the assessor was still including the land subject to the easement in A's property assessment.

Q5: Many cases raising the issue of whether a document conveys an easement or a fee simple estate involve deeds by which highways, railroads, canals, and pipelines acquire their routes. As background for considering problems involving more complete fact patterns, consider which of the following phrases, standing alone in the granting clause, indicate an intention to convey a fee estate? Which indicate an intention to convey an easement? Which are ambiguous?

    a.   "The grantor conveys to the grantee a strip of land, to wit: . . . [property description omitted]."

        A: A fee simple estate. The word "conveys" connotes the transfer of a fee simple; and the phrase "a strip of land" indicates the thing that the interest concerns. There is nothing to rebut, or even blur the presumption that something other than a fee simple absolute was transferred. That the document transfers a narrow band of land is insufficient to suggest that an easement was transferred.

b.   "The grantor conveys to the grantee a right of way over a strip of land, to wit: . . . [property description omitted]."

    A: An easement. This clause transfers a "right of way over" a thing, not the thing itself. "Right" is the direct object of the verb "convey." Direct objects answer the question "what"? Thus the "right" to pass over the land is what was conveyed.

        It is true that what is transferred is "a right of way" and that phrase has a double signification. However, this clause further modifies "right of way" as being "<u>over</u> a strip of land." This additional phrase removes any doubt that the "right of way" is a "right" and not the thing itself. It is also true that this clause "conveys" the interest, and the verb convey connotes the transfer of a fee estate. Use of the verb "grants" would make this document even clearer.

c.   "The grantor conveys to the grantee a strip of land for a right of way to wit: . . . [property description omitted]."

    A: Ambiguous. In this clause, "a strip of land" is the direct object of the verb, indicating that the thing itself was transferred. This intimates a fee simple estate. In some jurisdictions the phrase "for a right of way" would amount to no more than an indication of the purpose of the conveyance; it would not be sufficient to be construed as words of limitation confining the interest to an easement. In some jurisdictions, however, the phrase would be sufficient to limit the interest conveyed to a fee simple determinable if not an easement.

d.   "The grantor conveys to the grantee a strip of land for a right of way, for railroad purposes only, to wit: . . . [property description omitted]."

    A: An easement, in most jurisdictions. This variation involves the same principles discussed in part (c). As compared to the grant in part (c), the specific mention of railroad purposes would lead more states to find that this clause is ambiguous. Their view is that grants of narrow strips of land to railroads are normally intended be easements. A few states, however, would not find this clause ambiguous. Their position sticks to the view that "a strip of land" is the direct object of the verb, and, therefore, is what was conveyed. The recitation of purpose functions as a recital or as precatory language.

e.   "The grantor conveys to the grantee the following described strip of land, for railroad purposes only, to wit: . . . [property description omitted]."

    A: Ambiguous. This is another variation of the grant in part (c). Some courts would go so far as to hold that even the grant of a "strip of land," not specified to be a right of way, but limited to "railroad purposes" is sufficient to at least raise an ambiguity that the intent was to grant an easement and not a fee estate. Again, other courts would not agree.

[2] Determining whether the document transfers an easement appurtenant or an easement in gross

All too frequently, easements are created without sufficiently specifying whether they are appurtenant or in gross. The classic way that draftsmen indicate that an easement is appurtenant is to grant the easement to "A, his heirs and assigns." These words express the intent to create an easement appurtenant because in the early common law easements in gross were inalienable. Expressing an intent that the easement be alienable was the equivalent of expressing the intent that the easement be appurtenant.

Unfortunately, many easements are granted simply to "A" with no sufficient text indicating whether the easement is the personal right of the named party or annexed to some parcel of land that the named party owns or is being conveyed. When this occurs, there is an ambiguity that courts resolve by considering the circumstances surrounding the transaction and constructional preferences.

Courts prefer that easements be appurtenant; if land is burdened with an easement, courts prefer that it benefit other land. Accordingly, courts presume that easements are appurtenant. But sufficient extrinsic evidence concerning the parties' intent may overcome the presumption. For example, the presumption that a grant of an easement of way to "A" is appurtenant may be overcome by showing that A owns no land to which the easement may attach, or no neighboring land that would be benefited by having the easement annexed to it.

Q6:   O, owning a large tract of land, sells part of it to A. Although O's land has other means of ingress and egress, the deed of conveyance contains a clause that reads:

Reserving to the grantor, her heirs and assigns, the right to use as a driveway a strip of land fifteen (15) feet in width, to wit: . . . [property description omitted].

a.   Does this grant create an easement appurtenant or an easement in gross?

A: Appurtenant. The reservation clause contains words which all courts hold express the intention to create an easement appurtenant.

b.   Rediscuss part (a) on the assumption that the relevant clause reads

Reserving to the grantor the right to use as a driveway a strip of land fifteen (15) feet in width, to wit. . . [property description omitted].

A: Appurtenant. The deed is ambiguous in that the grant is simply to the grantor. This might be taken to mean that the grantor holds the easement as a personal right. If this were true, the easement would be in gross. However, courts presume that easements are appurtenant. In all jurisdictions, omission of the phrase "his heirs and assigns" is insufficient, by itself, to rebut that presumption.

Note, however, that one jurisdiction would hold that this grant is an easement appurtenant, but would do so through a different reasoning process which establishes that the deed unambiguously creates an easement appurtenant. See Burcky v. Knowles, 413 A.2d 585 (N.H. 1985).

c.   Evidence that is extrinsic to a deed—that is, any of the circumstances surrounding the transaction—is admissible only if the deed is ambiguous. If extrinsic evidence is available, would it be admissible if the deed is drafted as it is in part (a)? What if the deed is drafted as it is in part (b)?

A: If the deed is drafted as it is in part (a), the extrinsic evidence would not be admissible because the deed is unambiguously an easement appurtenant.

If the deed is drafted as it is in part (b), the extrinsic evidence would be admissible in almost all jurisdictions because the deed is ambiguous on whether the easement is appurtenant or in gross. But in New Hampshire, under Burcky v. Knowles, above, the extrinsic evidence would not be admissible because that jurisdiction thinks the deed in part (b) is not ambiguous.

Q7:   O, owning two adjacent lots oriented in an east-west direction grants the westernmost lot to A. The deed to A contains a clause that reads:

Reserving to the grantor, her heirs and assigns the right to use as a driveway the most northern fifteen (15) feet of the property herein conveyed; reserving also to the grantor the right to park motor vehicles on the most northeastern fifteen (15) square feet of the property herein conveyed.

a.   Is the parking easement an easement appurtenant or an easement in gross?

A: This is a close case; probably the easement is in gross. As explained in the answer to Q6(b), above, an easement given simply "to A" without mention of "his heirs and assigns" would be ambiguous but held to be an easement appurtenant due to the constructional preference for that type of easement. In this Question, however, there is a factor that is intrinsic to the deed that might overcome the constructional preference: in the reservation of the driveway easement, the draftsman demonstrated awareness of the appropriate words to use when creating an easement appurtenant. Omission of the words "her heirs and assigns" in the creation of the parking easement seems to be a knowing omission, indicating that the easement is personal to O.

b. If there were extrinsic evidence available, would it be admissible to help determine whether the parking easement is appurtenant or in gross?

> **A:** The extrinsic evidence would be admissible. Even though a court might rule that on balance a consideration of the words of the deed supports the conclusion that the easement is in gross, the reservation simply "to O" in the parking easement clause still would be considered ambiguous. See, for example, Mitchell v. Castellaw, 246 S.W.2d 163 (Tex. 1952). It seems that courts feel that granting, or reserving an easement "to A" is an ambiguous way of creating an easement.

[3] The ancient conveyancing rule that prohibits conveying a property interest to a "stranger to the deed"

According to the traditional common law, a property interest cannot be conveyed to a "stranger to the deed." Until the nineteenth century, the common law refused to recognize third party beneficiary contracts of any description. One expression of this policy that generally continues to this day was a rule prohibiting the transfer of any property interest to someone who was not a party to the transaction.

In application to the creation of easements, the rule does not prevent a grantor from granting to her transferee an easement in any land of which the grantor retains ownership. The transferee, after all, is not a stranger to the transaction. Nor does the rule prevent a grantor from reserving an easement to herself in the land she is transferring. The grantor also is not a stranger to the transaction. However, the rule does prevent a grantor from granting an easement in her retained land to someone other than the transferee, unless the grant to that other person meets the requirements of a complete grant (and, in effect, makes that person a transferee). Moreover, the rule entirely prevents a grantor from reserving an easement to someone other than herself in land she is transferring.

This conveyancing rule is based upon archaic, feudal-tenurial conceptions. Restatement (First) § 472 and Restatement (Third) § 2.6(c) refuse to adopt it. A few states have abolished it entirely, either by statute or court decision. Some states have elaborated sub-doctrines that undercut its scope. Nonetheless, it is a rule to be reckoned with: it is observed in most states.

Q8: O, owning three adjacent lots that are oriented in an east-west direction, grants the westernmost lot to A. One year later, O grants the middle lot to B. O's deed to B contains a clause that reads:

> Reserving to the grantor, her heirs and assigns the right to park motor vehicles on the most northeastern 50 square feet of the property herein conveyed; and reserving also to A, her heirs and assigns the right to park motor vehicles on the most northwestern 50 square feet of the property herein conveyed.

a. Does O have an easement appurtenant?

> **A:** Yes. When conveying property a grantor may "reserve" to herself an easement in the property conveyed. The easement O reserved has the classic words expressing the intent that it is appurtenant to O's adjacent retained property.

b. Does A have an easement appurtenant?

> **A:** In most jurisdictions, no. The part of the clause purporting to create an easement in favor of A violates the ancient conveyancing rule that no property interest can be granted to someone who is not a party to the transaction. Most jurisdictions still recognize this rule.
>
> A few jurisdictions have abolished the rule. In these jurisdictions, A would have an easement appurtenant.

For further discussion of Express Easements, see 4 Powell §§ 34.02–34.03; CSW §§ 6.2–6.3, 8.3; Restatement (First) §§ 471–72; Restatement (Third) §§ 2.2, 2.6.

[C]   Review Problems

PROBLEM 1

In the early twentieth century, the Redden Railroad Co. (RR) ran its track through Benton County. Most of its route was acquired through deeds which the RR supplied to the landowners. The relevant parts of the document read, in blank:

RELEASE OF RIGHT OF WAY

I, _____ of the County of _____ in the State of _____, in consideration of the advantages which will accrue to me in particular and the public generally by the construction of a railroad between _____ and _____ and for the purpose of inducing the construction of such a railroad and avoiding condemnation proceedings, do hereby release and quitclaim to _____ the right of way for such railroad as follows, to wit: A strip of land 400 feet wide, [legal description omitted]. . ..

Now the Coal Slurry and Natural Gas Pipeline Co. (CS&NGP) is looking for a route through Benton County. Because the County is somewhat developed, CS&NGP finds it most convenient to run its pipeline in, and at times underneath, RR's right of way. Construction and operation of the pipeline would not interfere with the conduct of RR's operations. Eager to sell CS&NGP the rights it needs, RR instituted a declaratory judgment action seeking a determination that it owns its route in fee simple. The successors of the original grantors claim that RR acquired only an easement.

a. Does the deed grant RR a fee simple interest or an easement?

b. One of the deeds by which RR acquired its route is different from the deed in part (a). When RR was acquiring its route, Hannah Holdout, who owned a strategic parcel of land, at first refused to grant any rights to RR. However, after some months of intense bargaining, Hannah wrote out and delivered to RR a deed, the relevant parts of which read:

This indenture witnesseth that Hannah Holdout. . . in consideration of $300. . . and covenants and agreements hereinafter stated. . . does hereby convey and quit claim unto the Redden Railroad. . ., for railroad purposes, the following real estate. . . to wit: A strip of land 400 feet wide. . . [legal description omitted].

Does Hannah's deed grant RR a fee simple interest or an easement?

ANALYSIS

a. As you may recall from the study of the creation of present estates and future interests, deeds—indeed all dispositive instruments—are construed according to the intent of the parties. That intent should be drawn from the document's words, and in appropriate cases from the transaction's surrounding circumstances and from the courts' constructional preferences and precedents. Construing a dispositive document requires considering all these factors to determine if it transfers a fee estate or an easement. Of course, as is true with the creation of present estates and future interests, extrinsic factors are inadmissible and need not be considered if the document is unambiguous.

Consideration of the document's words—The caption and granting clause of the deed refer to a "right of way." Courts generally hold that this term indicates an intent to transfer an easement. The conveyance is also made for nominal consideration, a factor generally taken to indicate the transfer of an easement.

Although the document, at one point, refers to a "strip of land," in context it is not a factor indicating the grant of a fee simple. The phrase "strip of land" is used in the property description clause. Reference to a "strip" in the property description clause should not be taken as evidence of intent to grant a fee title because that clause is supposed to describe the thing conveyed, not the type of interest that is conveyed. However, courts do tend to overlook the technically correct idea that reference to a "strip" in the description clause is inconsequential. When an easement is intended, it is dangerous to use the phrase; and out of an abundance of caution, one might even in the property description clause employ the phrase "an easement in a strip of land," or a "right of way over a strip of land."

Consideration of the transaction's surrounding circumstances—None are particularly important in this case.

Consideration of the courts' constructional preferences and precedents—This deed is a standard form prepared by RR and given to the landowners to sign. This seems a situation where the preference for interpreting documents against the grantor is inappropriate. This would support construing the document as creating an easement.

Construction of the document—This deed unambiguously conveys an easement. All of the intrinsic factors point in that direction—except for a very implausible argument based on the appearance of the phrase "strip of land" in the property description clause. There should be no need to consider extrinsic factors; but all of them point to the same conclusion.

b.   The analysis of Hannah's deed is substantially different.

Consideration of the document's words—There are many factors pointing towards an intent to transfer a fee simple interest. The document "conveys. . . for railroad purposes. . . [a] strip of land." Conveyances of "strips" of land generally are held to indicate an intention to transfer a fee interest. This is because, by statute, any transfer is presumed to be a transfer of a fee simple interest. When the "thing" is granted, with no indication that an interest less than a fee estate is intended, no factor rebuts the standing law's presumption.

Of course, as stated in the answer to part (a), the appearance of the phrase "a strip of land" in RR's deed was inconsequential. But that was due to the context. The phrase appears in the property description clause of both deeds. However, RR's printed deed, in the granting clause, describes the interest conveyed as a "right of way." Hannah's deed never does this. Thus the problem with Hannah's deed is not that it refers to "a strip of land" in the property description clause, but that it never limits the interest granted in the "strip."

In addition, the grant is made for more than nominal consideration. This is substantially more than the consideration given in RR's printed deeds. Without some notion of the market value of the property at the time of the conveyance, one cannot say with certainty that it indicates a fee conveyance. But $300 for this strip does seem like a large amount, indicating the intent to pass a fee.

Despite the foregoing, there is one factor in the document's words that may point to an intent to transfer an easement. The grant was "for railroad purposes." Many courts have held that in deeds to railroads, canals, or other similar companies, an expression of specific use is an indication of an intent to transfer an easement. Other courts, however, have taken the position that a grant "for railroad purposes" may express the motive for the deed; but the phrase, by itself, is legally insufficient to limit the ownership interest granted.

Consideration of the transaction's surrounding circumstances—As construed, all the rest of RR's route is an easement. It would be totally out of harmony with the surrounding land ownership pattern to construe this deed as transferring a fee interest. Moreover, RR has no need to hold Hannah's land in fee.

Consideration of the courts' constructional preferences—Hannah is the grantor and the drafter of the document. The preference for construing documents against her is applicable, but seems inappropriate. The policy preference not to carve the countryside up into little strips of land supports the finding of an easement.

<u>Construction of the document</u>—The only intrinsic factor opposed to the view that the document conveys a fee estate is the statement that land is granted "for railroad purposes." In some jurisdictions this would be insufficient to make the deed sufficiently ambiguous to allow for a consideration of extrinsic evidence. The phrase "for railroad purposes," in those jurisdictions, would be taken as an expression of motive and would be given no legal effect.

In other jurisdictions, the phrase "for railroad purposes" is given greater weight. It is taken as important evidence indicating an intent to grant an easement. The phrase, by itself, would make the document sufficiently ambiguous to allow consideration of extrinsic evidence.

The extrinsic evidence, if admitted, seems persuasive that the parties intended to convey an easement. RR holds no other part of its route in Benton County in fee. To hold that RR owns part of Hannah's farm in fee would create of small strip of land totally out of harmony with the surrounding pattern of landownership. RR has no need to own this parcel in fee. The size of the consideration RR paid may be large. But the surrounding circumstances indicate that it was a strategic piece of property. Hannah, it seems, was a good negotiator, but a poor draftsperson. This, at least, is how the court that adjudicated the case upon which this Problem was based felt. It held that Hannah's deed granted an easement. See <u>Richard S. Brunt Tr. v. Plantz</u>, 458 N.E.2d 251 (Ind. App. 1983). For an example of a jurisdiction that would construe the document as unambiguously conveying a fee estate, see <u>Cleary Petroleum Corp. v. Harrison</u>, 621 P.2d 528 (Okla. 1980).

PROBLEM 2

In January, 1905, Andy Andrews purchased 41 acres of land outside Spont City, Iowa for $120. The next year he granted rights to a 1000 x 100 foot strip running across the parcel to the Irrigation Ditch Co. (ID) by a deed which read:

That Andy Andrews of the County of Carlton in the State of Iowa, party of the first part, in consideration of the sum of Fifty Dollars in hand paid by the Irrigation Ditch Co., a corporation with its principal office at Spont City, County of Carlton,State of Iowa, party of the second part, the receipt whereof is hereby acknowledged, do hereby grant, remise, release and quit-claim unto the said party of the second part, its successors and assigns forever, all his estate, right, title, interest, claim, property and demand, of, in and to the following real property, situation in the County of Carlton, State of Iowa, and described as follows:

A Strip of land not exceeding 100 feet in width to be located by the surveyors of the Irrigation Ditch Co. to be used as a right of way for an irrigation ditch.

It is hereby agreed as a further consideration for payment of this right of way, that the party of the second part will furnish water at the regular established price fixed by said second party, for the purpose of irrigating all the land owned by the party of the first part, as soon as the ditch contains water that can be used for this purpose, and the party of the second part also agrees to place a bridge over said ditch at such place as the party of the first part may demand.

TO HAVE AND TO HOLD the same, together with all the hereditaments and appurtenances thereunto in anywise appertaining.

WITNESS my hand and seal this 14th day of November A.D. 1906.

_____(SEAL)

Andy Andrews

Recently, ID dissolved. In winding up its affairs, ID conveyed all its real property to a syndicate headed by Denise Developer. With regard to the 1000 × 100 foot right of way across the land once owned by Andy, Denise is aware that Spont City has grown since Andy's conveyance. Andy's land, except for the canal, has been further subdivided and has become a thriving residential, business and commercial area. Denise, accordingly, thinks it possible to fill the canal bed and construct business and commercial uses on it. Interested in establishing her ownership right to the 1000 × 100 foot right of way across the land once owned by Andy, Denise has instituted declaratory proceedings against Andy's successors-in-interest, seeking to quiet title to the 1000 × 100 foot right of way. Denise claims that she owns a fee simple absolute in the land; Andy's successors-in-interest claim that she owns only an easement.

In construing the 1906 deed to determine whether it grants a fee simple estate or an easement, what is your analysis of:

a. the document's words?

b. the circumstances surrounding the transaction?

c. the courts' constructional preferences?

d. how to construe this document?

ANALYSIS

a. <u>Consideration of the document's words</u>—The granting clause grants "all [the grantor's] estate, right, title,. . .." This phrase unambiguously intimates an intent to pass a fee simple estate.

However, other words intimate an intent to grant an easement. The land actually affected by the document is "to be located by the surveyors. . .." The affected land, in other words, is not described with particularity. Easements frequently are not described with the same particularity as fees. Easements—especially easements of way—frequently are "undefined." The subsequent behavior of the parties determines the specific location of the easement, within the boundaries of the general area set by the conveyance.

Finally, some words intimate the transfer of a fee or an easement, depending upon the jurisdiction. The description clause speaks of "A Strip of land. . . to be used as a right of way for an irrigation ditch." As was said in the analysis of Problem 1, <u>above</u>, mentioning a "strip of land" in the description clause should be of no account. But here the description clause also discloses the purpose of the grant. As discussed in Problem 1, such disclosure of purpose would, in many but not all jurisdictions, be taken as an important factor indicating that the parties intended to grant only an easement.

b. <u>Consideration of the transaction's surrounding circumstances</u>—Two extrinsic factors frequently found in fee/easement deed construction cases are present in this Problem. One points to a fee conveyance—the consideration was over 40% of the purchase price of the entire 41 acre parcel. The other points to an easement conveyance. ID has no need for a fee interest; ID's needs are met through the grant of an easement.

c. <u>Consideration of the courts' constructional preferences</u>—The preference for construing deeds in favor of the grantee favors conveyance of a fee interest; as does the preference for resolving any contradiction between the granting clause and latter clauses in favor of the granting clause. However, the preference for unitary ownership works, in this case, for the grant of an easement. This is because the result of construing this document as granting a fee is to create a narrow strip of land, separate from larger parcels.

d. <u>Construction of the document</u>—There are jurisdictions which would find this document insufficiently ambiguous to justify resort to extrinsic evidence. These jurisdictions would find that the words of the document, construed in light of the rules of construction, convey a fee simple estate. The granting clause, which is to be preferred over subsequent clauses, refers to an unlimited grant of the grantor's estate, right, title, *etc*. The language in the description clause restricting the grant to "a right of way for an irrigation ditch" would be construed as a statement of the purpose of the grant, not as a statement of what was granted.

Most jurisdictions, however, would find the document sufficiently ambiguous to require consideration of extrinsic factors. Some of these jurisdictions give great weight to clauses revealing that the purpose of the grant was to establish a right of way for a company, typically a railroad, that acquires tremendous lengths of narrow strips for transportation purposes. Others simply do not give much weight to the notion that deed interpretation should stay within the "four corners" of the deed; they do not require much ambiguity before saying a resort to extrinsic evidence is justified.

With regard to the extrinsic factors, the size of the consideration speaks very strongly in favor of a fee ownership. The idea that ID does not need more than an easement is not something very persuasive. It functions as a way of saying that if ID were confined to an easement it would lose no essential right.

With regard to the rules of construction, none of them are persuasive in this case. The preference for undivided ownership—which in this case is a policy against separate ownership of narrow strips—is persuasive when the strip is in a rural area. But Spont City has grown to encompass Andy's land; and a 1000 × 100 foot parcel might well be independently viable.

In sum, this a very close case. In the case upon which this Problem is based, the court held that the document granted an easement. But that court also had additional extrinsic evidence, such as that ID never paid taxes on the strip. You might be interested in reading the court's well considered opinion. It is Northwest Realty Co. v. Jacobs, 273 N.W.2d 141 (S.D. 1978).

PROBLEM 3

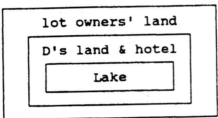

Some years ago, Denise Developer owned 200 acres of land entirely surrounding a lake. She platted most of the land into lots and sold them. None of the lots fronted on the lake because Denise retained the entire lake shore to a depth of 100 yards. On land fronting on one-quarter of the shore, Denise built a resort hotel with beach, swimming and boating facilities. She left the rest of the lake shore in its natural state.

At first, Denise allowed lot purchasers to use the lake and the hotel's facilities free of charge. However, when the development proved popular, Denise imposed usage fees equivalent to the charges made to hotel guests. When this occurred, most of the lot owners joined in instituting a declaratory judgment action challenging the validity of the usage fees. The lot owners' contention is that the lot owners have an easement appurtenant to use the lake and the hotel's facilities free of charge. Denise concedes that they have an easement, but argues that it is in gross. Accordingly, the usage fees are valid against her grantees' grantees.

Both sides to the controversy base their claims on a clause in the deeds issued by Denise that reads:

The grantor grants to the grantee and her immediate family only, the right to the free use of the lake and auxiliary recreational facilities constructed by the grantor.

a. Is the easement appurtenant or in gross?

b. Rediscuss part (a) on the assumption that another clause in the deed reads:

The grantee, her heirs and assigns agree to abide by all reasonable rules and regulations governing the usage of the lake and auxiliary recreational facilities that may be made, from time to time, by the grantor, her heirs and assigns.

c. Rediscuss part (b) on the assumption that the lot owners had been sold lake front lots, and thus, as littoral owners they had the right to use the lake without Denise's permission.

ANALYSIS

a. This is an easement appurtenant. The interpretation of the grant depends upon the intent of the parties, as shown by the words of the document, and if they are ambiguous, by the surrounding circumstances and constructional preferences and precedents. If the grant had been "to the grantee, her heirs and assigns, and their families only," then the easement would be unambiguously appurtenant. The absence of the phrase "her heirs and assigns" does not overcome the constructional preference for an appurtenant easement. Neither does the word "only," since the referent of "only" might be "family" as well as the entire preceding phrase. The clause is, therefore, ambiguous. It might grant an easement appurtenant that may be exercised by the lot owner and her family, but not the lot owner's invitees. It might grant an easement in gross limited to the immediate grantee and her family.

What might be drawn from the surrounding circumstances? The common sense view would be that the parties intended Denise's grantees to benefit as lot owners, but not to the extent of allowing their guests to use the lake and recreational facilities without charge. The desire to exclude guests from the benefits of free usage is perfectly understandable. The desire to limit the benefit to only the first purchasers is harder to understand. Such an understanding would diminish substantially the value of the lots on resale. There should be evidence of such an understanding, and a court would not presume it.

Finally, the constructional preference to construe the grant against the grantor, who assuredly drafted this document, points to the conclusion that the document should be construed to create an appurtenant easement. So does the preference to construe easements as appurtenant.

b.   The additional clause, properly interpreted, supports the conclusion that the easement is appurtenant. Usually the appearance of the words "her heirs and assigns" in one clause but not in another supports the inference that the draftsman knew their significance and knowingly put them in or omitted them. Thus absent other considerations, the clause without the words "her heirs and assigns" would be construed as an easement in gross.

However, in this case, the additional clause assumes that the grantees' heirs and assigns will be using the lake. The grantees' heirs and assigns have no right to use the lake unless the clause quoted in part (a) gave it to them. That clause gave it to them only if it was an easement appurtenant. Accordingly, the proper construction is that Denise granted an easement appurtenant, the use of which is limited to the easement owner and her family.

c.   Now the proper construction is that the easement is in gross. Under the additional facts, the grantees' heirs and assigns have the right to use the lake regardless of Denise's permission. Thus the assumption that they will be using the lake does not depend upon the clause quoted in part (a). Accordingly, the usual inference drawn from inclusion of the phrase "her heirs and assigns" in one clause but not another—the inference that was discussed in the answer to part (b)—should govern.

PROBLEM 4

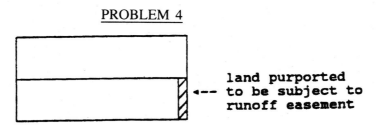

land purported to be subject to runoff easement

Some years ago, Denise Developer acquired a 20 acre parcel of land in the Metroville suburbs. Last year, she interested a group of investors in developing a shopping center on the northern half of it. Denise formed them into the Center Company (CC), a limited partnership with herself as the general partner. She then conveyed the northern half of her parcel to CC, and commenced construction.

Denise had always intended to develop the southern half herself, or at least control the company that developed it. But this year, Office Space, Inc. (OS) made her an attractive offer for the remainder of her parcel. Denise accepted it. Aware that shopping centers, by paving over large areas of ground, usually create water runoff problems, and aware that water in the area flowed south, Denise negotiated the following clause, which was inserted in her deed to OS:

> RESERVING to Center Company, a limited partnership, an easement appurtenant for the benefit of the real estate said Center Company owns adjacent to the real estate herein conveyed for the drainage of surface waters and waters discharged from the roof and floor drains of buildings constructed and to be constructed on said adjacent real estate, along and across the following described real estate, part of the land herein conveyed, to wit: [legal description of land subject to the easement omitted]. . ..

The price OS paid for the land reflected the presence of this clause. Nonetheless, when OS began site preparation, it regraded its northern border, blocking water runoff from CC's property. CC immediately instituted proceedings to enjoin OS's activity. CC acknowledges that the jurisdiction's standing law allows landowners to block water runoff from adjacent parcels. Any rights CC has derive from the above quoted clause. OS thinks CC has no rights, and has filed a motion to dismiss.

Does CC have an easement appurtenant to discharge its water runoff over the designated part of OS's land?

ANALYSIS

This Problem seems straightforward. OS is flagrantly disregarding an easement that was reserved unambiguously in its conveyance. Enjoining its activities, alas, raises a thicket of legal issues.

The quoted clause violates the traditional conveyancing rule that there may be no reservation in favor of a "stranger to the deed" because Denise no longer owned the dominant parcel at the time of her conveyance of the servient parcel. Reservation clauses, traditionally, were used to indicate the rights a grantor carved out of, and retained from, the otherwise complete bundle of rights her conveyance transferred. A stranger to the deed (more exactly, a stranger to the title being conveyed) had no estate out of which an interest could be reserved.

That reservation clauses could function only to retain rights for the grantor, and not to grant rights to a third party, was a consequence of archaic principles of medieval conveyancing. It has no contemporary rationale. You should also appreciate that had Denise, at any time prior to the OS deed, executed a separate deed granting to CC the easement contained in the OS deed, the easement would be effective. The reservation clause in the OS deed would have functioned as a "subject to" clause, putting OS on notice of prior rights and estopping it from denying their existence due to lack of notice. In addition, Denise could have drafted the deed to make separate grants—an easement to CC, and a fee estate to OS.

Thus this Problem arises as much from draftsmanship as from lack of foresight. The conveyancing rule violated here is totally and easily circumventable. Perhaps that is part of the reason for its survival. Unfortunately, it is violated all to often. Many lawyers simply do not know about or anticipate such an archaic rule.

Nonetheless, the rule is respected in most jurisdictions. In most jurisdictions, the quoted clause would be a nullity and CC's action would be dismissed.

This is a result that Restatement (First) § 472, Restatement (Third) § 2.6(c) and all scholarly commentators condemn. It exalts, they say, the historical conception of reservation clauses over the effectuation of the intent of the parties. Spurred on by this argument, a small—but growing—number of jurisdictions have abrogated the rule. England, whose jurisprudence gave rise to the rule, abolished it by statute in 1925. In these jurisdictions, CC would prevail.

Other jurisdiction have sought an accommodation between the demands of historical learning and the search for the draftsman's intent. They have elaborated a complex potpourri of subrules that, to a greater or lesser extent, undercut the vitality of the traditional rule. Some of them have no application here, but should be mentioned because of their frequent application: (a) the grantor's spouse is not considered a stranger to the deed; (b) reservations to the general public are effective by way of dedication.

Another subrule, however, is relevant here. It is the subrule that ineffective reservations may operate as exceptions. Exception clauses traditionally functioned as adjuncts to property description clauses. Exception clauses indicated the intent not to convey some physical part of the property generally described in the description clause. When reservations are allowed to operate as exceptions, they indicate the intent not to convey some of the rights to the property. The result is that the grantee does not receive those rights.

This subrule has two important limitations. One is that although the subrule prevents the grantee from obtaining the ineffectively reserved rights, it does not transfer them to the stranger. The rights remain where excepted property remains—with the grantor. The grantor may do with them as she wishes. In this Problem, under this subrule, CC's suit is premature; although a conveyance to it from Denise anytime before judgment may perfect its claim.

The other limitation is that the subrule operates only on uses being made of the transferred land at the time of the conveyance. It is said that because exception clauses traditionally apply to the physical property, and not to rights to that property, exceptions can be made only with regard to something existent at the time of the grant. In this Problem, under this subrule, OS has an interesting argument regarding whether, or the extent to which, its land was being used for runoff from CC's land at the time of the grant.

In sum, in the group of jurisdictions that has modified, but not abolished, the traditional rule, the outcome is uncertain. It depends upon which subrules have been adopted, and how they apply to the instant facts.

Whether the traditional rule should be retained, abolished or modified, is left to you, as is consideration of how the last mentioned modification ought to be applied. You might reconsider your response after our study of "quasi-easements" in § 1.03, below.

[D] Recapitulation

1. An express easement is an easement created by documents satisfying the Statute of Frauds and all other requirements for the transfer of real property interests.

2. Disputes over whether a transaction conveys an easement or some other property interest are decided by determining the parties' intent. Courts construe the parties' intent by considering the dispositive document, the transaction's surrounding circumstances, and the judiciary's constructional preferences. However, the surrounding circumstances and constructional preferences are considered only if the document is ambiguous.

3. In disputes over whether a transaction conveys a fee simple estate or an easement, courts seek to determine whether the parties intended to convey the general right to possess the property, or only a specific right to use it for certain limited purposes. Conveyance of a general right of possession indicates the conveyance of a fee simple estate. Conveyance of a specific right of use indicates the conveyance of an easement.

4. In disputes over whether a transaction conveys an easement appurtenant or an easement in gross, the courts seek to determine whether the parties intended the easement to be (a) annexed to some land, or (b) the personal privilege of the easement holder. If the easement is intended to be annexed to some land, it is an easement appurtenant. If the easement is intended to be the personal privilege of the easement holder, it is an easement in gross.

5. Granting an easement to "A, his heirs and assigns" is the classic way to express the intent to convey an easement appurtenant rather than an easement in gross.

6. As a limitation on the intent of the parties, many jurisdictions enforce an ancient conveyancing rule that prohibits granting an easement to "a stranger to the transaction." Restatement (First) § 472 com. (b) and the Restatement (Third) § 2.6(c) condemn this rule and a few jurisdictions have abrogated it.

§ 1.03 IMPLIED EASEMENTS

[A] Definitions

IMPLIED EASEMENT: An implied easement is an easement that is not sufficiently expressed in documents satisfying the Statute of Frauds or the other requirements for the transfer of real property interests. Because formal documents are not required for the creation of implied easements, implied easements are also known as informal easements.

EASEMENT BY IMPLIED GRANT: An easement by implied grant is an easement impliedly conveyed to the grantee in land retained by the grantor. See the definition of "grant" in § 1.02[A], above.

EASEMENT BY IMPLIED RESERVATION: An easement by implied reservation is an easement impliedly retained by a grantor in land she conveyed. See the definition of "reservation" in § 1.02[A], above.

QUASI-EASEMENT: No one can have an easement in her own land. When a landowner uses one part of her land for the benefit of another part, and the use could be an easement if the parcels did not have a common owner, the easement-like use is known as a "quasi-easement."

[B] Discussion and Questions

Implied easements ought not to exist. Implied easements ought not to exist because the parties to a transaction have the opportunity to document it completely. Implied easements ought not to exist, also, because they are property interests not evidenced by a writing. Their creation and preservation undercuts the policy of the Statute of Frauds and the Recording Acts. Yet implied easements do exist; and they are a frequent source of controversy between landowners.

On occasion, easements are implied from oral representations that are not incorporated into a deed. More frequently, easements are implied from the circumstances surrounding a transfer of property, unaided by written or parole evidence. Easements implied from oral representations are based on principles—primarily equitable estoppel and part performance—that are not unique to the law of easements. Equitable estoppel and part performance are important bases for the implication of real covenants and equitable servitudes; they will be discussed as part of the treatment of those servitudes. See § 2.03[B][1], below. Easements implied from oral representations are not the focus here. This section focuses on easements that are implied from the circumstances surrounding a transaction; they are based on principles that are unique to the law of easements.

Q9: O, owning two lots, grants one to A. At the time of the transaction, O orally promises A that A may have a right of way across the northern boundary of O's retained land. Assuming A has an easement, is it an express or an implied easement?

> **A:** A has an implied easement. In a sense the easement is as express as can be in that O orally said that A could have it. Nothing is left to conjecture. Nonetheless, express easements are only those easements that are embodied in documents that satisfy the Statutes of Frauds. All other easements are implied. Accordingly, express easements are sometimes called formal easements, and implied easements are sometimes called informal easements, because express easements are created by documents that are sufficiently formal to satisfy the Statute.

Why do judges imply easements from the circumstances surrounding a transaction? Consider the classic cases:

(1) a large parcel is divided, part is left landlocked, but no right of way is expressly provided for benefiting the landlocked part; or

(2) a large parcel is divided, the utilities serving one part run across the other part, but no easement for the utility lines is expressly provided for in the deed. In such situations, all courts and commentators

say that the circumstances surrounding the transaction support an inference that the parties themselves intended to create an easement. Some courts and commentators add that the policy favoring land utilization also supports the creation of an easement in favor of the needy parcel.

Q10: O, owning two adjacent lots, grants one of them to A under circumstances that would support the implication of a driveway easement burdening the lot conveyed to A. Does O have that easement if the deed from O contains a clause that reads "[i]t is understood that the grantor disclaims any right to further use of the driveway across the land herein conveyed"?

> **A:** No, O does not have the implied easement. Implied easements are grounded in the presumed intention of the parties. Express words can always rebut the required inference (as can the subsequent acts of the parties). The words in this deed are sufficiently explicit to rebut any inference of an easement in favor of O.
>
> The facts in this Question rebut the inference of an easement implied from prior use. The same comments apply to easements by necessity, except that courts find the inference of an easement by necessity rebutted only by the most explicit language.

As illustrated by the classic cases, the traditional doctrine of implied easements has two branches. One branch is easements implied by necessity. Easements are implied by necessity when (1) land in common ownership, (2) is severed into two or more parcels with separate ownership, (3) and the severance creates the necessity for the easement. In most situations the first two elements are not in dispute. Most controversy and confusion surrounds the third element.

Courts differ on whether the standard of necessity is "strict" or "reasonable" need for the easement. Courts also differ on their treatment of grantors and grantees. Some courts hold that their standard of necessity is the same whether a grantor or a grantee is the easement claimant (that is, whether the court is being asked to "reserve" or to "grant" an implied easement). Other courts hold that the standard of necessity is higher for grantor-claimants than for grantee-claimants. These courts hold that a grantee need only establish a reasonable necessity to establish an implied grant of an easement, but that a grantor must establish a strict necessity to establish an implied reservation of an easement. Confusion is added to the controversy over the standard of necessity by difficulties and differences in their application. The notion of strict or reasonable necessity is inherently vague. Courts that have adopted the same general standard may apply it differently.

Q11: O, owning two adjacent lots, grants one to A. Although the land retained by O is landlocked (i.e., it has no means of ingress or egress over a public road), the deed does not mention any easement over A's land in favor of O.

> a. If O claims an easement, will she be asking the court to create an easement by implied reservation or implied grant?
>
> > **A:** An easement by implied reservation. When grantors expressly retain easements in land they convey away, they do so through a part of a deed known as a "reservation" clause. They reserve an easement in the land conveyed. Hence, when a grantor retains an easement through implication, it is through an implied reservation.
>
> b. Assuming O had conveyed the landlocked parcel to A, and retained the parcel with access to a public road, if A claims an easement, will she be asking the court to imply an easement by implied reservation or implied grant?
>
> > **A:** A, as the grantee, would be asking the court to imply the grant of an easement
>
> c. Do courts make it easier to grant implied easements or reserve implied easements? What is the blackletter doctrine through which courts make one implied easement easier to imply than the other?
>
> > **A:** Some, but not all, courts make it easier to imply easements by grant. Through implied grants, grantors convey more than their deeds express; through implied reservations, grantors

convey less than their deeds express. Some courts to think that a grantor should not "derogate" from her grant.

In the courts that differentiate between implied reservations and implied grants, the doctrinal expression of their policy focuses on the standard of necessity. They require a higher degree of necessity for the implied reservation of an easement than they require for the implied grant of an easement. Typically, a court that makes the distinction demands a strict necessity to reserve an implied easement, but demands only a reasonable necessity to grant an implied easement.

Q12: O, owning two parcels of adjacent land, sells one of them to A. The parcel sold to A has no means of access to a public road.

    a.   Does A have an easement by necessity over O's land?

        A: Yes. All the elements for an easement implied by necessity are met. O's and A's parcels were severed from common ownership, and the severance created a strict necessity for an easement of way.

    b.   Rediscuss part (a) on the assumption that at the time of the O-A conveyance there was a public road adjacent to A's property, but that two years later the road was closed.

        A: No. No matter how great the necessity, the necessity did not exist at the time of the transaction that severed the two parcels. Because implied easements are said to be based upon the presumed intent of the parties, not upon the public policy favoring land utilization, the necessity must exist at the time the parcels were severed. Courts will not presume the parties intended to create an easement that they neglected to express in their deed when there was no need for the easement at the time of their transaction.

Q13: O owns two adjacent parcels of land. One of them is known as Blackacre, and the other is known as Whiteacre. Blackacre is landlocked in that it is surrounded on three sides by a river and on the fourth side by Whiteacre. Blackacre and Whiteacre are located in a remote area famous for its fishing and boating. Most landowners frequently access their land by boat, not car. O sells Blackacre to A.

    a.   Is there a strict necessity for implying an easement over Whiteacre in favor of Blackacre?

        A: Probably not. Strict necessity requires that the land may not be used for any valuable purpose without implying the easement of access. Given the nature of land-use in the area, Blackacre can be used for a valuable use—indeed, used in a fairly normal manner—without an easement over Whiteacre. See the famous, or infamous, case of <u>Littlefield v. Hubbard</u>, 128 A. 285 (Me. 1925) (holding that access by a navigable river prevents there being a strict necessity for an easement of way).

    b.   Is there a reasonable necessity for implying an easement over Whiteacre in favor of Blackacre?

        A: Maybe. In some jurisdictions, reasonable necessity requires no more than that the easement be a normal convenience that landowners usually expect. In other jurisdictions, reasonable necessity requires only that an alternate substitute for the easement cannot be obtained for a reasonable expense of labor and money. The facts here present a close case for reasonable necessity. Perhaps it would turn upon how frequently neighbors accessed their land by car rather than by boat.

    c.   Does Blackacre have an easement appurtenant, implied by necessity, over Whiteacre?

        A: Maybe. Some jurisdictions require strict necessity before they imply an easement by necessity. In those jurisdictions, the answer is no. Other jurisdictions require only a reasonable necessity. In those jurisdictions, there is a possibility that an easement would be implied.

d. Would Blackacre be more or less likely to have an implied easement appurtenant over Whiteacre if O had sold A Whiteacre instead of Blackacre?

> **A:** Less likely. Now the grantor, rather than the grantee, is claiming an implied easement. Grantors request courts to imply the reservation of an easement; grantees request courts to imply the grant of an easement. Some courts do not distinguish between the necessity required to imply or reserve an easement. But other courts do, and they increase the necessity requirement when they are asked to reserve an implied easement.

The other branch of the traditional doctrine of implied easements is easements implied from prior use. Easements are implied by prior use when (1) land in common ownership, (2) is severed into two or more parcels with separate ownership, (3) and before the severance part of the land was apparently, continuously and permanently used for the benefit of another part, (4) and continuation of the use is necessary for the enjoyment of the benefited part. In most situations the first and second elements are not in dispute. The third and fourth elements, however, lead to a large number of controversies. Courts differ over the meaning and application of the element of necessity in the doctrine of easements by prior use in the same ways that they differ over that element for the doctrine of easements by necessity. In addition, some jurisdictions impose different standards of necessity in easements implied by necessity and easements implied by prior use cases. Some, but not all, courts require strict necessity to imply the former, but only reasonable necessity to imply the latter.

Courts also differ over the application of the requirement of "apparent, continuous and permanent" prior use. Courts and commentators agree that "apparent" means reasonably discoverable. They also agree that "continuous and permanent" means that the use was not a temporary convenience creating no reasonable expectation of continuation after the land was conveyed. Nonetheless, courts vary significantly in their conclusions concerning when uses are reasonably discoverable or create reasonable expectation of future continuation.

Easements implied from prior use are also known as "quasi-easements." This term is a consequence of the legal theory that no one can have an easement in her own land. Easements are implied from prior use when the now separately owned parcels were held in common ownership and the common owner acted "as if" one part of her land was burdened with an easement for the benefit of the other part.

Q14: The facts are the same as in Q13, <u>above</u>, except that O usually gained access to Blackacre by driving a recreational vehicle over Whiteacre. Would A be more or less likely to have an implied easement?

> **A:** More likely. The additional fact raises the possibility that the doctrine of easements implied from prior use could be argued. Some courts have the same standard of necessity for both easements implied by necessity and prior use. But other jurisdictions relax the necessity requirement when an easement implied from prior use is involved.

Q15: O owns two adjacent parcels of land—Blackacre and Whiteacre. Although both Blackacre and Whiteacre are adjacent to public roads, O almost always gains access to Blackacre by driving across Whiteacre. After years of doing this, O sells Blackacre to A.

a. Does A have an easement implied from prior use across Whiteacre?

> **A:** No. There is insufficient necessity to support the implication of an easement from prior use. When land held in common ownership is severed, prior use, no matter how apparent, continuous and permanent does not give rise to an implied easement without some degree of necessity. The facts stated do not support a finding of necessity—even if necessity means no more than mere convenience. A, the easement claimant, has the burden of creating a record that supports a finding of necessity.

b. Two years after the conveyance from O to A, the public road bordering A's land is closed. Does A have an easement implied from prior use across Whiteacre?

> **A:** No. The necessity that now exists for an easement implied from prior use did not exist at the time of the transaction that severed the parcels. The discussion in the answer to

Q12(b), above, regarding the time when the necessity must arise applies to both easements implied by necessity and easements implied from prior use.

Q16: O owns two adjacent parcels of land—Blackacre and Whiteacre. Because Whiteacre's subsoil prevents adequate drainage, O digs an open drainage ditch around Whiteacre and across Blackacre to a pond. A few years later, O sells Blackacre to A.

    a.   Does O have a drainage easement implied by prior use over Blackacre?

        A: Yes. All the elements of an easement implied from prior use are clearly here. Land under common ownership was severed into two parcels under separate ownership. At the time of the severance, there was an apparent, continuous and permanent use of one parcel for the benefit of the other parcel. The continuation of that use is reasonably necessary and perhaps even strictly necessary for the utilization of the benefited land.

    b.   Rediscuss part (a) on the assumption that drainage across Blackacre was accomplished by means of a buried pipe that entered the pond beneath the surface of the water.

        A: No. The prior use is no longer apparent to the purchaser of the burdened land. A has no notice that the land she is purchasing has been used for the benefit of O's retained land.

    c.   Rediscuss part (b) on the assumption that access to the ditch was provided by manhole covers which were visible on Blackacre.

        A: Yes. A should have inspected the land. If she did, she should have seen the manhole covers and investigated their purpose. That O used Blackacre to drain Whiteacre is sufficiently apparent.

        This answer might lead you to reevaluate the answer to part (b). A, after all, may well have seen the open ditch around Whiteacre. If she did, shouldn't she have wondered how the water in the ditch drained from Blackacre? Some courts would say she should have. The difference between part (b) and this part, however, is that the facts that would put A on notice are located on the land that she is purchasing.

    d.   Rediscuss part (c) on the assumption that it was winter when O sold Blackacre to A, and snow covered the manhole covers.

        A: No. Now the facts that would put A on notice are not readily discoverable by a reasonable inspection of the land she is purchasing.

    e.   Rediscuss part (c) on the assumption that the buried pipe entered the pond above the surface of the water.

        A: Yes. The open pipe, poised above the lake, is readily apparent. It may not be much to see; but courts do not require very much to find that a purchaser had notice of a prior use of their property benefiting land that the grantor retained.

Q17: O owns two adjacent parcels of land—Blackacre and Whiteacre. Although a public road is adjacent to Blackacre, some years ago O built a gravel road across Whiteacre connecting Blackacre to another public road. Her reason for doing this was that the road adjacent to Blackacre is not kept clear of snow during the winter; the road adjacent to Whiteacre is. O used the driveway for access to Blackacre during the winter.

    Now O has sold Blackacre to A.

    a.   Does A have an easement implied from prior use across Whiteacre?

        A: Yes. All the elements for an easement from prior use are present. There is necessity during the winter when the road is effectively closed. Even though the driveway is used only during the winter, it is used continuously enough to satisfy the element that prior use be apparent, continuous and permanent. The driveway is used continuously in the sense that the use is appropriate to the need for it—it is used continuously during the winter.

(Matthew Bender & Co., Inc.)

b. May the easement be used during the summer?

A: No. The prior use was limited to the winter. The prior use burdened Whiteacre by a quasi-easement that authorized winter use only. The driveway easement is not a general right of way; it is a partial right of way limited to winter use.

The law of implied easements is complicated further by the rise of an alternate approach to the entire area. In the 1940s, the Restatement (First) adopted the position, which has had some influence on the courts, that there is only one kind of implied easement: an easement implied from the circumstances surrounding a conveyance. If easements are implied from the presumed intent of the parties, Restatement (First) § 474 argued, then courts must consider all the circumstances of a transaction. No particular consideration can be allowed to be decisive. Implied easements are inferred not from blackletter elements, but from a consideration and weighing of all relevant factors. Restatement (Third) § 2.11 carries forward this approach.

In detailing this conception, Restatement (First) § 476 listed eight factors it thought usually deserved consideration. They were: (a) whether the claimant is the conveyor or the conveyee; (b) the terms of the conveyance; (c) the consideration given for the property; (d) whether the claim is made against a simultaneous conveyee; (e) the extent of the necessity of the easement to the claimant; (f) whether reciprocal benefits result to the conveyor and to the conveyee; (g) the manner in which the land was used prior to its conveyance; (h) the extent to which the manner of prior use was or might have been known to the parties. These factors were not meant to be exhaustive. They were a listing of circumstances thought to recur frequently and be persuasive in implied easement controversies. See also Restatement (Third) §§ 2.12, 2.15.

The first and third Restatements' approach to implied easements differ in two important respects. The first is that the Restatement (First) § 476 com. (c) says it is proper to resolve doubts more readily in favor of grantees because "the grantor controls. . .the language of the conveyance. . .and has the power to make the language express the intention of the parties." In contrast, Restatement (Third) § 2.12 com. (a) advocates similar treatment of grantors and grantees except when the grantor "should have known of the need to continue the prior use, and it would be unfair to burden the grantee with the consequences of the grantor's neglect." In this circumstance, the Restatement (Third) says "the court may refuse to imply a servitude in favor of the grantor, even though it would have implied the servitude in favor of the grantee."

The second important difference between the first and third Restatements' approach to implied easements follows from the Restatement (Third)'s unification of servitude law. The traditional common law developed a unique doctrine for implying running covenants based on a "common scheme." This doctrine is discussed § 2.03[B][2][a], below. Under the traditional common law, this doctrine did not apply to easement. Under the Restatement (Third)'s unified approach to servitude law, easements may be implied from a common scheme. Similarly, under traditional common law, running covenants were not implied by necessity or prior use. Under the Restatement (Third), these doctrines extend to implying running covenants. See Restatement (Third) §§ 2.11, 2.12, 2.14.

Thus, the law of implied easements is rife with difficulty. Some of it stems from the multiplicity of approaches. But even when the approach is settled, further difficulty follows from the doctrine's inherent vagueness. The elements of the traditional approach clearly require clarification, clarification that can come only through concrete application. The meaning and weight of the first and third Restatements' factors similarly require clarification that, again, can come only from concrete application. Finally, difficulties arise from the interplay between the doctrine's conflicting conceptual bases in the parties' presumed intent and the policy favoring land utilization.

The Problems that follow are intended to further your understanding of, and facility with, the traditional and the Restatements' approaches to implied easements. The Problems analyze the application of the traditional doctrine's elements, and the Restatement's factors, in a variety of factual situations.

For further reading on Implied Easements, see CSW §§ 8.4–8.5; 4 Powell §§ 34.07–34.08; Restatement (First) §§ 474–6; Restatement (Third) §§ 2.11–2.12, 2.15.

[C] Review Problems

PROBLEM 5

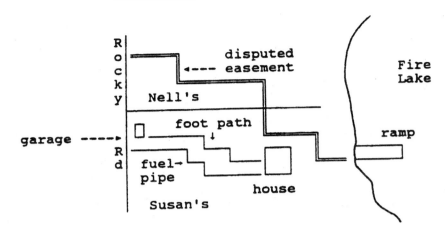

Four years ago, Susan Sailor bought a parcel of land bounded on the west by Rocky Road, and on the east by Fire Lake. From the road, the north half of the property gracefully slopes down to the lake; the south half descends more steeply. For most of the property, vehicular access to Rocky Road is over a gravel driveway that transits the north half of the property before ending on the south half. This was of no consequence until last year, when Susan sold the north half to Nell Neighbor. The deed did not reserve to Susan an easement over the driveway. Shortly after taking possession of her parcel, Nell forbade Susan to use the driveway. Susan sued, claiming an implied right of way.

At trial, Susan supported her claim by establishing, in addition to the facts mentioned above, that the first summer she owned the property, she built the gravel driveway and a boat launching ramp. The launching ramp is on the south half. The driveway runs by her house on the south half on its way to the launching ramp. During the time she owned both parcels, she frequently used the driveway to move boats on and off her land, to and from the launching ramp. Susan is an avid sailor. During the May to October sailing season she regularly sails on Fire Lake. She also sails for pleasure and in regattas on other lakes. She stores her boats off the land during the winter. Moving the boats to and from other lakes, and to and from storage, requires use of the driveway.

Susan also established that delivery and service vehicles used the driveway during the time she owned both parcels; that her house was winterized; and that she came there throughout the year for rest and recreation. Her retained land has a value of $40,000. Due to the slope, constructing a usable driveway, entirely on her retained land, would cost $10,000.

To rebut Susan's claim, Nell established that Susan usually did not use the driveway for personal access. Susan's predecessor in interest built the house on the south half because of the prospect. Since he used the property solely as an occasional summer retreat, he satisfied his access requirements by building a garage and parking area on the south half, just off Rocky Road, before the steep slope begins. He connected the garage to the house by a footpath down the slope. Susan continued his practice of parking at the garage and walking down the slope to the house when she needed personal access.

In addition, Nell established that the driveway is not used to fuel the house. The house uses oil heat that is supplied through a pipe that has an outlet off the highway, next to the garage. Nell also established that the driveway is not used for service and delivery vehicles all year. During the winter months, Susan never plowed the driveway, and snow frequently accumulated to such depths that vehicular access was impossible. Finally, Nell established that there are public boat launching and storage facilities located elsewhere on Fire Lake.

Based upon these facts:

a. Prior to the conveyance of the north parcel to Nell, was Susan's use of the driveway "apparent, continuous, and permanent"?

b. Is Susan's future use of the driveway "strictly necessary" to the enjoyment of the south parcel?

c. Is Susan's future use of the driveway "reasonably necessary" to the enjoyment of the south parcel?

d. In jurisdictions requiring strict necessity, does Susan have a driveway easement implied by prior use over Nell's land?

e. In jurisdictions requiring reasonable necessity, does Susan have a driveway easement implied by prior use over Nell's land?

f. In jurisdictions adhering to the first and third Restatements' approach, does Susan have a driveway easement implied by prior use over Nell's land?

g. If Susan had sold the southern half of her land to Nell, and then had prohibited Nell's use of the driveway, how, if at all, would the analysis of whether Nell had an easement implied from prior use differ from the analysis in parts (e) and (f)? (In parts (e) and (f) Susan sold the northern half of her land and then Nell had prohibited Susan's use of the driveway.)

ANALYSIS

a. Yes, for some uses; no, for others. The driveway crossing the north parcel is easily observable. It is apparent. The issue, however, is whether the driveway was used continuously and permanently; and if it was, whether it was used for general access or only for particular types of access.

The facts are clear that Susan's use of the driveway for general ingress and egress was not sufficiently permanent and continuous. In a sense, Susan's use of the driveway was not continuous for any purpose. Susan's use of the driveway for personal access was sporadic throughout the year. Her use for delivery and service vehicles was limited to months when it did not snow. Her use for moving boats was limited to the summer months.

Nonetheless, the function of the requirement that the use be permanent and continuous is to support the inference that the parties fairly understood and expected that a prior use would continue after severance. Courts tend to construe that understanding and expectation narrowly. Implied easements are not favored on the general policy grounds that they undercut the Statute of Frauds and the Recording Acts; moreover, they encumber the fee owner's use of her land. Courts especially tend to construe them narrowly when grantors attempt to obtain them, on the grounds that the grantor should not derogate from her grant, and that she controls the language with which a deed is written.

For these reasons, Susan's prior use was insufficiently permanent and continuous with regard to a personal right of access. However, Susan's use was sufficiently permanent and continuous with regard to the movement of the boats. Even though her use was not continuous throughout the year, it was continuous throughout the summer, the time during which the use was appropriate. Whether Susan's use of the driveway for deliveries was sufficiently permanent and continuous could go either way. It would be helpful to have more evidence on the difficulty of carrying deliveries down the footpath. Of course, since Susan has the burden of proof, any feeling that more evidence is needed intimates that the decision should not be in her favor.

b. No, Susan does not have a strict necessity to use the driveway for any purpose. Susan clearly has no necessity to use the driveway for personal access. The fact that she leaves the driveway unplowed during the winter is strong evidence that it is not that necessary for service and delivery vehicles. It may be convenient; but were it necessary she would keep the driveway clear during the winter.

Whether Susan has a strict necessity to use the driveway for the movement of her boats is a close case. Spending $10,000 to construct a driveway on a $40,000 lot is a significant expense. Nonetheless, it may not be sufficiently onerous given the relative unimportance to most people of the use desired (moving boats). The purpose of strict necessity is to allow the lot to be useful, not useful for every purpose.

In addition, Susan has not rebutted Nell's evidence that there are other boat launching and storage facilities on Fire Lake. Strict necessity is a stringent standard, and Susan has the burden of persuasion that for her to continue her boating activities there is no practicable alternative to implying an easement.

c. Regarding use for personal access, the facts do not meet even the weaker standard of reasonable necessity. But there does seem to be a reasonable need for a right of way for Susan's boats, and perhaps even for delivery and service vehicles. In some jurisdictions, the standard of reasonable necessity means no more than that it is convenient to the enjoyment of the benefited land, i.e., that the easement adds value to the dominant land. In these jurisdictions, Susan clearly has a reasonable need for the easement for delivery and service vehicles, and for boat moving. But in other jurisdictions the standard of reasonable necessity is more stringent. It means that a substitute cannot be furnished by reasonable labor and expense. In these jurisdictions, Susan might not be able to claim a reasonable need for the driveway.

In particular, with regard to the movement of boats, it is true that spending $10,000 to construct a driveway on a $40,000 lot may support a finding that a substitute cannot be furnished by reasonable labor and expense. But, as in part (b), Susan would be hurt by her failure to respond to Nell's evidence that there are alternative means of boat launching and storage. Without that evidence, it is impossible to determine if a reasonable substitute allowing Susan to boat on Fire Lake and other lakes could be obtained at reasonable cost. Thus, Susan may not have created a sufficient record even in jurisdictions that adhere to the more stringent version of the reasonable necessity standard.

d. No. According to the analysis in part (b) the facts do not meet the standard of strict necessity for any purpose.

Even if there were a strict necessity, two additional points should be borne in mind. Strict necessity is but one of four elements required before a court will imply an easement from prior use. Two elements, that (1) land in common ownership is (2) severed into two or more parcels with separate ownership, are clearly met here. The third, that before the severance part of the land was apparently, continuously and permanently used for the benefit of another part is not necessarily met. According to the answer in part (a), this element is met for some uses and not for others. Thus even if strict necessity were present, an easement implied from prior use could not be made out for the uses that were not apparent, continuous, and permanent before the severance.

The other point to bear in mind is that occasionally you may see a judicial opinion saying that a grantor should never be allowed to obtain an implied easement by prior use. Some judges still give voice to the old maxim that prohibits a grantor from derogating from her grant. Nonetheless, probably no jurisdiction takes such an absolutist view today. The jurisdictions are divided over whether the grantor must establish a strict or a reasonable necessity for the easement, but most, if not all, jurisdictions have no absolute bar to allowing a grantor to obtain such an easement. The strictest standard in force today for grantors is strict necessity.

e. Assuming that the other elements are met, an easement implied from prior use would be established in jurisdictions requiring only reasonable necessity. But the easement would not authorize general access to the south parcel.

The answer to part (c) concluded that there may be a reasonable necessity for continued use of the driveway for some uses. According to the analysis in part (c), Susan could not use the driveway for personal access. But she could use the driveway to move her boats, and perhaps, for access by delivery and service vehicles.

Of course, as was discussed in the answer to part (c), the jurisdictions adhering to the reasonable necessity standard differ among themselves regarding the stringency of the reasonable necessary standard. The different standards of reasonable necessity matter in this Problem. The outcomes in "reasonable necessity" jurisdictions might very well vary.

f. Yes, an easement implied from prior use would be established, but not for all uses. The easement would be limited to the movement of boats, and service and delivery vehicles at most. Thus, the result under the first and third Restatements would be similar to the result in jurisdictions requiring reasonable necessity. But, on the facts of this Problem, Susan would have an easier time making out her claim if the Restatement's approach were adopted.

The Restatement's approach does not divide the implication of an easements into various elements that function as independent hurdles. The Restatements weigh each persuasive fact. See Restatement (First) § 476; Restatement (Third) § 2.12. In general, the Restatement (First) says that courts should impose more stringent requirements on grantors. It argues that grantors, to a greater extent than grantees, "control both the language of the conveyance and the circumstances under which it is made." Restatement (First) § 476 com. (c). But, the Restatement (First) does not specify how much the scales of justice should be weighted against the grantor. Restatement (Third) § 2.12 com. (a) goes even further, saying

> Ordinarily, servitudes are implied in favor of the grantor as readily as in favor of the grantee. . .. However, the cases where the grantor should have know of the need to reserve a servitude to continue the prior use, and it would be unfair to burden the grantee with the consequences of the grantor's neglect, the court may refuse to imply a servitude in favor of the grantor, even though it would have implied the servitude in favor of the grantee.

In this case, under the approach of either Restatement, one has to weigh the degree to which Nell knew of Susan's prior use against the convenience for its continuation. Unlike the traditional approach, one can argue directly—assuming Nell had certain knowledge of Susan's avocation—that Nell's knowledge of it and of the driveway greatly lessens Susan's need to prove necessity. Given Nell's knowledge, and therefore, Nell's imputed expectation, all Susan needs to show is mere convenience.

g. Now Nell is attempting to establish an easement by prior use. Nell is a grantee. Under both the traditional and the Restatement's approaches, Nell has an easier case. However, under the traditional approach, the only element for which the analysis might change is the element of necessity.

Most, if not all, courts would hold that Nell need only establish a reasonable necessity. More courts would uphold her claim if it were merely convenient to her beneficial use. Given Susan's prior use, it is doubtful any jurisdiction would deny Nell the right to use the driveway for moving boats, if she has any. She even has a good case for use by delivery and service vehicles. This conclusion might depend specifically on whether she knew the driveway was not plowed during the winter. If she knew only of the summer use, she might reasonably have expected that the driveway was used by those vehicles throughout the year. In short, Nell is not bound by Susan's precise prior use. But the flexibility is affected by whether the underlying focus is on the grantor's presumed intention or the grantee's reasonable expectation. In any event, given the patent placement of the garage and footpath, it still would be unlikely that Nell would be able to establish a general right of access.

(On the general issue of the differential treatment of grantors and grantees, I tend not to accept the reasons usually given for it that were stated above. Grantors do not necessarily control the wording of their deed, nor understand it any better than grantees. See Problem 1, § 1.02[C], above. However, I do think that the grantor is, as a general matter, more intimately acquainted with the land; how it has been and can be used; and what appurtenant rights the land needs for those uses. For this reason, the grantor is in a better position to know what should be in the deed to protect her present and future use of the property. It is, therefore, less likely that an omission by the grantor was an innocent oversight. In sum, I approve differential treatment of grantors and grantees in these cases, but for the reason given by the <u>Restatement (Third)</u>. The issue is not control of the deed's language, as stated by tradition and the <u>Restatement (First)</u>, but knowledge of land-use.)

PROBLEM 6

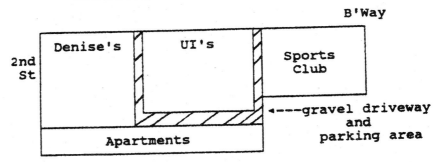

Part 1

Some years ago, Urban Investors (UI), a limited partnership, purchased a parcel of land in Pleasantville, bounded on the west by 2nd Street, on the south by a rental apartment complex, on the east by a sports club, and on the north by Broadway. The parcel is rectangular, 400 feet by 900 feet, with the longer frontage on Broadway.

Five years ago, UI developed a supermarket, fronting on Broadway, on the parcel's easternmost 300 feet. UI constructed a parking area on the first 200 feet in from Broadway, and the market building on the next 150 feet. UI paved the last 50 feet but left it open. The rear area was designed for deliveries, trash pickup and utility hookups. Access to the rear is over a gravel driveway, 15 feet wide, running along the west and east edge of the parking lot and market building.

Last year UI sold the rest of its parcel to Denise Developer. When Denise was contemplating the purchase, she surveyed the property UI was offering. A month after closing, Denise informed UI that its western driveway was located on land she now owned. Denise ordered UI to cease using it. UI immediately went to court to establish its rights to use the land for driveway purposes.

Both parties agree that the western driveway is located on land UI's deed conveyed to Denise. Both parties agree that UI did not reserve an express easement over that land.

a. In jurisdictions requiring strict necessity, does UI have an easement implied from prior use?

b. In jurisdictions requiring reasonable necessity, does UI have an easement implied from prior use?

c. In jurisdictions adhering to the first and third <u>Restatements</u>' approach, does UI have an easement implied from prior use?

Part 2

In addition to the above facts, UI establishes the following at trial:

Since the supermarket opened, deliveries have been made through the rear, and the traffic pattern has been to approach the rear area through the east driveway and depart through the west. The reason for taking deliveries through the rear is simple: that is where the loading dock and facilities for storing items and preparing them for sale are located.

Accepting deliveries through the front of the store would require a number of changes. Many deliveries are made on pallets that forklifts carry through the loading dock's extra wide doors. None of the building's front doors are wide enough to accommodate the pallets. Were one door to be widened, then one or two shopping aisles would have to be set aside for forklift traffic. An alternative, of course, would be to break down the pallet deliveries outside the building. But that would require a good deal of extra work.

The reason for the two driveway traffic pattern is that an average of 20 trucks a day make deliveries; five of them are semi-trailers. The width of the rear area is 1 and 1/2 trailer lengths. If no other trucks are in the rear area, it is possible to turn a semi-trailer. around with a good deal of jockeying. If other trucks are present it is impossible. Delivery trucks follow no set schedule. They overlap, and at times as many as 5 delivery trucks are in the rear and east driveway.

    d. In jurisdictions requiring strict necessity, does UI have an easement implied from prior use?

    e. In jurisdictions requiring reasonable necessity, does UI have an easement implied from prior use?

    f. In jurisdictions adhering to the first and third Restatements' approach, does UI have an easement implied from prior use?

ANALYSIS

a.   No. All the elements for an easement implied by prior use are present except strict necessity. UI has the burden of establishing sufficient necessity. The facts state that UI has a driveway on the east as well as on the west. There is no showing that the east driveway is insufficient to support the beneficial use of UI's land.

b.   No. Again, all the elements for an easement implied by prior use are present except reasonable necessity. UI has the burden of establishing sufficient necessity. Since UI has two driveways, there is no showing that the driveway on the west is more than just a mere convenience and that a material part of the value of the UI's parcel depends upon it.

c.   No. All the factors which Restatement (First) § 476 and Restatement (Third) § 2.12 deem important in determining whether easement should be implied from prior use are present, except the factor of necessity. Restatement (First) states that prior use alone does not justify the "implication of a corresponding easement unless some necessity for the continuance of the use exists." Id. at § 476 com. (i). The Restatement (First) says that prior use, and the extent to which that use is known to the other party are important factors "strengthening" the inference that an easement was intended by the parties. Apparent and continuous prior use reduces the degree of necessity required to infer an easement. But, prior use alone is insufficient. Restatement (Third) § 2.12 illus. (7) implies a similar stance by denying an easement where the prior use is not reasonably necessary to the full utilization of the dominant property.

    (Consider, as an alternative, the doctrine of reformation of deed. There may be a mistake by UI that Denise inequitably took advantage of. We will not investigate that doctrine.)

d.   Possibly. These additional facts put into the record facts upon which a finding of strict necessity might be predicated.

    Of course, UI has not established the cost of building larger doors in the front of the store. Similarly, UI has not detailed the consequences of having delivery trucks wait in the parking area when one semi-trailer enters the rear area. In this sense UI is like Susan in Problem 5, above. Recall that Susan failed to establish the inconvenience of storing and launching her boats other than from her land. But even if the doors could be constructed at minimal expense, the cost or inconvenience of frequently running forklifts down a shopping aisle should speak for itself. Permanently closing off a shopping aisle indicates a good degree of cost and inconvenience. Also, the consequences of asking other delivery trucks to wait while one semi-trailer enters the rear area, unloads, and completes an arduous turning process are fairly clear.

    In short, UI's case would be stronger if the record contained direct evidence of the amount of inconvenience and cost. But unlike Susan's case, here we can draw justifiable inferences from the facts that are on the record.

    From them, it certainly is arguable that UI has a strict necessity for the easement. Strict necessity does not require absolute need; there is some flexibility in its scope. Another way of expressing the stringent standard is whether the claimed easement is required for the claimant to make effective use of the land. It is a close case whether UI meets this standard. In jurisdictions requiring strict necessity, UI is at risk for not adducing evidence on the total cost of redesigning the store or adopting a "no other truck when a semi delivers" rule. But even without direct proof, one can almost definitely conclude that UI's ability to make effective use of the property is in jeopardy.

Obviously, the additional facts make this a close case on the element of strict necessity.

e.   Yes. As discussed in the answer to part (c), even with the additional facts there still are shortcomings in the record developed by UI. But if we indulge reasonable inferences, there is little doubt but that the second driveway is reasonably necessary. The driveway adds a good deal of value to the benefited land, making its use significantly more convenient. Thus whether the standard of reasonable necessity is the material addition of value, or that a substitute cannot be furnished by reasonable labor and expense, UI has it.

f.   Yes. In contrast to the traditional approach, under the approach of the first and third Restatements, Denise's certain knowledge of UI's open prior use directly balances against the required degree of necessity. This could only help UI, and make it certain to prevail even where strict necessity is required.

PROBLEM 7

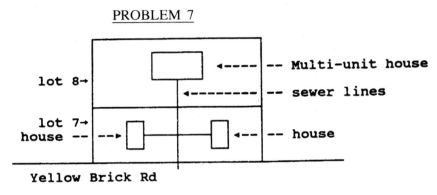

Block 12 in Emerald City is oriented in an east-west direction, and is bounded on the south by Yellow Brick Road. On block 12, lot 7 fronts on Yellow Brick Road for 100 feet and extends north for 100 feet. Lot 8 adjoins lot 7, generally on the north. But lot 8 is connected to Yellow Brick Road by a 20 foot by 100 foot strip immediately west of lot 7.

Ten years ago, Toto Terrier purchased lots 7 and 8. After purchasing the lots, Toto demolished the existing structures. She built two single-family dwellings on lot 7, one on the east half and one on the west half. Toto also repaved lot 8's 20 foot-wide strip, turning it into a driveway, and constructed a multi-unit house on the bulk of the lot.

Toto ran all the buildings' water, sewer and gas lines out to Yellow Brick Road, where they joined the municipal mains. The lines were exposed in the basement of all the buildings. The lines in the house on the east half of lot 7 entered and exited in a western direction; the lines in the house on the west half of lot 7 entered and exited the house in an eastern direction; the lines in the multi-unit house on lot 8 entered and exited in a southern direction. All three lines joined a larger line that Toto placed 12 feet underground on lot 7, between the two houses. This line ran south into the mains on Yellow Brick Road.

For nine years, Toto rented the houses and the apartments in the multi-unit house. Last year Toto sold lot 8 to Cowardly Lion. This year, when lot 7's plumbing backed up, Toto decided to terminate lot 8's use of the lines under her land. When she informed Cowardly Lion of her plans, he made a feasibility study of running new pipes out to Yellow Brick Road under his driveway. His study showed it would cost $15,000. In light of this, Cowardly Lion exercised his new found courage and sued Toto, claiming an easement implied from prior use.

a. Is Toto's prior use of lot 7 for the benefit of lot 8 sufficiently "apparent" to support the implication of an easement?

b. Rediscuss part (a) on the assumption that Toto sold Cowardly Lion lot 7 (instead of lot 8), and a year later, when Cowardly Lion discovered that lot 8's pipes ran under his land, he decided to disconnect them.

ANALYSIS

a. Yes. In the traditional approach to implying easements from prior use, one of the elements is that the prior use must be apparent; in the approach of the first and third Restatements, it is a factor. Usually this element or factor is applied without difficulty. Prior uses often leave physical marks upon the servient premises that are readily visible by casual observation. As discovery becomes more difficult, so does the application of this element or factor. Underground uses are the most frequent fact pattern giving rise to difficult cases—many of which turn on their particular facts as viewed through the prism of the jurisdiction's policy on implied easements.

Prior uses that are not casually observable, even underground uses, may be sufficiently apparent because apparent does not mean visible. Courts and commentators agree that apparent means known or capable of being known, i.e., discoverable through a careful inspection of the premises by someone conversant with land-use patterns and construction techniques.

Were the underground utility lines apparent to Toto? Clearly so; having built them she knew, or should have known, their location. Were the utility lines apparent to Cowardly Lion? That depends upon the function that this element or factor serves.

If this requirement served the function of fairness, i.e., of providing the burdened party with notice of the encumbrance on her title, Cowardly Lion's knowledge would be irrelevant. Cowardly Lion could ground his easement on Toto's knowledge. If this requirement was part of a doctrine focused on promoting the efficient utilization of land, Toto's knowledge would again seem sufficient.

But most courts, commentators and the Restatement (First) say that this requirement (and the doctrine of which it is a part) serves the function of construing the intent of the parties to the transaction. Toto's knowledge allows a court to infer her intent and expectation to convey an easement. But what evidence is there that Cowardly Lion expected, and thus intended, to receive the easement?

Most, if not all, courts would accept the argument that Cowardly Lion intended and expected to receive an easement burdening lot 7 from the fact that he knew or could have known that the utility lines in his basement entered and exited in a southern direction. Undoubtedly, acceptance of this argument seems a facade for a policy determination favoring fairness or efficient land utilization. But courts and commentators have attempted to forge some legitimate connection between this argument and an "intent of the parties" rationale. Cowardly Lion, they would say, knows that his utility lines go somewhere. He may not know where specifically, but he knows that the building receives service and he presumably intends and expects to receive all the rights that make that service possible. Cowardly Lion has a general intent to accept an easement, not a specific intent to accept a particular one. For these reasons, the Restatement (Third) § 2.12 advocates implying an easement for underground utility lines without regard to whether they are apparent.

b. Yes, in some jurisdictions; no, in others. Now the situation of the parties is reversed. Toto, the grantor, is attempting to claim an implied easement. Considerations of fairness and notice to the burdened party are dramatically different. Cowardly Lion is the burdened party, and unlike when Toto (the builder-grantor) was the burdened party, he may be unfairly surprised.

Nonetheless, the overall issue remains the same as in part (a); but this time the question is whether there are facts that reasonably might have alerted Cowardly Lion to the prior use, and from which we can infer that he expected an easement to be reserved in favor of lot 8. The information that he reasonably may be expected to have is that the utility lines from the two houses point toward a pipe running between the houses. Is that enough to alert him to the possibility that another line runs down from lot 8?

Courts split over the inference they draw from these facts. Some courts apply the argument that worked in favor of Cowardly Lion in part (a) against him in part (b). The mere fact that a Cowardly Lion knew the buildings he was purchasing had modern utilities that must connect with larger mains is sufficient to alert him to the possibility that lines from other lots run under his land. Other courts would not accept this inference. The Restatement (First) § 476 com. (h), illus. 10 enigmatically indicates that if Cowardly Lion "had reasonable opportunity" to learn the facts a holding that an easement by prior use was created "is proper." The Restatement (Third) § 2.12 com. (g) simplifies the argument by saying forthrightly: "Parties buying and selling developed land expect existing utility arrangements to be part of the package."

You might think it proper to give some benefit to Cowardly Lion in that he purchased from a grantor-builder who had actual knowledge of the placement of the pipes yet did not inform her grantee. Yet, in jurisdictions that employ the traditional approach this consideration is irrelevant. Under the traditional approach, the stringency (or looseness) of the element that the prior use be apparent remains unchanged. The only element that is different in implied grant and implied reservation cases is the element of necessity.

This consideration is relevant, however, in jurisdictions that employ the first and third Restatements' approach. Restatement (First) § 476 com. (b) says that its listing and discussion of factors is illustrative and not exhaustive. Under the first and third Restatements' approach, every case should be plumbed for its own persuasive factors.

PROBLEM 8

Part 1

Twenty years ago, Vista Development Co. (VD) purchased 60 acres of land on a bluff overlooking the Big Muddy River Valley. The parcel included not only the land on the top of the bluff, but the face of the bluff as well. At the time, the area was undeveloped. Aside from agricultural uses, the only development was the BMRV Electric Co.'s (BMRVE) high power transmission lines that ran along the base of the bluff. VD warehoused the land, anticipating future demand for second homesites.

Ten years ago, VD, facing financial reverses, sold half of its land on the top of the bluff to Ridge Townhomes Development Co. (RTD) for $500,000. After the sale, RTD contacted BMRVE to establish electrical service. BMRVE informed RTD that for $20,000 it could place a transformer just off the high power lines at the foot of the bluff and run wires up its face to RTD's property. Establishing service from the next most convenient point would cost $60,000.

RTD had not purchased the face of the bluff. When VD demanded $10,000 for the right of way, RTD sued, claiming it had an implied easement for its electrical lines.

a. Was there a sufficiently "apparent, continuous and permanent" prior use of the bluff for the benefit of the parcel sold to RTD to support the implication of an easement from prior use?

Part 2

Four years later, VD filed a plat subdividing its remaining land on the top of the bluff into 15 spacious lots, each with a gorgeous vista overlooking the valley. Over the succeeding five years, VD sold nine of the lots. The lot purchasers were able to establish electrical service at minimum cost because VD allowed BMRVE to run wires up the face of the bluff to them.

Last year, the nine lot owners became concerned that VD planned to subdivide and sell the bluff face. Demand for homesites had increased to the point where the extra cost of cantilevered construction was justified. As development of the bluff face would detract from their view, the lot owners purchased it for themselves.

This year, VD sold another of the bluff top lots to Alice Andrews. The purchase price was $50,000. After closing, Alice contacted BMRVE to establish electrical service. BMRVE said that given existing facilities, service from the transmission lines at the foot of the bluff could be established for $100; service from another point would cost $2,000. At about that time, the neighboring lot owners informed Alice that they would not allow her to run a line up the face of the bluff, unless she agreed to pay a share of the property's cost.

Alice refused their demand, and sued to established an implied right of way for her electrical lines.

b. Was there a sufficiently "apparent, continuous and permanent" prior use of the bluff face for the benefit of the parcel sold to Alice to support the implication of an easement from prior use?

ANALYSIS

a. No. Prior to the sale to RTD, VD did not make use of face of the bluff for the benefit of the land that RTD purchased on the top. BMRVE's high power transmission line is apparent. It is temptingly close. RTD may have wished or hoped, or even expected to connect to it. But the mere existence BMRVE's high power transmission line does not mean that the land that separates it from RTD's parcel was used as a quasi-servient estate for the benefit of the parcel that RTD purchased. Clearly, the bluff face was not so used.

b. Yes. The additional facts are sufficient to support a finding that prior to Alice's purchase there was an "apparent, continuous and permanent" use of the face of the bluff for the benefit of the lot she purchased. It is true that the face of the bluff has not been used for the benefit of the very parcel that Alice bought. It is also true that VD never used the bluff for the benefit of land at the top of the bluff as long as the land was in VD's ownership. Each prior use of the bluff face was initiated after VD sold the land benefiting from the use.

But this is too narrow a focus. The requirement of apparent prior use serves the function of indicating the understanding and intent of the burdened and benefited parties to create an easement when the land is severed. Authorities say that the requirement of continuous and permanent prior use serves the function of supporting the specific understanding and intent that the prior use should continue after severance.

Before the neighbors purchased the face of the bluff, VD, on nine occasions—every occasion it had—had allowed the bluff face to be used for the benefit of the lot it sold. VD's actions support an inference that should the occasion arise, it intended to establish a similar burden on the bluff for the benefit of all the land it owned at the top of the bluff. The neighbors clearly knew of VD's course of conduct; they had clear notice that VD intended to reserve easements in favor of the land it retained (after the sale of the bluff face) to be asserted when the occasion arose.

In other words, when VD sold the bluff face to the neighbors, it impliedly reserved an easement down the bluff face for the benefit of its retained land. Part of that land passed to Alice; she has all VD's appurtenant rights.

[D] Recapitulation

1. Implied easements are easements which are not sufficiently expressed in documents that satisfy the Statute of Frauds or the other requirements for the transfer of real property interests.

2. Courts say they imply easements based upon the presumed intent of the parties. Commentators suggest that courts also are motivated by a concern for efficient land utilization.

3. The law of implied easements has two distinct branches: easements implied by necessity and easements implied from prior use.

4. Easements are implied by necessity when (a) land in common ownership, (b) is severed into two or more parcels with separate ownership, (c) and the severance creates the necessity for the easement.

5. Easements are implied from prior use when (a) land in common ownership, (b) is severed into two or more parcels with separate ownership, (c) and before the severance part of the land was

apparently, continuously and permanently used for the benefit of another part, (d) and continuation of the use is necessary for the enjoyment of the benefited part.

6. Courts differ over the standard of necessity required to imply an easement. Some courts require a "strict" necessity; other courts require only a "reasonable" necessity. An easement is strictly necessary when the land is nearly useless without it. An easement is reasonably necessary, in some jurisdictions, when a substitute for the easement cannot be furnished by reasonable labor and expense. But in other jurisdictions the standard of reasonable necessity is even less stringent, requiring only that the easement is convenient to the enjoyment of the benefited land.

7. Restatement (First) § 474, in a departure from tradition, proposes a single category of implied easement: "an easement implied from the circumstances surrounding the transaction." Restatement (First) § 476 discusses eight factors that frequently arise in implied easement disputes, but the Restatement (First) also urges the consideration and weighing of all persuasive evidence in determining whether or not to imply an easement. Restatement (Third) §§ 2.11–2.12, 2.15 carries forward and refines this factor-based approach.

§ 1.04 SCOPE

[A] Definitions

SCOPE: The scope of an easement refers to the uses the easement owner may make of the servient land, and the restraint upon the fee owner's use the easement owner may insist upon, due to her ownership of the easement. Because scope determines the limits of an easement's use, the scope of an easement is also known as its "extent."

SURCHARGE: Most frequently, the term "surcharge" describes using an easement in a manner that is authorized, but to an extent that is unduly intense. Occasionally, "surcharge" describes using an easement in a manner that is unauthorized.

UNDEFINED EASEMENT: An undefined easement is an easement whose location on the servient land is not yet specified.

[B] Discussion and Questions

Easements are acquired for a great variety of purposes; questions and conflicts over their scope are equally as diverse. Accordingly, the legal doctrine by which disputes over an easement's scope are analyzed and resolved can be stated only in general form.

Except for prescriptive easements, easements are volitional interests. Their scope is governed by the intent of the parties. In other words, the transaction which creates the easement also fixes its scope. Determination of the extent of express easements focuses on the wording of the deed. Determination of the extent of easements implied from prior use or necessity focuses on the prior use or necessity from which the courts inferred the parties' intent to create the easement. Obviously, construction of the parties' intent may be difficult and somewhat artificial.

In determining an easement's scope, questions or controversies involving matters that are clearly covered by the deed, prior use or necessity that created the easement may be resolved easily. Unfortunately, the deed, prior use or necessity that created the easement frequently does not precisely cover the question or controversy at hand. Deeds creating easements are often vague or incomplete; inferences from prior use or necessity are no more precise than the frequently ambiguous circumstances surrounding the transaction. In such cases the parties' intent is uncertain and must be construed.

When the deed, prior use or necessity does not directly address the issue at hand, courts construe the parties' intent through a balancing approach. Courts understand that both the easement and the fee owner have rights to use the servient land. They acknowledge that the rights of the easement owner may not be abridged or denied. But the easement holder, courts point out, is not a fee owner; she may not exercise all of the rights that literally come within the general or vague terms of the easement.

Consequently, the general doctrine is that an easement holder is entitled to a reasonable use of the servient land to support reasonable uses of the dominant land. She is not entitled to burden the servient land "materially" and "unduly." Conversely, the fee owner may make any use of the servient land that does not unduly interfere with the easement holder's use of the easement.

In other words, the easement owner's use of the servient land must be within the general authorization of the grant; and the fee owner can not interfere with a specifically granted right. But for questions and controversies beyond the clear terms of the agreement, all the guidance that doctrine gives is that "the rights of the easement owner and of the landowner are not absolute, [unrelated], and uncontrolled, but are so limited, each by the other, that there may be a due and reasonable enjoyment of both the easement and the servient estate." 25 Am. Jur.2d, Easements and Licenses 478 (1966).

In sum, the clear terms of the deed, or the clearly established prior use or necessity that created the easement governs the uses that may be made by the easement and fee owner—no matter how reasonable or capricious they may seem. But where the deed, prior use or necessity speaks ambiguously, a balancing approach that gives recognition to the reasonable needs and expectancies of both parties is adopted to govern their relationship.

Q18: A and B own two adjacent lots improved with single-family residences. A grants B "an easement of way over the most northern 6 feet of my property." After receiving this grant, B discovers that she cannot make effective use of the easement unless it is 8 feet wide.

    a.   Can B use the most northern 8 feet of A's property?

        A: No. The easement specifically limits the easement to the northern 6 feet.

    b.   Rediscuss part (a) on the assumption that A granted "an easement of way over the land immediately adjacent to the northern border of my property."

        A: Possibly. The easement is undefined. B's rights extend to all land that is reasonably necessary to accomplish the purpose of the grant. An easement 8 feet wide might be necessary.

    c.   Rediscuss part (a) on the assumption that there was no express easement in the document, but that A had always used only the northern 6 feet of her property for access to the parcel she sold to B, and the land bearing the effects of this use was no more than 6 feet wide.

        A: No. The prior use of the land that is subject to the easement was limited to an easement of way 6 feet in width. That is all the use A made, and needed to make, of the land that she retained for the benefit of the land she sold. Accordingly, an easement 6 feet in width is all that B had reason to expect was implicitly conveyed to her.

Some commentators say that the inherently flexible "reasonable use" approach to resolving conflicts over the scope of easements is designed and used by the courts to promote economically efficient and productive land-use by maximizing the different interests of the fee and easement owners and minimizing their conflicts. But the courts say that the parties to the agreement, whether the agreement is express or implied, presumably intended to allow themselves reasonable rights of use, rights that allow both of them to benefit from the land subject to the easement.

Whatever the ultimate policy basis, in controversies over the scope of easements, the rights of the parties are absolute where the deed, prior use or necessity is clear. Within the constraints of public policy, the parties may fashion their relationship as they see fit. But where the deed, prior use or necessity is unclear, the rights of the parties are not absolute; they are correlative. As some courts and commentators say, neither the easement owner nor the fee owner is entitled to unlimited use of the servient land; each is entitled to unlimited reasonable use.

Although controversies over the scope of easements are as diverse as the purposes for which easements are acquired (multiplied, perhaps, by the failure to anticipate and resolve them clearly in the deed), many questions and conflicts fall into three broad categories. The character and intensity of the easement or fee owner's use of the land subject to the easement is a frequent cause of conflict. Maintenance and repair obligations are also a fertile source of controversy. The third broad category of frequent questions and conflicts involves the location of easements that are not specifically situated by the conveyances creating them.

Character and Intensity of the Use of the Servient Land

Q19: A and B own adjacent lots, which are improved with single-family dwellings. A grants B an easement of way across the northern 20 feet of her property.

a.   Can B use the northern 20 feet of A's property

1. for access to B's property by motor vehicle?

A: Yes. An easement owner may use the easement for all purposes that come within the specific terms of the grant; and for all uses that reasonably come within the general terms of the grant.

Access by motor vehicle is not specifically mentioned in the grant; but in contemporary society it is a reasonable means of access. A court would hold it to be among the means of access intended by the parties.

It is possible that the parties intended only a footpath. But that is unusual in contemporary society and the limitation is not normally contemplated in a general grant of an right of way.

2. for a shuffle-board court?

A: No. Use of the servient land as a game court of any kind is not reasonably within the terms of a general grant of a right of way.

3. to park cars?

A: No. Parking and crossing are separate activities. Parking creates a permanent occupancy of the servient estate. Courts do not construe general easements of way as including rights of parking.

b.   Can A use the northern 20 feet of her property

1. for access to A's property by motor vehicle?

A: Yes. The owner of the servient estate may use her land for all purposes that do not unreasonably interfere with the easement. Using the servient land for access to her lot would not seem to interfere with B's right of access.

2. for a shuffle-board court?

A: Yes. In the typical residential setting, the frequency of the easement owner's use of a right of way would not be all that frequent. Thus the servient owner's use of the servient land as a shuffle-board court would not unduly interfere with the dominant owner's right of access. (This answer might vary if the right of access were frequently used, as in a commercial setting.)

3. to park cars?

A: Possibly. Parking cars narrows the right of way remaining to the easement owner. If the right of way were 10 feet wide, it would be clear that the easement would be totally blocked and this would unduly interfere with the dominant owner's rights. But if cars are parked along one side of a twenty foot wide easement of way, there is, in the normal situation, still sufficient room for the dominant owner to use the servient land conveniently. When there is a conflict between authorized rights of the easement owner and the residual rights of the fee owner, the rights of the easement owner are paramount. Nonetheless, in this situation, there is no conflict in convenient use.

Q20: A and B own adjacent lots that are improved with residential uses. A grants B an easement of way across the northern 20 feet of her property, giving B additional convenient access to the public road.

    a.   May B improve the easement by

        1. paving it with asphalt?

        A: Yes. The easement owner may improve the easement in a manner that is reasonably necessary to support her use if the improvement does not impose an undue burden on the servient landowner. Normally, an asphalt driveway would aid the dominant owner's use of an easement of way and impose a minimal burden on the servient landowner.

        2. building a fence along the border between the servient land and the remainder of A's lot?

        A: No. A fence may define the easement better and even make it more attractive. But it is difficult to see how the fence aids the dominant owner's use of an easement of way this wide. Moreover, the fence may interfere with the servient owner's use of the servient land. On balance, this is likely to be an unreasonable improvement that imposes an undue burden on the servient landowner.

        3. building a gate at its junction with the public road?

        A: Probably. A gate tends to prevent entry by unauthorized individuals. This is beneficial to the easement owner (as well as the servient owner). Gates can be constructed so that they are easy to manipulate. Thus a gate can be a de minimis burden on the servient landowner.

    b.   May A improve the easement by

        1. paving it with asphalt?

        A: Yes. The servient owner may make any use of the easement that does not interfere with the rights of the easement owner. Paving a right of way with asphalt, in the normal situation, would not interfere with the use by the servient owner.

        2. building a fence along the border between the servient land and the remainder of A's lot?

        A: Yes. It is hard to imagine that fencing a 20 foot wide right of way interferes with the easement owner's use of the easement. It is part of the servient owner's residual rights to use the servient land as she sees fit.

        3. building a gate at its junction with the public road?

        A: Probably. As stated in the answer to part a(3), gates tend to prevent entry unauthorized individuals. This is beneficial to the servient owner. This benefit can be achieved with de minimis inconvenience to the dominant owner. It does not unreasonably infringe upon the rights of the easement owner.

Q21: A and B own adjacent lots that are improved with single-family residences. A grants B an easement of way across the northern 20 feet of her property.

    a.   B subdivides her lot into 2 lots and sells them. Do B's grantees have the right to use the easement across A's property?

        A: Yes. This Question raises the issue of whether the use of an easement may be increased through increases in the use of the dominant estate. That the words of the grant are general does not mean, on the one hand, that any and all increases in the burden imposed on the servient estate are permitted. Nor does it mean, on the other hand, that no changes are permitted. In line with their policy to promote land utilization, courts presume that the parties contemplated evolutionary, not revolutionary, changes that are in harmony with the natural, and normal development of the dominant parcel.

        It would be hard to imagine that this change in use of the dominant parcel is not to be expected; it is also hard to imagine that the increased use of the servient land imposed an unreasonable, uncontemplated burden.

b.   B builds a highrise condominium with 500 apartments and a garage space for every apartment. B sells the apartments. Do B's grantees have the right to use of the easement across A's property?

   A: Probably not. This may well be a revolutionary change, imposing a burden on the servient landowner that was not contemplated when the easement was granted. The only factors that might prevent such a ruling are a) that highrises were typical land-uses in the area at the time the easement was granted; and b) that the increase in use of the easement is due to a change in the intensity of use of the dominant parcel (i.e., increased residential density) rather than a change in the type of use of the dominant parcel (i.e., from residential to commercial).

c.   B builds a shopping center on her parcel. It is estimated that the shopping center will attract about 500 cars a day over the easement. Do the shopping center tenants and their customers have the right to use the easement across A's property?

   A: No. Now the change in the intensity of the use of the easement is due to a change in the type of use of the dominant estate. That factor does not preclude a court from allowing the increased use. But it does make it more likely that the court will hold that it is a revolutionary change not contemplated by the parties.

d.   B remodels her residence into a combined medical office and residence. Do B and her patients have the right to use the easement across A's property?

   A: Probably. Although the change here is semi-commercial, it probably does not increase the use of the servient estate all that much. It probably is an evolutionary development of the dominant parcel, imposing only a reasonable increase in burden.

e.   Rediscuss parts (a) and (d) on the assumption that the easement said "this easement grants rights of ingress and egress for the single-family residential use of the dominant property."

   A: Now B's grantees, in part (a), do not have the right to use the easement. Neither do B's patients, in part (d). The specific terms of the grant control. The doctrine of reasonable use, the doctrine that allows reasonable increases in the use of the easement, is a judicial presumption that applies in the absence of express intent.

f.   Rediscuss parts (a) and (d) on the assumption that the easement was implied by necessity or from prior use.

   A: Easements by necessity and from prior use result from the presumed intent of the parties. The courts presume that the parties' intent included allowance of reasonable development of the property. But courts limit the scope of the reasonable development to the necessity or prior use that gave rise to the easement. In other words, the use of easements implied by necessity and from prior use have some room for development—but less than the room allowed to express easements.

   Applying these principles here, the subdivision in part (a) seems well within the scope of the original necessity or prior use that supported the creation of the easements. B's grantees would be allowed to use the easements. The combined residence and medical office use contemplated in part (d), however, is substantially different from the necessity (basic access to residential property) or prior use (access to residential property) that created the easement. It would not be allowed. This outcome is less certain for an easement implied from prior use than for an easement implied by necessity. Courts are more generous to easement holders in regard to the former than in regard to the latter.

Q22:   A and B own adjacent lots. Both lots are improved with 6 story commercial buildings. A grants B an easement across the back of A's lot to allow B a more convenient means of receiving and shipping.

a.   B builds another 6 floors onto her building, doubling her floor space. Does B have the right to use the easement across A's property for shipping and receiving from her newly constructed space?

A: Yes. The law relating to development of the dominant parcel, discussed in Q21, <u>above</u>, applies here. A doubling of floor space by adding onto the existing building is a reasonable development.

b. Instead of building up, B doubles her floor space by purchasing another adjacent lot and building a 6 story building that is fully interconnected with her original building. Does B have the right to use the easement across A's property for shipping and receiving from her newly constructed space?

A: No. Easements may not be used for the benefit of nondominant land. (But see the discussion in the analysis of Problem 10, part 4, § 1.04[C], <u>below</u>.) Benefitting nondominant land is considered a <u>per se</u> unreasonable increase in the burden on the servient land because the burden is extended to land that the parties never contemplated benefiting.

Q23: A and B own adjacent lots. Both lots are improved with 6 story commercial buildings. A grants B an easement across the back of A's lot to allow B a more convenient means of receiving and shipping. A decides to increase her floor space by building over the land subject to B's easement, turning B's easement into a tunnel-like alley. May A do this, and if so, how much headroom must A leave for B's use.

A: Yes, A may build over the land subject to the easement. Servient landowners are entitled to make any use of their land that does not interfere with rights of the dominant landowner. A must leave a reasonably sized passage for B to use. The specific height would depend upon the foreseeable height of vehicles that would be using the easement.

Q24: O, owning two adjacent lots, sells one of them to A. The lot sold to A was improved with a 6 story commercial building that was heated by a furnace burning oil heat. Although the building on the lot sold to A fronts on a public road, the only convenient access to the furnace's fuel pipe is across the back of O's lot. O had always routed fuel delivery trucks across the back of the lot that she retained. Nonetheless, no easement to use the back of O's lot was expressed in the deed from O to A.

Despite the absence of an express easement, A routes all deliveries over the back of O's lot. Because of the doctrine of easements implied from prior use, O concedes that A may use the back of her lot for fuel oil delivery purposes. However, O claims that A has no right to route other deliveries over O's property.

a. Is O's claim correct?

A: Yes, O's claim is correct. Easements implied from prior use are created due to the presumed intent of the parties. Their presumed intent is based upon the prior use of the land when still in unitary ownership. Thus the scope of the prior use determines the scope of the implied easement. O did not use the back of her retained property as an all purpose quasi-easement of way. Rather, it was used for the limited purpose of fuel delivery. Presumably, the intent of the parties was to continue the quasi-easement limited to that purpose.

b. On the assumption that A doubled her fuel oil deliveries by building another 10 floors onto her building, would A have the right to use the back of O's lot for all the fuel oil deliveries?

A: Yes. The intensity of the use authorized by easements implied from prior use may develop along with the foreseeable development of the dominant property. The parties are presumed to have intended an easement that allows reasonable changes in the use of the dominant estate.

c. On the assumption that nuclear technology progressed to the point that small furnaces could be powered safely by nuclear fuel, if A changed over to a nuclear heated furnace and still could only conveniently receive fuel over the back of O's lot, would A have the right to receive the nuclear fuel over that route?

A: Probably. The issue in this question is whether the changes in the use of the dominant estate that the easement presumably is authorized to support is limited to technologies that existed at the time the easement was created. The parties could not have anticipated the specific technology that was later developed, and thus could not have specifically authorized its support.

Nonetheless, courts rule with regard to express easements that the parties presumably intend to support modern uses. This is consonant with the policy favoring the efficient utilization of land. The same policy applies with equal force to implied easements.

Of course, this answer presumes that the delivery of nuclear fuel across O's land presents no safety hazard. If it did present a safety hazard greater than the delivery of oil fuel, then the burden on the servient land would be significantly, and perhaps unduly, changed.

Maintenance, Repair and Improvement of the Servient Land

Q25: A and B own adjacent lots that are improved with single-family residences. There is a gravel path across A's land leading from a public road to B's parcel. A never uses the path. A grants B an easement of way over the path. Due to B's heavy use of the path, it becomes rutted and pitted.

a. Is A required to restore and maintain the path?

A: No. The servient owner who does not use the servient land has no active obligations. Her responsibility is negative: to refrain from interfering with the easement owner's use of the servient land.

b. Is B required to restore and maintain the path?

A: Yes. The dominant owner has the duty of making sufficient repairs to allow the servient owner to make a reasonable use of the servient land.

c. May A restore and maintain the path? And if she does, may she charge the cost, or some share of it, to B?

A: Yes, A may restore and maintain the path. The servient owner has the privilege of restoring and maintaining the servient land. And if the servient owner—A in this case — acts after the dominant owner has neglected her maintenance obligations, she may charge all appropriate costs to the defaulting dominant owner. She may also collect all damages flowing from the dominant owner's breach of her duty.

d. May B restore and maintain the path? And if she does, may she charge the cost, or some share of it, to A?

A: Yes. Not only may B restore and maintain the servient land, but B must do so to fulfill her obligations as the easement owner. See the answer to parts (a) and (b). Accordingly, she cannot charge any of the cost to A, the fee owner.

e. May A improve the path by paving it with asphalt? And if she does, may she charge the cost, or some share of it, to B?

A: A can improve the servient land by paving it with asphalt. The fee owner may make any use of the servient land that does not unduly interfere with the easement owner's use. Improvement is a use of the servient land. It would be hard to imagine that paving the path with asphalt would interfere with B's use. (However, if such a case occurred, then A could not do it.) Indeed, paving the path is likely to benefit B.

Nonetheless, A cannot charge any of the cost of improvement to B. Even though the paving benefits B, the common law generally does not impose on nonconsenting parties the cost of elective expenditures. Improvement is an elective expenditure.

f. May B improve the path by paving it with asphalt? And if she does, may she charge the cost, wholly or partially, to A?

A: B can probably improve the servient land by paving it with asphalt. The easement owner has the privilege of making all improvements that reasonably promote the purpose of the easement, so long as the improvements do not unduly interfere with the uses the servient owner makes of the land. It is difficult to imagine that paving the road interferes with A's use of the servient land. But if such a case arose, then B could not pave the path.

Nonetheless, B cannot charge any of the cost of the improvement to A. The reason is the same as that expressed in the answer to part (e).

g. Rediscuss parts (a), (b), (c) and (d) on the assumption that A uses the path and part of its deterioration is due to her use.

A: Now A, the servient owner, shares some responsibility for restoring and maintaining the easement. Although most treatises say that the servient owner has no maintenance obligations, they must be thinking of situations where the servient owner does not in fact use the easement, and does not in fact contribute to its wear and tear. The few precedents on the issue support the rule that the fee owner who uses the easement bears a pro rata share of the maintenance costs. The reason, as expressed by one court, is that if the fee owner's rightful use rendered the easement unusable, it would be inequitable to compel the easement owner to repair only to have to repair again when the fee owner's rightful use rendered it unusable again. See Bina v. Bina, 239 N.W. 68, 71 (Ia. 1931).

h. Rediscuss parts (a), (b), (c) and (d) on the assumption that an unusual flood left the servient land rutted and impassable.

A: Now neither party has a duty to restore the land. The servient landowner who does not use the easement has no affirmative obligation to maintain the servient land. In this situation, neither does the dominant landowner. Natural forces, not use by the easement holder have caused the deterioration of the servient land. B's responsibilities do not extend to injury due to Acts of God or even ordinary obsolescence. In other words, the easement owner is responsible for repairing injury due to her use, not the ravages of time or natural forces.

Q26: A and B own adjacent lots in an urban area. Their lots are improved with adjacent buildings. The buildings share a common entrance which is entirely located in A's building. B has an easement of way over the entrance and stairs in A's building up to the second floor where there is an entrance to B's building.

a. Is A or B, or both of them, responsible for the maintenance and repair of the common entrance and stairs.

A: A and B share responsibility. A uses the servient land as well as B, the dominant owner. A is liable for a share of the maintenance expenses. See the discussion in the answer to Q25(g), above, which is the same issue set in a different fact pattern.

b. If A maintains the common entrance and stairs, may A charge any or all of the cost to B?

A: A is partially liable. A may charge B a share of the costs, based upon B's proportion of use. See the reasons for this that were discussed in the answer to Q25(g).

c. A wants to redesign the entrance to her building to make it more stylish. May she do so? And may she charge all or part of the cost to B?

A: A may redesign the entrance, but may not charge any of the cost to B. Redesigning the entrance is an improvement. Improving parties may not charge any of the cost to nonconsenting parties.

d. A's building burns down, but not due to any fault of A's. Is A wholly or partially responsible for reconstructing her building, or at least so much as will provide B's building with an entrance and stairs as before.

A: No. A, the servient owner, is not responsible for deterioration due to natural forces beyond her control. A has no liability for problems to the servient owner's use of the easement due to their effects. See the answer to Q25(h), <u>above</u>, which is the same issue set in another fact pattern.

Location of "Undefined" Easements

Q27: A and B own adjacent lots improved with single-family residences. A grants B an undefined easement "for ingress and egress to B's property across my property."

    a.   Does B have rights of ingress and egress over all of A's property, so that one time she crosses at one point, and another time at another?

        A: No. Literally read, the grant allows B to cross anywhere. But courts presume that the parties did not intend such a result. Rather, they presume the parties intended that B have the right to cross A's land, but did not specifically locate the path. The term for such a grant is an "undefined" easement because a future agreement or action of the parties is necessary to locate it.

    b.   If A wants to locate the easement on the northern 10 feet of her property, and B wants to locate the easement on the southern 10 feet of A's property, whose wishes will prevail?

        A: If A's wishes provide a reasonable location for the easement, A's wishes will prevail. The easement in this Question is "undefined" in that the exact land that is subject to it is not specified. When this occurs, the servient owner has the right to locate the easement, as suits her convenience, provided that the location is convenient for the purposes of the easement.

    c.   A and B agree that the easement is to be located on the northern 10 feet of A's property. Two years later, A wants to move the easement to the southern 10 feet. Will the easement be moved without B's consent?

        A: No. Once located, the easement is defined. The courts presume that the location of the easement specifies the intent of the parties that was ambiguous in the document. It requires the consent of both parties to move an undefined easement once it has been located. <u>Restatement (Third)</u> § 4.8 rejects this rule. Arguing that development of the servient estate may be promoted by allowing relocation, the <u>Restatement (Third)</u> allows the servient landowner reasonably to relocate an easement if doing so has minimal impact on the easement owner's use or maintenance of the easement.

    d.   Rediscuss part (a) on the assumption that the deed specified that the land subject to the easement was the middle 8 feet of A's property?

        A: Neither party's subsequently announced individual desire prevails. The deed specifies the location of the easement, and its width. The deed controls until modified by the unanimous consent of the parties.

Because the overall standard for resolving disputes over the scope of easements involves a balancing test where the deed, prior use or necessity is unclear, it would unnecessarily extend this introductory essay to state and discuss additional issues. The preceding Questions have focused on issues and fact patterns that repeatedly arise. For these issues and fact patterns, the vague reasonable use test has achieved some degree of concreteness.

Other issues and fact patterns, however, arise less frequently and turn entirely on their discrete facts. The Problems that follow focus on these issues and fact patterns. The goal of the Problems, as with the Questions, is to provide the understanding and intuitive feel for the resolution of Scope disputes that can only come from seeing the inherently vague balancing approach in action. Coming to terms with the concept of reasonable use, the central concept in so many controversies over the scope of easements, requires concrete application.

For further reading on the Scope of Easements, see 4 <u>Powell</u> §§ 34.12–34.14; 25 Am. Jur.2d, <u>Easements and Licenses</u> 478–99 (1966); <u>CSW</u> § 8.9; Annot., <u>Extent and Reasonableness of Use of Private Way in Exercise of Easement Granted in General Terms</u>, 3 A.L.R.3d 1256 (1965).

[C] Review Problems

PROBLEM 9

Part 1

Pecheur's Pond is a small body of water that is used primarily for swimming, fishing and boating with small boats—mostly canoes, sailfishes and a few small outboards.

Donna Dominant and Serge Servient own neighboring cottages at Pecheur's Pond. Serge's cottage is located on the shore of the pond. Donna's cottage is located across a roadway, to the rear of Serge's property. A few years ago, Serge granted Donna a

> right of way over a 10 foot wide strip on the westerly side of the grantor's land for the purpose of reaching the pond.

For the first month, Donna used the right of way to walk to the lake to go swimming. Then Donna bought a canoe which she began portaging to the lake across Serge's land. The land which is subject to the easement has trees on it, but Donna was able to maneuver fairly easily around them. Nonetheless, Donna tells Serge that she intends to provide herself with easier access by cutting and removing some of the trees. Serge objects, claiming that Donna has neither the right carry her boat across his land, nor the right to cut and remove his trees.

 a. Is carrying her boat across Serge's land within the scope of Donna's easement?

 b. Is cutting and removing some of the trees on the servient land within the scope of Donna's easement?

Part 2

Pecheur's Pond is a large body of water upon which many people run fairly sizable power boats. Within a month of receiving the easement—under the grant quoted in Part 1—Donna purchased a power boat that was about average size for use on the lake. The boat is too large to maneuver around the trees that are on the land subject to the easement. Donna claims the right to cut and remove the trees.

 c. Is cutting and removing the trees on the servient land within the scope of Donna's easement?

 d. Assume that the answer to part (c) is that Donna has the right to cut and remove the trees to make a path for her power boat. However, assume further that Donna has bought only a canoe that can be portaged easily around the trees. Now can Donna cut and remove the trees?

ANALYSIS

This Problem involves determining the specific rights of use that are authorized by an express easement of way. Although express easements are governed by the document that creates them, the document involved in this Problem created the easement of way in only the most general terms. Because courts view the relationship between the fee and easement owners as involving correlative rights of use, they do not interpret a general grant as authorizing any use that literally comes within its vague scope. Where the grant does not speak specifically to the issue at hand, the rights of the parties are construed with regard to their reasonable interests and expectations.

The reasonable use doctrine is a balancing approach that weighs all persuasive factors. Certainly the circumstances surrounding the easement's creation are important; so are the benefit to the easement holder and the harm to the fee owner of the contemplated use. The following is how these and other factors apply in this situation.

 a. Yes, carrying her boat across Serge's land is within the scope of Donna's easement. The easement is for the purpose of enabling Donna to "reach the pond." Reaching the pond must be for some purpose. The transaction's surrounding circumstances show that the pond commonly is used for boating with small boats. In this area, bringing small boats to the pond is a normal use of a path. It is presumable that Donna had a reasonable expectation of this beneficial use. At the same time, the additional burden on the fee owner is <u>de minimis</u>.

b. No, cutting and removing the trees is not within the scope of Donna's easement. Removing the trees benefits Donna's use of the easement only minimally, while, at the same time, it is a significant additional burden on the fee owner's use of the servient land for shade, ornament or quiet enjoyment.

c. Cutting and removing the trees may be within the scope of Donna's easement. But it is a close case. Now the facts show that the transaction's surrounding circumstances support the expectation that boating with larger power boats is a normal use of the pond. Cutting and removing the trees is necessary to allow Donna, the easement owner, to use the easement to accomplish that use once she "reaches the pond." Nonetheless, cutting and removing the trees is a significant additional burden on the servient land that is not specifically authorized by the document creating the easement.

It would be helpful to have at least one other factor to consider—the factor of consideration. Did Donna receive a gratuitous easement; or did she pay a substantial amount for it? If the easement was granted for minimal consideration, then it would be more likely that cutting and removing the trees is not within the scope of the easement. If it were for a substantial consideration, then it would be almost certain that cutting and removing the trees is within its scope.

d. No, Donna may not cut and remove the trees—at this time. A facet of the reasonable use doctrine is that the fee owner may make any use of the servient land that does not materially and unduly interfere with the easement owner's use. Until Donna purchases the larger boat, she does not need to cut the trees. Until that time, Serge's use of the servient land for ornamental trees does not interfere with Donna's use. Donna's rights are paramount, but only when she requires their exercise.

This illustrates the dynamic aspect of the doctrine of reasonable use. The question shows how the doctrine not only integrates the parties' uses at the present time but flexibly shifts over time as the most efficient, productive and harmonious use of land, within the confines of the general privilege granted, shifts.

PROBLEM 10

Serge Servient and Donna Dominant own adjoining three story buildings on adjacent lots in Metropolis. Between the buildings is a tunnel-like passageway, which is four feet in width and nine feet in height. Each building is over one-half of the passageway. Thirty years ago, when the buildings were constructed and the passageway formed, the owners of the lots granted each other mutual rights to the passageway in a deed that described it as:

a right of way, forever, over and through an alley four feet wide, to wit: . . ..

The buildings were built as single-family townhomes.

Part 1

Until now the buildings have been used as single-family townhomes, and have been owner occupied. The alley has been used mainly by trash collectors and meter readers for access to the rear yards where the trash cans and meters are located.

Unfortunately, the neighborhood has been deteriorating for a while. It no longer is an exclusive residential area. Accordingly, Donna decided to renovate her building into a three-flat, with one rental apartment per floor. When Serge was informed of Donna's plan, he viewed it as deterioration that he wished to prevent. Knowing that all of Donna's tenants would have to use the tunnel for access to the yard (both for recreational use and to dispose of their trash) Serge sued to prohibit what he regarded as a surcharge of the mutual easement.

a. Discuss and resolve Serge's claim that the potential increase in the use of the easement is an impermissible surcharge.

Part 2

Due to the change of the neighborhood, both buildings eventually were renovated into three-flats. Now the area is gentrifying. Some of the buildings are being turned into upgraded residential properties. Others are being turned into art galleries and commercial boutiques. Mixed use buildings abound.

Three years ago, Donna converted her building to commercial uses. This year, she announced plans to construct a four story commercial building on the rear of her lot, whose shops will be open 7 AM to midnight almost every day of the year.

Serge, concerned about the extent to which commercial use of the neighboring property and the easement will disturb his tenants' quiet enjoyment, immediately sued to prohibit her use of the easement for commercial purposes. Serge claims, accurately, that until Donna's renovation, the alley had been used only by the building's residential tenants for access to the trash bins and dumpsters that are kept in the rear.

b. Discuss and resolve Serge's claim that the potential increase in the use of the easement is an impermissible surcharge.

Part 3

Donna has changed her plans. Using new "sliver" construction techniques, she decided to remove the old structure and build a thirty story residential condominium. She plans to retain the alley, as she must, and use it to allow deliverymen, meter readers and trash collectors access to the rear area.

Serge immediately sued. He argues, accurately, that when the buildings were constructed trash was collected once a week; after conversion to three-flats, collection increased to twice a week. He complains that the new building will generate much more trash than the prior uses of the dominant land. The trash collectors will drag more garbage bins, more often through the alley, disturbing his tenants. Donna agrees, saying that she has contracted for daily trash collection at 6 AM. But she says that this use of the easement is within her rights.

c. Discuss and resolve Serge's claim that the potential increase in the use of the easement is an impermissible surcharge.

Part 4

Donna has changed her plans once again. She has bought the parcel that adjoins her on the other side. She intends to tear down both buildings and build a new residential building with four stories. She intends to use the alley she shares with Serge for access by deliverymen and meter readers. Trash collection will occur once a week and involve very little because the new building will have modern compactors. Still, Serge has sued to prevent her use of the easement for this purpose.

d. Discuss and resolve Serge's claim that the potential change in the use of the easement is an impermissible surcharge.

ANALYSIS

This Problem involves the easement holder's rights to increase the intensity of use of the servient land due to changes in the intensity of use of the dominant estate. The easement whose scope is at issue is express; its scope is governed by the document creating it.

The deed, however, grants "a right of way" but is not at all specific about the rights of use. No court would interpret this general grant as encompassing anything that may be physically or usually done on rights of way; no court would allow the easement owner to take the words to their literal limit. Courts construe such a grant according to the rule of reason, as they hold that reasonable use is the presumptive intent of the parties.

In fashioning the rule of reason, and in rendering it more concrete through repeated application, all courts have held that the reasonable use of an easement, though influenced by the circumstances surrounding the easement's creation, is not frozen by the uses made at that time, or even by the uses that would have been reasonable at that time. All courts have adopted the position that changes in the intensity and character of the use of an easement that are convenient to serve the "normal development" of the dominant estate are contemplated and intended by the parties. Accordingly, new uses of easements that serve "normal development" of the dominant land are permitted unless they unduly increase the burden on the servient land.

Applying this slightly more concrete idea of the reasonable use doctrine to the Problem at hand:

a.   Serge does not have a valid cause of action. The dominant estate was used residentially; after renovation it will still be residential. The character of use of the dominant estate has not changed; its intensity has been increased somewhat. This change has led to change in the intensity of the use of the easement. The increased intensity is in keeping with the evolution of the locale. This is the easiest case to bring within the "normal evolution" subdoctrine.

If Donna's was the first building to be subdivided, and/or if the neighborhood was not changing then Serge's complaint would be stronger. Still, the increase in intensity is so slight that it is doubtful any court, absent words in the document, would find the contemplated use of the easement "unreasonable."

b.   The change in the facts changes the balance. The use of the dominant estate has changed from residential to commercial. Conceptually, both the intensity and the character of the use of the dominant estate have changed. In a sense, the character of the use of the servient land has not changed; it is still used as a footpath by individuals. But the intensity is significantly greater. Not only are more people likely to use the alley, but the hours of use are greater, as will be the noise that will accompany the use.

When the dominant estate changes from residential to commercial use, courts are much more hesitant to find that the parties intended to authorize the concomitant change in the use of the easement. This is particularly true when the character of the use of the servient land changes. But this is not the case here; and the change to commercial use is not a per se bar under the reasonable use doctrine. In favor of upholding Donna's contemplated use of the easement is the fact that it is in keeping with the general development of the locality. This fact, however, does not necessarily mean that Donna should prevail. Taken to its fullest, allowing any development that is in character with the locale would allow the easement to be devoted to practically any purpose that was currently fashionable, no matter how burdensome or unexpected by the parties who created the easement. For that reason, courts consider whether the development was "normal" at the time the easement was created, not when the case is brought.

The resolution of this Problem involves, in other words, a conflict between the policy bases of the reasonable use doctrine. The more it is dedicated to promoting balanced and harmonious land-use, the more likely it is that the general neighborhood development means that Donna will prevail. The more the policy is the effectuation of the intent of the original parties, which limits changes in use to those that they might have foreseen and desired, the more likely it is that Serge will prevail.

The court that adjudicated the case upon which this Problem is based, Wheeler v. Lynch, 445 A. 646 (D.C. App. 1982), upheld Donna's use of the easement for commercial purposes. However, the court, exercising its equitable powers in pursuit of the reasonable use doctrine, limited the hours of such use to 8 AM to 8 PM. You should be aware of the possibility of courts striking such a fine balance between the contending factors, and of their power to issue decrees adjusting the parties' correlative rights.

c.   It is difficult to predict how a court might balance the factors in this case. On the one hand there is no change in the character of the use of the dominant estate or the easement; the change is entirely in its intensity. Indeed, the use of the easement is identical to what it was originally: access for trash collection. Yet the change involves more than a seven-fold increase that is quite disturbing.

Perhaps the resolution is to allow it, but, as was done in part (c) limit the hours during which trash may be collected.

d.   Most, if not all, courts would enjoin Donna's use of the easement (if not terminate it entirely, see § 1.06[B][4], <u>below</u>). The blackletter doctrine is that any use of the servient land to service land that is not part of the dominant parcel is an undue burden on the servient land and <u>per se</u> unreasonable.

Analytically, one could argue that the rule of reason does not apply. The deed itself unambiguously grants the right of way for the benefit of the dominant parcel. No rights of use were granted to any other land. The parties to the transaction, therefore, have spoken on the matter. It may be reasonable for the easement owner to use the easement to benefit other land that he owns; but the parties' clear, express agreement governs, whether it is reasonable or unreasonable, so long as it is within the bound of public policy.

Yet, there are a few cases which allow the continued use of an easement even though part of its use serves non-dominant land. In none of these cases was there an increase in use due to the extension to non-dominant land. This fact allowed one court to argue that the easement's use was still no more than what the parties contemplated; it allowed another court to conclude that the proper remedy for the misuse was damages, but not an injunction. See <u>Carbone v. Vigliotte</u>, 610 A.2d 565 (Conn. 1992); <u>Brown v. Voss</u>, 715 P.2d 514 (Wash. 1986).

PROBLEM 11

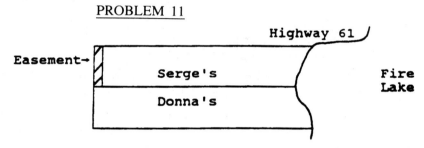

At the time of Oscar Owner's death, twenty years ago, he owned a 160 acre parcel of property that he used as a vacation home. The property was bordered on the north by Highway 61, on the west and south by farms, and on the east by Fire Lake. In his will, Oscar devised the north half of the parcel to his nephew, Serge Servient, and the south half to his niece, Donna Dominant. The south half of the property fronted on a road that eventually connected with the highway. But that road was fairly circuitous, so Oscar included in his will a devise of

an easement for a right of way, benefiting the property herein devised to my niece, Donna, over and across the westernmost 20 feet of the property herein devised to my nephew, Serge.

For a few years after Oscar's death, Serge and Donna used their respective parcels for vacation homes. A few years ago, Donna turned her parcel into a year round mobile-home park and vacation camp ground, with beach privileges open to the general public on a daily, weekly and seasonal basis.

Serge was displeased by Donna's development. When it proved popular, his displeasure increased. Serge was concerned about the fact that the general public not only uses the easement, but also that people often speed down the lane. He is also concerned that teenagers run noisy dirt-bikes up and down the road all day and, sometimes, at night.

To curtail these activities, Serge erected two heavy gates at the turn-off from Highway 61 onto the easement, and at the border between his parcel and Donna's. He also placed five-inch high concrete "speed breakers" on the easement.

After protesting Serge's activities, Donna sued seeking an injunction compelling Serge to remove the gates and the speed breakers. Serge countersued for an injunction banning motor cycle riding on the easement.

At trial, Serge conceded that given other land-use in the area, Donna's present use of her land is a "natural" development of the land and within the scope of the grant. Nonetheless, he insisted that the speeding and noisy dirt-bike riding are misuses that surcharge the easement.

Also at trial, several vacation and day-users of Donna's land testified that the gates were extremely heavy and inconvenient to open and close, and that their cars had been injured by the speed breakers even though they went over them at slow speeds.

Write the trial court's opinion:

a. discussing Serge's contention that the speeding and dirt-bike riding are activities that surcharge the easement;

b. discussing Donna's contention that Serge's defensive measures are not appropriate uses of the servient estate by the servient owner; and

c. disposing of the case.

ANALYSIS

Opinion of the Court—

a.   Discussion of whether the speeding and dirt-bike riding surcharge the easement:

Serge Servient, the defendant, does not attempt to justify the obstructions he has placed in the lane on the grounds that any use of the lane to serve the commercial use of Donna Dominant's land is unreasonable. There is nothing in the record to indicate that Donna's converting her property to a mobile-home park and public beach is not a normal development, consonant with land-use patterns in the locale.

Rather, Serge defends on the grounds that certain uses of the lane have materially increased the burden on the servient land; that they are outside the user privilege devised to Donna in Oscar Owner's will.

Oscar devised a general right of way. Speeding and dirt-bike riding were not specifically authorized. Thus the initial issue is whether speeding on the lane, and frequent riding of noisy dirt-bikes (when the object in their use is not to go anywhere) are reasonable uses of the easement.

I do not think they are reasonable uses. Cars and even dirt-bikes are a normal means of ingress and egress; their use must be suffered by the servient landowner. Speeding cars are not reasonable. They threaten the safety of the servient landowner and the public. Speeding cars are of no benefit to the dominant parcel, and they burden the servient parcel substantially.

Similarly, recreational dirt-bike riding on an otherwise quiet country lane is an unexpected use. I do not believe that easement's grantor intended to authorize this use. Permitting it benefits the dominant parcel only in the remotest degree; permitting it burdens the servient land substantially.

Accordingly, I would enjoin both activities as unreasonable uses of the servient land. (Note that I am not saying that the recreational riding of dirt-bikes in these circumstances is so unreasonable that it would support a finding of nuisance that would justify an injunction between fee owners. If Donna owned the lane in fee she would have greater freedom in her use of it, though even then her rights of use would not be absolute and exercisable without any concern for the convenience of her neighbors. But the rights of an easement owner are more limited than a fee owner. What is reasonable for a fee owner is not necessarily reasonable for an easement owner.)

b.   Discussion of whether Serge's defensive measures are appropriate:

The issue becomes, therefore, whether the servient landowner's defensive measures are reasonable, or whether they are an undue intrusion into the uses allowed to the dominant landowner. Though some counter-measures must be permitted, the specific measures adopted might go too far and impermissibly disturb Donna's rights of user.

I think that in this context gates and speed breakers are an efficient means to combat the problem. But the gates and speed breakers chosen are unnecessarily intrusive. Gates, I believe, will serve their purpose even if they are constructed of light-weight material. Speed breakers will also work if they are lower and unlikely to damage cars driven at an acceptable speed.

However, there is no evidence in the record upon which to predicate a decision as to what size or type of speed breaker will serve its function without improperly damaging cars. Moreover, there is no evidence that the gates will not be sufficient to remedy the problem. The rights of the easement owner are paramount. The burden of proof is on the servient landowner to establish that the easement owner's uses are unduly burdensome, and that his counter-measures are reasonable. Otherwise, the fee owner's counter-measures are obstructions and a disturbance of the easement owner's rights.

c.   Disposition of the case:

Consequently, I order the removal of the speed breakers and the gates; but I authorize the erection of light-weight gates at the places where the gates are at present.

PROBLEM 12

Over the past forty years, the Trans-America Pipeline Co. (TAP) has established an extensive network of oil and gas pipelines. The rights to its routes were established by numerous conveyances by fee owners. The conveyances were all printed forms, given by TAP to the fee owners' that said that the fee owner

granted to the grantee the right to construct, test, reconstruct, renew, operate, maintain, inspect, alter, repair and remove a pipe line for the underground transportation of oil and gas through the following described 30 foot wide strip of real property, to wit: . . . [property description omitted].

After constructing its lines, TAP patrolled them, searching for leaks or other dangerous conditions, through monthly visual inspection conducted on horseback or by motor vehicle. Last year, in order to achieve substantial savings in inspection expenses, TAP discontinued surface inspection in favor of airplane patrols.

In general, the land subject to the easement is readily visible from the air. At some places, however, adjacent trees overhang the easement, obscuring the view of the surface from the air. Because aerial inspection requires an unobstructed view of the ground, TAP informed the fee owners that it intended to prune away overhanging limbs.

a. Upon being informed of TAP's plan to prune away overhanging tree limbs, several servient owners protested. Among them were Fannie Farmer, Fred Fruit-Farmer, and Homer Homeowner. Fannie's overhanging trees are of no commercial value; Fred's overhanging trees are commercial fruit trees; Homer's overhanging trees are ornamental elms. Do Fannie, Fred and Homer have valid protests?

b. Good Samaritan owns land through which TAP's easement runs, but he did not protest TAP's decision. Good had just begun constructing a warehouse on his land that will abut the border of the easement. After receiving notice of TAP's intention to prune away overhanging limbs, Good cut down the trees, benefiting himself and TAP. Good then sent TAP a pro rated bill for the expense. TAP files a motion to dismiss his claim, not protesting the quantum of the bill but the validity any claim. What result?

ANALYSIS

a.   The deed creating the easement expressly granted TAP the right "to inspect" the easement. But because the right is phrased generally, its implementation is subject to the rule of reason. That the document expressly mentioned the right of inspection does not alter the parties' common law relationship.

(Even if the deed were silent on the subject of inspection, the common law allows the easement owner to maintain and repair the easement. This privilege may even become a duty, if the failure to repair impairs the servient landowner's use of the land. A corollary of the privilege and duty to repair is the right to inspect. It is a "secondary easement," implied as necessary for the enjoyment of the primary easement. TAP has the right, by common law, to inspect the easement. The inspection, however, must be done reasonably, with reference to the interests of both the easement and fee holder.)

TAP, therefore, has the right of inspection, so long as it does not unreasonably interfere with the rights of the fee owner. Aerial inspection is permitted. Cutting down overhanging tree limbs helps aerial inspection. But aerial inspection is not necessary. It has become more convenient for TAP; but it increases the burden on the fee owner. How does the overall balance come out?

If the easements had been granted recently, and aerial inspection was a known custom of the pipeline industry, TAP would have a strong argument that aerial inspection, and its necessary incident of maintaining a clear line of sight, was contemplated by the parties at the time of the agreement. That the easement is 40 years old, and aerial inspection was not the norm weakens its case. That the parties' contemporaneous conduct was not aerial searches also weakens its case. But the absence of aerial inspection until now is not fatal. Once again, the courts hold that the parties contemplate all normal evolutionary changes in the use of an easement; and this concept applies to modes of inspection.

The question recurs—how does the balance come out? In the case upon which this Problem was based, Sun Pipe Line Co. v. Krikpatrick, 514 S.W.2d 789 (Tex. App. 1974), the court thought it was obvious that the easement owner had the better right. The fee owner, in fact, conceded the right. (The case involved destruction of overhanging limbs through aerial spraying of herbicide and that was the focus of his protest.) The case did not describe the use of the trees being destroyed, or give us facts of relative value. Nor was there a discussion of the history and extent of aerial inspection in the pipeline industry at the time the easements were created. And do not forget that the easement was granted through the use of forms supplied by the easement holder. But you should feel that Fannie has the weakest case; Fred and Homer have a better one.

b.   TAP's motion should be granted. Cutting the trees entirely is not ordinary maintenance of the easement. It is an improvement. Although repair and maintenance expenses that benefit both the servient and dominant owner may be pro rated, improvement expenses are not apportionable.

[D] Recapitulation

1.   The scope of an easement refers to the uses the easement owner may make of the servient land, and the restraints upon the fee owner's use that the easement owner may insist upon, due to her ownership of the easement.

2.   The intent of the parties determines the scope of an easement.

3.   When the intent of the parties is ambiguous, the courts presume the parties intended that both the easement owner and the servient landowner could make a reasonable use of the land subject to the easement. "Reasonable use" is a balancing approach that gives recognition to the needs and expectancies of both parties. The easement holder may make any authorized use that does not burden the servient land "unduly." The fee owner may make any use of the servient land that does not "unduly" interfere with the easement holder's use of the easement.

4.   The courts presume that the parties intend the scope of an easement to change with the normal development of the dominant estate, the development of the surrounding locale, and the progress of technology.

5.   The courts also presume that the easement owner, not the fee owner, has the obligation to maintain and repair the land subject to the easement. The easement owner, or the fee owner, may improve the land subject to the easement, so long as so doing does not prejudice the rights of the other party.

§ 1.05 TRANSFER: ALIENATION AND APPORTIONMENT

[A] Definitions

ALIENATION: Alienation of an easement is a transfer that totally divests an easement holder of her ownership interest. The transfer may be inter vivos or at death. Because most transfers involve inter vivos conveyances, some courts and commentators refer to the alienation of an easement simply as its assignment.

APPORTIONMENT: Apportionment of an easement is a transfer that results in a division of an easement among several owners who use it independently of one another. Apportionment occurs when an easement owner transfers her ownership interest to two or more owners, as when an easement holder dies, and the easement passes to her children as tenants in common. Apportionment also occurs when an easement owner transfers less than her complete ownership interest, as when a telegraph company grants permission to a telephone company to string telephone wires along the telegraph's right of way. Some courts and commentators refer to apportionment as division.

EASEMENT APPURTENANT: See § 1.01, above.

EASEMENT IN GROSS: See § 1.01, above.

COMMERCIAL EASEMENT IN GROSS: A commercial easement in gross is an easement in gross that is created primarily for economic benefit.

NONCOMMERCIAL EASEMENT IN GROSS: A noncommercial easement in gross is an easement in gross that is created primarily for personal satisfaction.

EXCLUSIVE EASEMENT IN GROSS: An exclusive easement in gross allows the easement owner the sole right to enjoy the privileges granted by the easement without competition even from the servient landowner.

NONEXCLUSIVE EASEMENT IN GROSS: A nonexclusive easement in gross allows the servient landowner to exercise, or to grant to others, the same right she granted to the easement owner.

PROFITS A PRENDRE: In the traditional common law, a profit a prendre was a nonpossessory right to use the land of another that authorized the severance and removal of some part of the substance of the servient land. The right to mine, timber, or pasture cattle, are examples of nonpossessory rights which traditionally were called profits a prendre, not easements. The modern common law makes no distinction between nonpossessory rights that allow the severance and removal of some part of the servient land and nonpossessory rights that do not allow such use. In the modern law, both types of nonpossessory rights are called easements.

SURCHARGE: Most frequently, the term "surcharge" describes using an easement in a manner that is authorized, but to an extent that is unduly intense. Occasionally, "surcharge" describes using an easement in a manner that is unauthorized.

[B] Discussion and Questions

The common law on alienation and apportionment of easements reflects a balance of a variety of concerns. In general, the common law assumes that society is best served if property interests are freely alienable. Free alienability includes apportionment. But easements burden land. An easement may clog the marketability and utilization of the servient estate. To the extent that easements are felt to fetter commerce in land, permitting their free alienation aggravates the problem. After all, an interest that is inalienable lasts no longer than the life of its original owner. To the extent that free alienation is perceived as a problem, permitting apportionment aggravates the problem even more. Multiplying the people entitled to use an easement usually increases the burden on the servient land, increasing the risk of surcharge. This further decreases the value of the fee interest.

The extent to which common law courts have felt easements, or particular types of easements, threatened commerce in land has varied over time. Thus the common law of assignment and apportionment of easements is one of continual change. In addition, the courts have felt that easements appurtenant and easements in gross differ markedly in the extent to which they threaten to burden rather than benefit commerce.

In general, common law courts felt that easements appurtenant did not raise the problems discussed above but that easements in gross did. With easements appurtenant, for every parcel of land that is burdened, there is another parcel that is benefited. This is not so for easements in gross. This difference is very significant in agricultural economies where land is the preeminent source of economic wealth. In addition, due to their necessary connection with neighboring land, the owners of easements appurtenant are over time far more easily identifiable and multiply less rapidly than owners of easements in gross. This significantly affects a servient landowner's ability to negotiate a release should an easement become a clog on her title.

In consequence, the law regarding the alienation and apportionment of easements appurtenant and easements in gross developed differently, and will be discussed separately.

(The topics concerning alienation and apportionment of easements focused on in this section assume that the easements have already been properly identified as appurtenant or in gross. Obviously, the determination of whether an easement is appurtenant or in gross is a condition precedent to the application of the rules concerning alienation and apportionment. Determination of whether an easement is appurtenant or in gross was discussed in § 1.02[B][2], above.)

[1] Easements appurtenant

The common law on the alienation of easements appurtenant is straightforward. Easements appurtenant are incidents of the possession of the land. Transfer of that possession transfers the easement. Of course, the easement does not have to be alienated with the land to which it is attached. The parties may provide expressly that the easement is not to pass with the land. In this case, the easement is said to have been "severed." But the judicial presumption is that the parties conveying the possession of the land intend to convey all easements appurtenant; and the rule is that if the conveyance is silent on the matter the easement is conveyed.

The judicial presumption also is that an easement appurtenant is extinguished when it is not conveyed with the land to which it is incident. A severed easement appurtenant can be converted into an easement in gross, but only if the parties, authorized that outcome when they created the easement.

Q28: O owns Blackacre, which has an easement appurtenant to camp on Whiteacre. A owns Whiteacre. O conveys Blackacre to B.

    a.   The deed makes no mention of the easement. When B camps on Whiteacre, A objects, claiming that O's right was never transferred to B. Is A correct?

        A: A is incorrect. Courts presume that easements appurtenant are conveyed with the dominant land.

    b.   Assume O's conveyance to B "excepts" the right to camp on Whiteacre. After the conveyance, A objects to O's camping on Whiteacre. Is A correct? What if B camped on Whiteacre and A objected?

        A: A is correct; O can no longer camp on Whiteacre. O's conveyance severed the easement from Blackacre. O could camp on Whiteacre only if the terms or manner creating the easement authorized its transformation into an easement in gross. The presumption is against this, and no facts are given which overcome the presumption.

        A also may successfully object to B's camping on Whiteacre. The word "excepts" is sufficient to express the intent that B not receive the easement. It is severed from Blackacre. In this case, O's severance of the easement extinguished it.

The common law on the apportionment of easements appurtenant is also straightforward. Easements appurtenant are apportioned by the subdivision of the dominant land. Courts presume that the parties intend to attach the easement to every parcel carved out of the original estate. Limitations on the apportionment of easements appurtenant must be expressed by the parties, or clearly implied by the circumstances surrounding their transaction. Limitations also arise from the courts' efforts to prevent easement owners from surcharging the servient land. This has been treated previously under the topic of Scope, § 1.04, above.

[2] Easements in gross

The common law on the alienation of easements in gross is complex and controversial. The traditional common law refused to permit the transfer of easements in gross. Indeed, the common law did not permit easements in gross at all. Easements in gross were recognized as contract rights, not as property rights, and were enforceable only so long as both the original easement owner lived and the original servient owner owned the land.

The traditional rule prohibiting the transfer of easements in gross was significantly tempered in one respect. Many agreements which today are called easements were then called profits a prendre. Any agreement that authorized not only the nonpossessory use of the land of another, but also authorized the severance and removal of some part of the substance of that land was a profit, not an easement. For example, the right to mine, timber or pasture cattle, rights which today are denominated easements, were then denominated profits. The reason for the distinction was the commercial value of profits a prendre. The importance of this distinction is that profits were alienable, both inter vivos and at death.

With the development of railroads and other utilities, the traditional common law on the assignment of easements in gross began to crumble. Railroads and utilities frequently acquired routes through easements in gross. To hold their routes nonassignable was economically undesirable. Courts first responded by ruling that easements in gross were assignable when they effectively gave the easement holder the virtual possession of the servient land. Eventually, however, at the urging and under the influence of the Restatement (First) §§ 489-92, the whole rule structure was reformulated.

The Restatement (First) reformulation melded easements and profits into a single concept, denominated easements. The Restatement (First) then changed the key to the law on the alienation of easements in gross from the distinction between easements and profits to the distinction between commercial and noncommercial easements in gross. Commercial easements in gross are those created primarily for economic benefit; noncommercial easements in gross are those created primarily for personal satisfaction. As the Restatement (First) § 491 com. (a) says, noncommercial easements in gross "contribute to pleasure rather than financial well-being."

According to the Restatement (First), both commercial and noncommercial easements in gross are freely alienable if that is the intent of the parties. But the modern common law presumes that the parties intend a commercial easement in gross to be alienable. The parties may limit its alienability, but they must clearly indicate their intent (and even then the general rules protecting the alienability of property may override that limitation). In contrast, the modern common law does not presume that the parties intend a noncommercial easement in gross to be alienable. As the Restatement (First) says, noncommercial easements in gross are inalienable unless "the manner or the terms of their creation" support a different conclusion. The Restatement (First) suggests that when the "terms" creating a noncommercial easement in gross are ambiguous, significant factors in construing whether the parties intended it to be alienable include (a) the personal relations between the grantor and grantee; (b) the probable increase in the burden on the servient land resulting from alienability; and (c) the consideration paid.

More recently, the Restatement (Third) suggested a further simplification of the presumptions on the alienability of easements in gross. Abandoning the commercial/noncommercial distinction, Restatement (Third) § 4.6 says that easements in gross are presumptively alienable unless they are "personal." Restatement (Third) § 4.6 considers easements in gross to be "personal" when "the relationship of the parties, consideration paid, nature of the servitude, or other circumstances" indicate that the parties did not expect the easement to be transferrable.

Q29: Rediscuss Q28(a), above, on the assumption that O's right to camp on Whiteacre was founded on an easement in gross.

A: Now A is correct. The nature of an easement in gross is that it is not incident or attached to dominant land. The transfer of Blackacre does not imply a transfer of O's personal right to camp on Whiteacre.

Q30: O grants "to A" the right to camp on O's land. A owns no land in the vicinity. A assigns her right to B.

    a.   When B camps on Blackacre, O objects, claiming that A's right was not assignable. Is O correct?

A: O is correct. A's easement is an easement in gross because there is no land to which it is incident. A personal right to camp seems to be one that is for "personal gratification," not financial "well-being." It is a noncommercial easement in gross. Presumptively, it is not alienable.

    b.   Assume A is a for-profit corporation that teaches interested members of the public environmentally sound camping techniques. A used O's land as a "school" site. Now is O correct?

A: O is incorrect. A grant to a for-profit corporation engaged in teaching environmentally sound camping bespeaks a business purpose. The easement is, therefore, a commercial easement in gross. Presumptively, the parties intend a commercial easement in gross to be alienable.

Q31: Rediscuss Q30(a), <u>above</u>, on the assumption that the grant was "to A, her heirs and assigns."

A: O is incorrect. The words "her heirs and assigns," (or "its successors and assigns" when the grantee is a corporation) are classic words expressing the intent that the easement in gross is alienable. The presumption that the parties did not intend the easement to be alienable is overcome.

Q32: Rediscuss Q30(a), <u>above</u>, on the assumption that O granted "to A"—who owned no land in the vicinity—the right to hunt on O's land, that A assigned her right to B, and that O objected when B went hunting on O's land.

A: In most jurisdictions O would be correct. Under the <u>Restatement (First)</u> formulation, noncommercial easements in gross are presumptively inalienable, having been created for personal pleasure, not financial gain. Under the <u>Restatement (Third)</u> approach, easements in gross intended to be the personal privilege of the original grantee are inalienable. A privilege to hunt on someone's land sounds in personal gratification. Of course, facts extrinsic to the grant may well rebut this presumption. In the absence of evidence rebutting the usual judicial presumption, an easement to hunt is inalienable. See <u>Restatement (First)</u> § 491 com. (a); <u>Restatement (Third)</u> § 4.6.

Nevertheless, a right to hunt on someone's land involves the right to remove something from the land of another. Before the <u>Restatement (First)</u> reform, it was a <u>profit a prendre</u>. As a profit, it was alienable. There are jurisdictions that would continue to hold a noncommercial "easement in gross of the profit type" assignable because of their old precedents. These jurisdictions have not fully integrated the <u>Restatement (First)</u>'s reforms into their law.

The common law on the apportionment of easements in gross is equally perplexing. Under the traditional common law, easements in gross were not apportionable. (How could they be? They were not assignable.) Profits were apportionable. However, a distinction was drawn between the apportionment of an exclusive and a nonexclusive profit. An exclusive profit is one in which the profit holder was granted the sole right to remove the object of the profit, without competition even from the servient land owner. A nonexclusive profit contemplates that the servient land owner retains the right to remove the object of the profit, or to authorize other people to do so.

Exclusive profits were apportionable; nonexclusive profits were not. The reason for the distinction was that apportionment generally increases the rate of exploitation of the servient land. The grant of an exclusive profit was a grant of the right to take all of the profit's object; the grant of a nonexclusive profit was a grant of the right to take whatever part of the profit's object that had not been taken by the servient landowner or other profit holders. Clearly, the rate at which a profit holder exploited her interest mattered less for exclusive than for nonexclusive profits. Apportionment was less likely to be a means to "milk" the servient land when exclusive, as opposed to nonexclusive, profits were involved.

The apportionability of exclusive profits and the nonapportionability of nonexclusive profits were subject to two important caveats. On the one hand, nonexclusive profits were alienable to two or more people if the multiple owners did not exploit the profit independently. In the words of an old case, the multiple owners had to work as "one stock." Mountjoy's Case, 123 E.R. 488 (C.P. 1583). On the other hand, the owners of exclusive profits did not have a totally uncontrolled ability to apportion them. Particular apportionments could so increase the exploitation of the servient land as to amount to a surcharge. For example, apportionment could result in a scale of exploitation that interfered with the servient landowner's reasonable enjoyment of the underlying fee. Regardless of the fact that apportionment was permitted, the servient landowner retained her right to bar unreasonable increases in the scale of use by the profit holder or holders.

The Restatement (First) § 493 retained this rule structure, but changed the irrebuttable rules into rebuttable presumptions. Under the Restatement (First) formulation, exclusive easements in gross are presumptively apportionable; nonexclusive easements in gross are presumptively nonapportionable. These presumptions may be overcome if the "terms or manner" of an easement's creation indicates that the parties had a contrary intent. But the Restatement (First) suggests, at least for the presumption that nonexclusive easements are nonapportionable, that courts require a "clear indication" of a contrary intent.

The Restatement (Third) essentially carries forward the formulation of the Restatement (First), while perhaps making it more likely that easements in gross will be found to be apportionable. Restatement (Third) § 5.9 adopts the rule that benefits in gross are presumptively apportionable. However, in subsequent commentary, it also says reasonable expectations about the intent of the parties counsel that "exclusive [easements in gross] are more likely to be apportionable than non-exclusive [easements in gross]." Id. at com. (b).

Finally, although neither the first nor the third Restatement discusses the matter, the traditional and still dominant judicial presumption is that easements in gross are nonexclusive; a clear indication of a contrary intent is required to overcome it.

Q33: O grants A an assignable, but nonexclusive, easement in gross to camp on O's land.

    a.   A takes B camping with her. O objects to A and B camping together, claiming that A had a personal easement. Is O correct?

    A: O is incorrect. Easements in gross are personal easements in the sense that they are not appurtenant, i.e., they are not owned in the capacity of occupant of some parcel of land. Easements in gross also may be personal in the sense of being inalienable, i.e, no one other than the named grantee may own the easement.

    Here, O is claiming the easement is personal in yet another sense. O claims not that only A can own the easement, but that A may not bring guests. This is really a question of scope. Since the grant of an easement to camp usually allows the grantee to bring a reasonable number of guests, O would have to present additional evidence to rebut the presumed scope of her grant.

    b.   A tells B that B may go camping on O's land on weekends that A remains at home. O objects to B's camping without A. Is O correct?

    A: O is correct. Apportionment occurs when a transfer of an easement results in it being held by two or more individuals who then make an independent use of it. Apportionment does not occur through transfers to two or more individuals who exercise their rights as a single entity. This is the "one stock" rule.

    The grant of a right to camp usually does not intend that the grantee allow guests to enjoy the easement in her absence. Such use is beyond the scope of the grant. A has moved from enjoying the easement herself (by bringing a guest with her) to apportioning her easement. A has not alienated her easement to B. By giving permission to B to camp on O's land in A's absence, A has, in effect, licensed B to camp on O's land. Since A still retains the right to camp, yet has authorized B to use it independently of her, she has apportioned her easement. Since A had a nonexclusive easement, it is presumptively not apportionable.

c.   A dies, devising all her property to B and C. Even though B and C always camp together on O's land, O objects. Is O correct?

    A: O is incorrect. A's easement was assignable. It survives A's death and may pass to B and C. If B and C camped separately, they would be enjoying the easement independently. In that case the easement would have been apportioned and O could object to their activity. However, B and C, by camping together, are using the easement as "one stock." (B and C camping together is little different than A bringing a guest.) As long as they use the easement for joint camping trips, the easement is not considered apportioned. The reason for this is that as compared to independent use, it is less likely that joint use will surcharge the servient land.

d.   A dies, devising all her property to the American Scouts, a not-for-profit corporation that trains children in citizenship and outdoor activities. The American Scouts uses O's land for camping, bringing up to 100 scouts to the land. O objects. Is O correct?

    A: O is probably correct. A's easement is assignable and may pass to the American Scouts. Thus O may not object to the assignment _per se_. However, it is likely that camping by 100 people at a time is beyond the degree of use that O and A contemplated when they created the easement. O can object to the surcharge. She can enjoin the extent of the American Scouts' use of her land, but not the fact of their use.

Q34: O grants A a nonexclusive easement in gross to cut timber on O's land.

a.   A, while continuing to cut timber herself, authorizes B to cut timber on O's land. O objects to B's cutting timber.

    A: O is correct. A's commercial easement in gross is presumptively assignable but not apportionable. Because A's easement is not exclusive, O retains the power to grant more timbering rights. Merely by authorizing B to timber, A has withdrawn a potential customer from O. A has interfered with the exercise and value of O's retained rights. She has surcharged O's servient estate.

b.   A takes in B as a partner, and together they cut timber for their partnership business. O objects to B's cutting timber.

    A: O is incorrect. Apportionment occurs when a transfer of an easement results in it being held by two or more individuals who then make an independent use of it. Apportionment does not occur through transfers to two or more individuals who exercise their rights as a single entity. This is the "one stock" rule. But for the "one stock" rule, descent of an easement in gross to two or more heirs, and assignments to partnerships, would be barred. By compelling multiple owners to act as a single entity, the "one stock" rule serves to inhibit multiple owners from racing against each other to deplete the land of the resource that is the object of the profit. The "one stock" rule, in theory, turns an apportionment into a _de facto_ assignment.

    O might still prevail, however. In the unlikely circumstance that O could show that A's partnership with B results in an uncontemplated increase in the scale of timbering, O could object based upon a violation of the scope of the easement. O has the right to object to an increase in A's scope of operation even if A had not entered into a partnership with B. O should always be aware of the possibility of this objection; but it is essentially different from an objection based upon the mere fact of apportionment.

c.   Rediscuss part (a) on the assumption that O granted A an exclusive easement.

> **A:** O is incorrect. An assignable easement that is exclusive is presumptively apportionable. O has granted A all the rights to the resource on her land. Now when A authorizes B to timber, she is not withdrawing a potential customer from O. The mere fact of apportionment has not surcharged O's retained estate.

Q35: O grants A an exclusive easement in gross to cut timber on O's land. After receiving the easement, A sues to enjoin O from cutting timber on O's land. O defends by arguing that an exclusive easement means that the grantor will not make the same grant to another, not that the grantor is precluded from removing the object of the easement. Is O's contention valid?

> **A:** O's contention is incorrect. An exclusive easement precludes the fee owner, as well as any other subsequent grantee of the fee owner, from making the same use that was the subject of an exclusive easement.

Q36: Does each of the following phrases suggest the grant of an exclusive easement or a nonexclusive easement?

a.   O grants to A "a right to camp. . .."

> **A:** This suggests a nonexclusive easement. The indefinite article "a" and the single "right" suggests the grant of permission, but not exclusive permission, to camp.

b.   O grants to A "the camping rights. . .."

> **A:** This suggests an exclusive easement. The definite article and the plural "rights" indicate a grant of all the rights to the particular activity. When the easement holder has all the rights to the particular activity, the servient landowner is excluded. The easement is therefore exclusive.

c.   O grants to A "the right to camp. . .."

> **A:** This phrase is ambiguous. Grammatically, it can be read as granting the entire corpus of rights to the particular activity because of the use of the definite article. However, common usage of the definite article does not support this reading. The judicial presumption is that easements are nonexclusive. This language should be held insufficient to overcome the presumption.

Q37: In the following deeds, the parties do not expressly say that they intend the easement to be apportionable. Nor do the parties expressly say that they intend the easement to be exclusive, thereby presumptively intending it to be apportionable. Yet, do you see an argument that the terms of the deed nevertheless support an inference that the easement is apportionable?

a.   Serge Servient grants the Petroleum Company the "right to explore and remove oil and gas from the following described lands, <u>viz</u>. . . [property description omitted]. The grantee herein shall also enjoy the free and uninterrupted access over and upon said land, except portions of said land used or needed by the grantor for the purpose of farming the same. . .."

> **A:** The second clause guarantees the Petroleum Co. uninterrupted access to the servient land except when it is used for farming. This implies that no other use of the servient land may impede the easement owner's exploration and drilling activity. Since exploration and drilling by the grantor or another party would bar the Petroleum company from parts of the tract, the grant must be exclusive.
>
> This is not the only reading of the clause. It might be taken to mean that the easement owner understands that the servient landowner's farming activities are not to be disturbed. However, in <u>Chandler v. Hart</u>, 119 P. 516, 521 (Cal. 1911), the clause was taken as strong evidence that the grant was intended to be exclusive.

b.   Serge Servient grants the Petroleum Company the "right to explore and remove oil and gas from the following described lands, <u>viz</u>. . . [property description omitted]. The grantee herein is to pay grantor a royalty of 12.5% of the value of all oil, gas and other such minerals produced and saved from the above described real property, less reasonable costs of exploration and production. . .."

A: Many courts hold that when the grantor of an easement in gross of the profit type is recompensed through royalties, apportionment is allowed.

The reasoning behind this is that the common law allows apportionment of easements in gross whenever the parties intend that it be allowed. The parties are presumed to have intended that a nonexclusive easement in gross is nonapportionable. This presumption may be overcome by sufficient words or circumstances indicating a contrary intent.

Payment based upon royalty frequently is held to be a circumstance that indicates the intent that the easement be apportionable. When payments are based on royalties, many courts say that the owner of the servient estate is benefited, not harmed by an increase in scale of operations, because her income is increased. The fact that the owner of the servient estate is benefited by the apportionment is taken as evidence that she intended to allow it.

Of course, one can object that the owner of the servient estate could claim to be harmed by not being able to negotiate a higher royalty from the easement holder's licensee. But many courts have not accepted this argument. Yet, if the servient landowner could show that the initial easement was granted for an unusually low royalty, that grant should be held not apportionable, the amount of consideration being insufficient to support the conclusion that the parties intended all the presumptive consequences of a royalty-based easement.

Q38: O grants "to A, the exclusive right to camp. . ." on Blackacre. A is O's close friend and pays no consideration for the grant. A takes B camping with her, but also tells B that she may go camping alone. O objects to B's camping without A. What is O's argument that this exclusive easement in gross is not apportionable?

A: According to blackletter doctrine, the parties are presumed to intend exclusive easements to be apportionable. However, the terms or the circumstances surrounding the transaction creating the easement may rebut the presumption. O may argue that the terms and the circumstances surrounding the creation of this exclusive easement in gross indicate that the parties intended it to be nonapportionable.

O may argue that A's easement is personal, not only in the sense that it is not incident to a dominant estate, but also in the sense that only A is to enjoy it. A's easement is certainly not alienable. The circumstances show that it is noncommercial and that it was granted for no consideration. An easement that is not alienable is, <u>a fortiori</u>, not apportionable, as that is a partial alienation.

Moreover, O may argue, exclusive easements in gross are usually granted in commercial situations. The presumption that an exclusive easement in gross is apportionable reflects the expectations of parties seeking profit from the commercial exploitation of the land. But O's grant was for personal satisfaction. It was a gift to a close friend. In such a case, the expectation of commercial exploitation that supports the presumption that an exclusive easement is apportionable is inapplicable.

In sum, the common law on assignment and apportionment of easements is complex. The Questions should have helped you to master its basics. The Problems that follow will further explore the major areas of current litigation:

(1) whether an easement in gross has a commercial or noncommercial character;

(2) the words or surrounding circumstances that overcome the presumption that

(a) the parties intend a noncommercial easement in gross to be inalienable;

(b) the parties intend an easement in gross to be nonexclusive;

(3) the uses of an apportioned easement in gross that surcharge it.

For further reading on the Transfer of Easements, see Restatement (First) §§ 487–96; Restatement (Third) §§ 4.6, 5.9; CSW §§ 8.10–8.11; 4 Powell §§ 34.15–34.16; 2 ALP §§ 8.71–8.86; Annot., Assignability and Divisibility of Easement in Gross or License in Respect of Land or Water, 130 A.L.R. 1253 (1941).

[C] Review Problems

PROBLEM 13

For many years, Bette Builder, a contractor doing about $5 million dollars worth of construction a year, owned a large tract of land from which she mined sand and gravel for her construction projects. Three years ago, Bette sold the land to Serge Servient, reserving an exclusive easement to excavate sand and gravel from the property for a term of 10 years.

a. Last year, Bette assigned her easement to MegaCorp, one of the nation's largest builders. MegaCorp began using Serge's land to supply sand and gravel for over $26 million worth of construction projects. On what ground, if any, may Serge object to Bette's assignment to MegaCorp?

b. This year, Bette retired from business and assigned her easement to MinorCorp and MiddlingCorp, two different construction companies, each of which does $1 million worth of construction a year. MinorCorp and MiddlingCorp use Serge's land to supply sand and gravel for their separate construction projects. On what ground, if any, may Serge object to Bette's apportionment of her easement to MinorCorp and MiddlingCorp?

c. Rediscuss part (b) on the assumption that MinorCorp and MiddlingCorp each do over $13 million worth of construction a year, and that they each use Serge's land to supply all their projects.

d. Rediscuss part (b) on the assumption that Bette reserved a nonexclusive easement to remove sand and gravel from Serge's land.

e. Rediscuss part (d) on the assumption that MinorCorp and Middling Corp use Serge's land only for projects in which they are joint venturers.

ANALYSIS

a. Serge may not object to the assignment per se. As a commercial easement in gross, Bette's easement is presumptively freely assignable. Even in a jurisdiction that denies the alienability of easements in gross, this one involves a profit a prendre, which would be held assignable.

Serge may object, however, based upon surcharge. The assignment is valid, but MegaCorp may be enjoined from using the servient land as extensively as it does. A five-fold increase in the amount of sand and gravel removed may well be beyond the degree of usage contemplated by the parties at the time the easement was created. The type of use is the same as originally intended; but the increase in scale may substantially interfere with Serge's use of the servient land. Substantial interference might indicate that the parties could not have contemplated it. Serge would have to develop these facts in order to prevail. In short, this case would be determined by the principles discussed in the section on Scope, § 1.04, above.

b. Serge has no grounds for objection. He could not object based upon the apportionment. Exclusive commercial easements in gross are presumptively apportionable. No facts are given that might overcome that presumption. In theory, Serge could object if the apportionment in fact results in an overuse of the servient land. Clearly, this is not the case here since the scale of use has decreased.

c. With the change in facts, Serge might have a valid objection based upon surcharge of the servient land. It is important to note that the objection would not be based upon the apportionment per se; and that the evidence Serge would need to prove surcharge is the same as in part (a) where there was an assignment to one large corporation.

   d.   Serge could successfully object based upon the apportionment <u>per se.</u> Nonexclusive easements are presumptively not apportionable. This is true even where the purported apportionment clearly does not threaten an actual over use of the servient land.

   The rationale for this position, given by the first and third <u>Restatements</u>, is that when nonexclusive easements are granted, the servient landowner retains the power to grant the same interest to others. The mere fact that the nonexclusive easement holder divides her holding among others does not necessarily physically surcharge the land. But it does withdraw a potential customer from the servient landowner; it surcharges her remaining rights—which include not just the physical use of the land but the power to permit others to make use of the land.

   Of course, the logic of this position can be pushed to argue against allowing the holder of a nonexclusive easement in gross to assign her interest. After all, when the easement holder makes an assignment she is withdrawing a potential customer from the servient land owner. But this would diminish the economic value of the easement far more than a rule that prevents her apportioning it. The presumption against apportionment of nonexclusive easements is, a prophylactic rule that through an easily applicable test attempts to achieve the more or less just balance. What it lacks in justice arguably is made up for in efficiency.

   e.   Serge has no grounds for objection. The apportionees are using the easement as "one stock." One could say that there is no apportionment because the assignees are not using their privilege independently. Most courts would say that there is no violation of the rule against apportioning nonexclusive easements in gross when the assignees act together. Either way, the point is that without independent activity an assignment to two or more is more or less the equivalent of an assignment to a single entity.

PROBLEM 14

As part of its environmental work, the Conservation Club of Clayton County (CCCC) has been using club funds to purchase "conservation" easements intended to prevent environmentally damaging development. Most of the easements are for wetland and scenic preservation, but a few require the preservation of the county's historic structures.

The following document is typical of the operative language in the deeds through which CCCC acquires its easements:

   Whereas _____ of Clayton County, the GRANTOR, has received $_____ dollars and other good and valuable consideration, the GRANTOR, for herself, her heirs, successors and assigns, conveys to the Clayton County Conservation Club, the GRANTEE, an easement in the following described real property, to wit:

   _____
   _____
   _____
   _____
   _____

The easement is for the purpose of conserving, maintaining and returning the above described real property in or to its natural state; provided that activities, such as farming, hunting and fishing, that at present are conducted upon the land may continue. . ..

Last year, strapped for funds and lacking the resources needed to enforce effectively the rights it has acquired, CCCC dissolved and assigned all its conservation easements to the State Conservation Society (SCS).

When they discovered that CCCC had dissolved, several conservation easement grantors decided that they no longer were bound by their grants. SCS commenced a declaratory judgment action seeking a determination of whether SCS acquired CCCC's rights, and may enforce the conservation easements.

At trial, the defendant servient landowners claimed that SCS acquired no rights because CCCC's easements were not assignable. The landowners' specific argument is that CCCC's easement is a noncommercial easement in gross and that noncommercial easements in gross are not assignable.

You have been retained by SCS.

a. Can you argue that CCCC's easements are commercial? If so, make the argument.

b. On the assumption that CCCC's easements are noncommercial, can you nevertheless argue that they are assignable? If so, make the argument.

ANALYSIS

a. The argument that CCCC's easements are commercial follows: CCCC's conservation easements are commercial as that term is used in the commercial/noncommercial dichotomy. Literally, the easement is not commercial; it is entered into to prevent commercial exploitation. The Restatement (First) describes a commercial easement in gross as one that is entered into for "economic benefit" rather than "personal satisfaction." The grantees may be said to have entered into this transaction for personal satisfaction, not economic gain. For the grantors, the reverse may well be true. There was consideration, and there are federal tax incentives, for this transaction.

At a more basic level, however, the function of the commercial/noncommercial dichotomy is, according to the Restatement (First), to distinguish easements in gross which are, from easements in gross which are not, presumptively worth permanently burdening land. See Restatement (First) §§ 489 com. (b) and 491 com. (a). Easements in gross limit the utilization of land without correspondingly increasing the utilization of other land. They burden commerce in land. For this reason, unless there is an alternate economic rationale, the social policy that usually supports the alienability of property interests is lacking. In addition, without an economic rationale, it is likely that the transaction was intended by the parties to inure to the sole benefit of the named grantee.

Nevertheless, although conservation easements do not promote the market exploitation of land, they still have a social policy rationale that supports finding them permanent, rather than transitory, interests in land. Conservation easements have noneconomic reasons for their creation that support a presumption that they were intended to outlive the named grantees. If the function of the commercial/noncommercial distinction is to separate those easements in gross which presumptively should be of limited duration (either due to social policy reasons or the probable intent of the parties), conservation easements are commercial.

In other words, a commercial rationale for an easement in gross is the usual way that an easement in gross is found consonant with the social policy favoring alienability of property interests; it is the usual way that an easement in gross is found consonant with the presumptive intent of the parties that its existence outlive the named grantee. An environmental rationale is another.

b. The argument that CCCC's noncommercial easements are nevertheless assignable follows: The argument for holding conservation easements "commercial" indicates another argument. Even if the easement is held noncommercial, this does not mean that the easement is not alienable. Noncommercial easements in gross are presumed inalienable. The presumption may be overcome by the circumstances surrounding the easement's creation. Usually this is through the presence of words in the document that indicate the intent that the easement be alienable. In the instant Problem, however, there are no such words. Nevertheless, unlike most noncommercial easements in gross, conservation easements probably are entered into with an expectation that they are permanent, and will, accordingly, outlive the named grantee. The circumstance that the easement is a conservation easement, granted for a rather large consideration, should raise the presumption that it was not intended to be impermanent and perish with the named grantee. The presumed intent of the parties is, with regard to this particular noncommercial easement, that it has permanency that can be achieved only if it is alienable.

The <u>Restatement (Third)</u>'s decision to drop the commercial/noncommercial distinction recognizes the arguments in parts (a) and (b). The <u>Restatement (Third)</u>'s presumption that easements in gross are alienable unless they are "personal," in the sense of granted solely for the benefit of the grantee, easily supports the conclusion that CCCC may transfer its easement to SCS.

PROBLEM 15

Cable Television, Inc. (CTV) is seeking rights of way through the suburbs. Its coaxial cable can be strategically located for minimal cost if CTV can run the cable along the Electric Power Co.'s (EP) established route, and attach it to EP's poles. To obtain the necessary authorization, CTV would prefer to negotiate only with EP and not with EP's innumerable servient landowners. CTV has retained your law firm to determine whether or not EP's authorization alone will suffice.

EP acquired its route through a variety of deeds, all drafted by EP. Under these deeds, EP's rights of way clearly are assignable easements in gross.

a. You have been asked to determine if EP's easements in gross are apportionable, either because they are exclusive, or because the parties intended EP's nonexclusive easement to be apportionable. The relevant language in the various deeds follows:

1. "The grantor hereby grants to the grantee a right of way to construct, operate and maintain a line of poles and wires for the purpose of transmitting electric power and messages. . .. The grantee is granted also the right to convey to other utility companies an interest in the rights granted under this agreement."

2. "The grantor hereby grants to the grantee, its successors, assigns, lessees and tenants a right of way. . . to construct, operate and maintain a line of poles and wires for the purpose of transmitting electric power and messages. . .."

3. Same grant as in part (a)(2), only the grant is to "the grantee, its successors and assigns. . .."

b. On the assumption that EP's easements in gross are apportionable, you have been asked also to determine whether attaching CTV's coaxial cable to EP's poles would surcharge the servient estate, either because CTV's cable is not within the type of uses authorized by the grant, or because the attachment is an impermissible increase in degree of use of the servient estate.

On the issue of surcharge, the relevant language in the deeds set forth in part (a) is that the grant is "for the purpose of transmitting electric power and messages. . .."

ANALYSIS

a.   (1) The easement in gross conveyed by this grant is apportionable. There is a constructional preference against finding easements in gross apportionable because apportionment usually increases the burden on the servient estate. There is also a constructional preference for interpreting ambiguities against the drafting party, which is EP.

Nonetheless, the last sentence in the grant says that the grantee may convey "an interest," as opposed to "the interest," to other utility companies. This wording expresses the intent that the totality of EP's rights may be divided with sufficient clarity to rebut the constructional preferences mentioned above. The only objection that might be raised is whether CTV is a utility. Most, if not all jurisdictions, would say cable TV is a utility.

a.   (2) Whether or not this grant creates an apportionable easement is debatable. The grant is to the grantee, its assigns, "lessees and tenants." A lease might be of the entire right, for a period of time shorter than the duration of EP's interest in the easement (like the lease for 10 years of an entire building that is owned in fee). This type of lease is like an assignment for a term. It involves none of the problems of abuse that the law on apportionment is designed to prevent because the leasing easement owner is as interested in preventing abuse of the leased easement as the servient landowner. Moreover, there is but one occupant at any one time.

But a lease might also be of part of EP's interest (like the lease of the third floor of the building owned in fee). This type of lease does raise the problems of increased use which the common law of apportionment was designed to inhibit because it threatens to multiply the parties utilizing the servient estate.

The lease CTV is seeking is this latter type of lease. According to the ALP and the Restatement (First), both products of legal thinking in the 1940s and 1950s, the presumption against apportionability can be overcome only by a "clear indication" or an "affirmative showing." Under this standard, an appellate court in Ohio ruled that the connotation of the words "lessees and assigns" was insufficiently strong to overcome the constructional preference against apportionability. Yet, the Ohio Supreme Court reversed this judgment. "The words' lessees and tenants indicate. . . that it was clearly intended by the parties. . . that [the grantee] could lease some portion of its interests to third parties. Such language (its . . . lessees' obviously means its. . . sub-lessees,' in the absence of any restrictive definition of 'lessee' in the easements—and there is none) is open to no other interpretation." Joliff v. Hardin Cable Television, 269 N.E. 2d 588 (Ohio 1971). The Restatement (Third)'s presumption that easements in gross are apportionable, and its accompanying commentary that power line easements generally are intended to be exclusive, supports this conclusion. Restatement (Third) § 5.9 com. (b).

Nonetheless, an abundance of caution leads to their regular inclusion so that the presumption need not be relied upon. This is the understanding with which servient landowners would read this deed; any other colorable meaning would be, therefore, insufficient to indicate clearly an intent to make the easement apportionable.

However, appellate courts in several states have held that this grant clearly intends an apportionable easement in gross. The argument is not drawn from the words, and the claim is not that the words "successors and assigns" overcome the usual constructional preference against apportionment. Rather, the leading opinion on this type of deed said, "the very nature of [the] easements obtained [by these deeds] indicates that they were intended to be exclusive." Hoffman v. Capitol Cablevision System, Inc., 383 N.Y.S.2d 674, 676 (App. Div. 1976). The court supported its conclusion by pointing out that there was no indication that the landowner or his predecessors in title had ever sought to treat the easement at bar as nonexclusive, invoking the principle that "the construction which the parties have placed upon the grant may be considered, and indeed, is of considerable importance in determining its meaning." But, at bottom, the court more or less found that the "nature" of the transaction — a grant of a right of way to an electric utility—reversed the traditional presumption against construing easements in gross as exclusive. In short, the circumstances surrounding the transaction rebutted the constructional preference for construing easements in gross as nonexclusive.

Having determined that the easement was exclusive the court concluded that it was apportionable. Subsequent courts have cited this opinion as persuasive.

b. Cable TV "transmit[s] electrical. . . messages" and therefore is a use contemplated by the grant. Cable TV may not have been invented when the easements were granted, but servient landowners are subject to the "natural" development of "progressive" inventions. See § 1.04[B], above, on the scope of easements. A wire for transmitting cable TV does not surcharge the easement in the sense of being an unauthorized use.

Nor does the stringing of a coaxial cable surcharge the easement in the sense of unreasonably increasing the degree of use. A coaxial cable is much larger than most electric wires, and block that much more of the servient landowner's view. But this is a minor burden. Moreover, in the usual case access to cable TV benefits the servient landowner, undercutting any claim of surcharge.

PROBLEM 16

Fifty years ago, when Sam Subdivider platted the Shady Grove addition to Midale Township, he dedicated the streets to the public. But he also noted on the plat that "the exclusive right to construct, maintain and operate over, under, and upon said streets gas and water pipes and mains is reserved to Sam Subdivider." The Midale Township government accepted Sam's dedication.

Twenty years ago, Sam died, leaving all his property to his daughters, Sammie and Samantha Subdivider.

Neither Sam, Sammie nor Samantha has ever provided gas or water service to Shady Grove. The residents obtain water from wells on their lots and heat from electricity provided by the electric company.

Now, the Midale Water Co. wishes to extend service to the Shady Grove addition area.

a. Is Sam's reserved easement appurtenant or in gross?

b. On the assumption that Sam reserved an easement in gross, did it descend to Sammie and Samantha?

c. On the assumption that the easement descended to Sammie and Samantha, if Sammie authorizes the Water Co. to lay its pipes in the streets of Shady Grove, may either the township government (which owns the fee interest in the street) or Samantha object?

ANALYSIS

a. Sam's easement is in gross. Sam reserved the easement for himself. Courts prefer to find easements appurtenant. But in this case there is a problem as to the land to which the easement could be annexed. Sam has no retained land that the easement could attach to. It is arguable that Sam reserved the easement on behalf of the lots he sold, and, accordingly, the owners of these lots share in the easement as tenants in common. That, however, would make an exceedingly complex property right to administer. The only sensible interpretation is that Sam reserved an easement in gross.

b. The easement in gross did descend to Sammie and Samantha. This is a commercial easement in gross. Presumptively, it is alienable. There is nothing to rebut the presumption.

c. Whether the township government or Samantha could object is unclear. The easement in gross is exclusive. Presumptively, it is apportionable. This means that Sammie and Samantha may exploit the easement independently of one another. Sammie alone may authorize the Water Co. to lay its pipes.

Nonetheless, the township government, as owner of the servient land, may object to an apportionment that in fact surcharges the servient land. Midale may argue that the possibility that the streets will be dug up by more than one water company is in itself a surcharge. Normally, there is but one water company in an area. Allowing Sammie and Samantha's exclusive easement in gross to be apportioned raises the specter that two water companies might eventually operate in the Shady Grove area. Since two water companies operating in the same area clearly is a surcharge, Midale may argue that even though Sammie and Samantha's easement in gross is exclusive, it is not apportionable.

Another way to make Midale's argument, is that the circumstances surrounding the creation of the easement, i.e., the nature of an easement to provide water service, rebuts the presumption that the right to provide water was apportionable.

Samantha would have the same grounds to object as the township government. If the easement cannot be apportioned, then Samantha can enjoin Sammie's independent activity.

[D]   Recapitulation

1. Alienation of an easement is a transfer that totally divests an easement holder of her ownership interest. Apportionment of an easement is a transfer that results in a division of an easement among several owners who use it independently of one another.

2. The parties' intent determines whether an easement is alienable and apportionable.

3. An easement appurtenant is presumptively alienable and apportionable.

4. A commercial easement in gross is an easement in gross that is created primarily for economic benefit and is presumptively alienable.

5.   A noncommercial easement in gross is an easement in gross that is created primarily for personal satisfaction and is presumptively inalienable.

6.   An exclusive easement in gross allows the easement owner the sole right to enjoy the privileges granted by the easement, without competition even from the servient landowner. An exclusive easement in gross is presumptively apportionable.

7.   A nonexclusive easement in gross allows the servient landowner to exercise, or to grant to others, the same rights she granted to the easement owner. A nonexclusive easement in gross is presumptively not apportionable.

§ 1.06 TERMINATION

[A] Definitions

<u>TERMINATION</u>: An easement terminates when the easement owner's right to enforce it ends.

<u>ABANDONMENT</u>: Abandonment is the cessation of the use of an easement accompanied by the intent to relinquish the right of use.

<u>MERGER</u>: Merger is the fusion of two or more separately owned property interests into a single consolidated interest brought about by their transfer to a single owner.

<u>MISUSE</u>: Misuse is any unauthorized use of an easement.

[B] Discussion and Questions

Under the traditional common law, there are seventeen ways to terminate an easement. They are grouped and listed below. A good number of termination doctrines are either self-evident or straightforward applications of doctrines discussed elsewhere in the typical property course. They will not be discussed further. The doctrines that are unique, or have applications that are unique, to easements are marked with an * and will be focused on in this section.

I.   Termination by express limitation

   1.   End of time period specified by the terms of the easement's creation

   2.   Breach of condition to which the easement was subject

  *3.   Purpose for which easement was created is accomplished or becomes impossible of accomplishment

II.   Termination due to subsequent events

   1.   Acts of easement owner

     a.   Severance of easement appurtenant that does not permit severance

     b.   Release

    *c.   Abandonment

    *d.   Misuse which cannot be prevented even by an injunction

   2.   Acts of owner of servient estate

     a.   Prescription

     b.   Transfer to a bona fide purchaser

    *c.   Voluntary destruction of servient estate

   3.   Acts of both easement owner and servient owner

     a.   Merger

     b.   Estoppel

4. Acts of God or other parties

    a. Eminent domain

    b. Mortgage foreclosure

    c. Tax sales

    d. Statutory enactment

  *e. Involuntary destruction of the servient estate

[1] Purpose for which easement was created is accomplished or becomes impossible of accomplishment

At times easements are created expressly to accomplish a particular purpose. Even in the absence of express termination clauses, courts presume that the parties intend an easement to terminate when its express purpose is accomplished. In addition, even if the purpose of an easement is not fully accomplished, courts presume that the parties intend to terminate the easement when its purpose ceases to be accomplishable.

Q39: A owns a parcel of land that is bordered on the south by Ramble Road and on the north by a parcel owned by B. Five years ago, A granted B an easement of way over the westernmost 20 feet of A's land, from B's parcel to Ramble Road. This year the city permanently closed Ramble Road.

  a. Is B's easement terminated?

    A: Yes. Easements are terminated when the purpose for which they were granted becomes impossible to accomplish. Closing Ramble Road means that B's easement can no longer serve the purpose of providing B's property with access.

  b. If five years later the city reversed itself and reopened Ramble Road, would B's easement revive?

    A: No. Once an easement terminates, it is gone forever.

Q40: Several years ago, O, owning two parcels of adjacent land, sold one of them to A. Because A's parcel had no means of access to a public road, O and A agreed that A had an easement by necessity over O's land. They disagree over whether the easement has been terminated. Has A lost the easement implied by necessity if:

  a. This year, the county opened a public road immediately adjacent to A's land, providing her with access.

    A: Yes, the easement has been terminated. Easements last only so long as their purpose is accomplishable. Regarding easements implied by necessity, courts take this to mean that the easements last only so long as the necessity that gave rise to them. Because A's land has other means of access, her easement by necessity no longer serves the purpose of making her unaccessible land accessible.

  b. A few years after the O-A conveyance, the county opened a public road immediately adjacent to A's land, providing her with access. This year, the county permanently closed that road.

    A: Yes. Once terminated easements do not revive. This applies even to easements by necessity. In a sense, this is an application of the implied easement rule that the necessity must arise at the time common ownership is severed. The necessity that now exists arose subsequent to the severance.

  c. For 25 years, A's friend B allowed A to reach A's land over a private road on B's land. This year, B sold her land to C, and C refuses to allow A to use the road.

    A: No, the easement has not terminated. On the one hand, A's use of B's land was permissive, not of right. Because A had no rightful means of access, the necessity that gave rise to the easement never ended. See, e.g., Finn v. Williams, 33 N.E.2d 226 (Ill. 1941). On the other hand, no matter how long continued, non-use does not terminate an easement. See

Pencader Associates, Inc. v. Glascow Tr., 446 A.2d 1097 (Del. Supr. 1982), where an easement implied by necessity was not terminated despite non-use for 178 years.

    d.   Rediscuss part (a) on the assumption that A's easement was implied from prior use.

        A: No, the easement has not terminated. Easements by prior use are not created solely by necessity. Accordingly, the necessity that gave rise to the easement was not its only purpose. Convenience was a purpose also.

[2] Merger

According to legal theory, one cannot have an easement in one's own land. Consequently, an easement appurtenant is extinguished when ownership of the dominant and servient land unite in a single owner. The easement merges into the larger fee. Subsequent transfer of the parcels into separate ownership does not revive the easement that was terminated. (Of course, a new easement may be created at that time by express act or implication.)

Similarly, an easement in gross is extinguished when ownership of the easement and ownership of the servient land pass to a single owner. The easement in gross also is not revived should the easement owner transfer either the land or her incorporeal right to another party.

Q41: Ten years ago, the city condemned an easement through A's land for street purposes. Development of the street was postponed pending development of the surrounding land. Two years ago, when she subdivided her surrounding land, A dedicated the land that was subject to the easement to the city in fee on the condition that the city maintain the road for pleasure vehicles and ban usage by trucks weighing over 3 tons. The city accepted the dedication.

        This year when the city developed the road, it did not ban usage by trucks weighing over 3 tons. When A, and the people who purchased lots from her, protested that the city was violating the terms of the dedication, the city responded that it had developed the road pursuant to the easement it had condemned which had no limitation as to usage. May the city rely on its easement?

        A: No, because the city's easement was extinguished through merger. When the city accepted the dedication in fee, its preexisting easement merged into the fee. Even though the fee was subject to a defeasing condition, it is a fee estate. Thus the city owns only the fee subject to the defeasing condition that ban vehicles over 3 tons. (If the city wants to violate the condition, it must acquire that right through purchase or condemnation and pay compensation for it.)

[3] Abandonment

In property law, abandonment is defined as the giving up of possession accompanied by the intent to give up title. Since easements are nonpossessory, the easement holder cannot give up its possession. Nonetheless, she may cease using it. Thus, abandonment of an easement involves the cessation of use accompanied by intent to relinquish the right of use.

Neither intent nor non-use separately amounts to an abandonment. Words incorporated in a sufficiently formal document satisfying the Statute of Frauds may effect a release. But unless incorporated in such a document, words declaring an intent to abandon an easement, no matter how unambiguous, do not terminate the easement. However, the words may aid in interpreting subsequent actions. And words, accompanied by a period of non-use, may be sufficient to support a finding of abandonment.

Similarly, mere non-use no matter how long continued does not, by itself, support a finding of abandonment. In many jurisdictions non-use may be evidence that supports a finding of intent to relinquish the easement. In a few jurisdictions this is carried so far as to hold that non-use for the period of the statute of limitations raises a presumption of abandonment. But in general, to support a finding of abandonment, non-use must be accompanied by words or action that is inconsistent with the intent to make further use of the easement.

Courts, however, do not favor a finding of abandonment. They require a clear manifestation of intent, although the manifestation may be made by acts as well as words.

Q42: A and B are adjacent land owners. B has an easement of way over A's land. B has other means of access, and for the past 5 years has not used the easement over A's land.

    a.   Is B's easement terminated?

        A: No. By itself, non-use does not support the finding of abandonment.

    b.   Rediscuss part (a) on the assumption that B has not used the easement for 25 years.

        A: Probably not. Nonuse does not terminate an easement. In a few jurisdictions, however, non-use for the period of the statute of limitations for real property actions creates a presumption of abandonment.

    c.   Rediscuss part (a) on the assumption that grass, bushes and trees have grown on the easement making it difficult if not impossible to use.

        A: Probably not. In many jurisdictions, allowing underbrush and trees to grow is not an affirmative act indicating an intent to abandon an easement. In some jurisdictions, however, allowing natural growth to make the easement impossible to use would be recognized as having some probative force on the question of intent to abandon.

    d.   Rediscuss part (a) on the assumption that 5 years ago B built a fence around her land and there is no gate in the fence at the point where the easement enters her property.

        A: Probably not. The dominant owner's erection of an impermanent, easily removable obstruction to using her easement is not held to indicate an intent to abandon it. In the majority of jurisdictions, fences would be found to be an impermanent obstruction.

    e.   Rediscuss part (b) on the assumption that 5 years ago B constructed a building on her lot, one wall of which occupies the area where the easement enters her property.

        A: Yes. The dominant owner's erection of a permanent, difficult to remove obstruction to using her easement is held to indicate an intent to abandon. All jurisdictions would find that the wall constitutes a permanent obstruction.

[4] Misuse which cannot be prevented even by an injunction

Misuse of an easement, that is, a use not within the scope of the easement, usually does not terminate it. The misuse can be enjoined. But the authorized use of the easement survives.

However, in some situations the misuse of an easement cannot be separated from the authorized use. The classic example is a parcel with an easement of way over adjacent land. Should the dominant landowner connect the easement to an adjacent public road, affording access to the easement from adjacent nondominant land, the traffic from the dominant and nondominant land cannot be separated; and the use of the road by nondominant landowners cannot be enjoined. In this case, an injunction cannot restrain the easement's excess use yet permit the authorized use.

In such situations, in order to protect the servient landowner from excessive use of her land, all courts enjoin the use of the easement for authorized as well as unauthorized purposes. Theoretically, many of these courts would lift the injunction if the status quo ante was ever re-established. Recognizing that this is unlikely to be done, and perhaps reasoning from abandonment doctrine, some courts go further and terminate the easement. These courts do so reluctantly, and only if the authorized and unauthorized uses cannot be separated. The increase in the marketability of the servient land from the removal of the cloud on title caused by the existence of the easement whose use is probably permanently enjoined justifies the extinguishment of the easement.

Q43: A owns a large parcel of land that is bordered on the south by Ramble Road and on the north by land that is owned by B. A's parcel has an easement of way over B's land to another road. In subdividing her parcel, A developed a street pattern that allows traffic to enter and leave the subdivision either through Ramble Road or the easement over B's land. When A recorded her subdivision, she dedicated its streets to the public.

a.   Is A's easement over B's land terminated?

> **A:**   Yes. Land outside A's subdivision is nondominant land. A's layout of the subdivision's street pattern makes it possible for nondominant land to use the easement. This is a misuse. Moreover, use by the nondominant land (the misuse) cannot be separated from use by the dominant land. Thus not only may the use of the easement be enjoined, it may be terminated.

b.   Rediscuss part (a) on the assumption that A did not dedicate the subdivision's streets to the public and has not yet sold any lots from her subdivision.

> **A:**   No. The use of the easement for ingress and egress from B's land may be enjoined, but the easement cannot be terminated. As in part (a), B's layout of the subdivision's street pattern makes it possible for nondominant land to use the easement. This is a misuse. Because the misuse cannot be separated from the authorized use, the use of the easement may be enjoined.
>
> But unlike in part (a), B still retains ownership of the streets. By a simple measure—such as a gate—B may alter the current state of affairs to prevent the misuse. Since courts hesitate to declare a forfeiture, they would only enjoin B's use of the easement until she remedied the situation.

[5]   Voluntary or involuntary destruction of the dominant or servient estate

At times an easement is not in land or on behalf of land, which rarely can be destroyed, but in or on behalf of a structure on the land. (For example, a staircase in a building providing access to an adjacent building.) Reasoning that an easement requires both a dominant and servient estate, courts agree that the involuntary destruction of either the dominant or servient structure terminates the easement. Once terminated, the easement cannot be revived even by reconstruction of the purportedly dominant or servient structure. Typically, involuntary destruction occurs through nonnegligent casualties, such as acts of God or fire. But since the servient estate owner is under no obligation to keep the easement in repair, the natural physical deterioration of a structure terminates an easement. Easements in structures, the courts say, impliedly are intended to last only as long as the structures themselves.

Courts also agree that the voluntary destruction of a dominant structure supports a finding of termination. The reasoning employed shows that this outcome is appropriately classified as a form of abandonment.

Courts do not agree on the consequences of a voluntary destruction of a servient structure. Massachusetts has ruled that the intentional destruction of the servient structure by its owner extinguishes the easement. Massachusetts' view is based on the theory that an easement requires a dominant and servient estate; it is also based on the belief that the rule promotes the efficient use of land by allowing more rapid redevelopment of decaying structures. But Massachusetts is alone in taking this position. The other courts that have ruled on the point refuse to allow a servient owner to extinguish an easement in her structure by voluntarily destroying it when it becomes economically (as opposed to physically) obsolete.

Q44:   A and B own adjacent lots developed with buildings that share a common entry and stairway. The entry and stairs are entirely in B's building. When the buildings were originally constructed, B's predecessor in interest granted A's predecessor in interest an easement of ingress and egress through B's building. A fire has destroyed B's building.

a.   Is A's easement terminated?

> **A:**   Yes. A's easement is in B's adjacent building, not the adjacent lot. The building has been destroyed without B's fault. The easement is terminated.

b.   Rediscuss part (a) on the assumption that there was no fire but that B wishes to tear down her building to construct a larger building in its place.

A: In most jurisdictions, no. In most jurisdictions the courts do not allow the servient owner to terminate an easement in a structure through the voluntary destruction of the structure. However, at least one jurisdiction, Massachusetts, allows servient owners to terminate easements by the voluntary removal of a sound structure.

[6] The <u>Restatement (Third)</u> and the termination of easements

In general, the <u>Restatement (Third)</u> adopts the traditional termination doctrines discussed in this section. The <u>Restatement (Third)</u> also suggests important reforms to termination doctrine. These reforms follow from the <u>Restatement (Third)</u>'s unification of servitude law. They chiefly involve the extension to easements of a unique doctrine developed to terminate running covenants—the changed conditions doctrine. They also involve the extension to easements of a flexible approach to judicial selection of remedies. These reforms are not be discussed here. The <u>Restatement (Third)</u>'s reforms are discussed as part of the analysis of the termination of running covenants. See § 2.07[B][5] & [6], <u>below</u>.

For further reading on Termination, see 4 <u>Powell</u> §§ 34.18–34.20; <u>CSW</u> § 8.12; 2 <u>ALP</u> §§ 8.87–8.108; <u>Restatement (Third)</u> §§ 7.1–7.12; Simonton, <u>Abandonment of Interests in Land</u>, 25 Ill. L. Rev. 261 (1930); Annot., <u>Abandonment, Waiver or Forfeiture of Easement of Ground of Misuse</u>, 16 A.L.R.2d 609 (1951); Annot., <u>Loss of Private Easement by Nonuser or Adverse Possession</u>, 25 A.L.R. 1265 (1952)

[C] Review Problems

PROBLEM 17

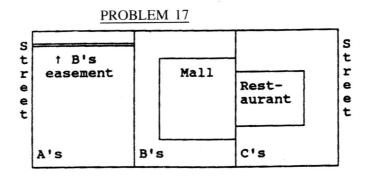

In a commercial subdivision Ann Able, Bette Benson, and Charles Chew own adjacent lots. Bette's parcel lies between Ann's and Charles'. Bette's parcel is developed as a mini-shopping mall. The primary means of access to the mall is an easement of way over Ann's property.

Last year, Bette acquired Charles' property and built a restaurant. Bette connected the restaurant building with the mall building. Although Charles' property had access to a public street, Bette designed the restaurant so that its main entry was through the mall.

When the restaurant opened, Ann sued for a declaratory judgment that Bette's easement over her land was terminated due to misuse. At trial, the evidence showed that most of the restaurant customers enter the complex over Ann's land, and park and shop in the mall either before or after dining at the restaurant.

a. Is Bette's easement terminated?

b. Rediscuss part (a) on the assumption that there was no pedestrian interconnection between the mall and restaurant, but that the restaurant delivery and service vehicles reached the restaurant over Ann's easement.

c. Rediscuss part (a) on the assumption that the mall and restaurant are heated by a furnace located in the mall's basement. Oil for the furnace is delivered over Ann's easement.

ANALYSIS

a.   No. Before an easement can be terminated for misuse there must be a misuse. There is no misuse in this Problem. Patrons of the restaurant do use the easement to reach the nondominant land on which the restaurant stands. But the evidence is that most of the customers are also using the mall. In other words, most of the customers use the easement as part of the authorized use, i.e., reaching the dominant land on which the mall is built. Once they are in the mall, they have every right to proceed from there to the restaurant land.

Of course, the implication of saying that most restaurant customers have business in the mall is that some do not. Thus, there is a misuse. But the evidence does not show that it is more than de minimis.

b.　No. The evidence now indicates a clear misuse. However, termination requires more than a misuse, it requires a misuse that an injunction is incapable of preventing. There seems to be no problem in simply enjoining Bette's use of the easement for servicing the restaurant. Moreover, given that the parcel on which the restaurant stands has street access, it is likely that Bette could redirect her delivery and service vehicles. Depending upon the design of the restaurant, redirecting the delivery and service vehicles might involve some redesign. But the point is that it is well within Bette's power to stop the misuse of the easement should she be enjoined. The injunction can separate the authorized from the unauthorized uses. A termination is not required.

c.　Probably not. There certainly does appear to be a misuse of the easement. Part of the oil delivered to the furnace over the easement is used to heat nondominant land; and the oil that creates heat for the nondominant parcel cannot be separated from oil that heats the dominant parcel.

Nonetheless, most courts would simply look to where the furnace physically is located to determine if the use of the easement was to service activity on the dominant or nondominant land. This is a close case that could go either way.

PROBLEM 18

Entry and Stairs to Bob's Building

Ann Aronson and Bob Benson own adjacent lots that are developed with buildings that are served by a common entry and stairs. The entry and stairs are entirely in Ann's building. Bob's building has an easement of way over the entrance and stairway.

A few months ago, a fire swept through Ann's building, destroying most of it but leaving the entrance and stairs it shares with Bob's building largely unharmed. Now Ann has begun the reconstruction process. Her plans call for her to tear down the burned hulk of her building, including the sound entrance and stairs, and to rebuild without providing any access to Bob's building. Upon learning of Ann's plans, Bob sued to prevent her from removing the old entry and stairs without providing a new one that services his building.

a. Should Bob prevail?

b. Rediscuss part (a) on the assumption that there was no fire. Rather, for a number of years, Ann had not maintained her building. Bob always objected to this and did what he could to keep the entryway and stairs in decent condition. But due to Ann's lack of maintenance, the rest of her building became physically dilapidated. Now, Ann has announced plans to tear down her building and replace it with another. Her plans do not include providing Bob's building with any access.

(c) Rediscuss part (a) on the assumption that there was neither a fire nor physical dilapidation. Rather, Ann wishes to redevelop her lot with a taller and more modern building.

ANALYSIS

a. No. Easements in structures are terminated when the structure is destroyed without the fault of the servient owner. Ann's structure has been destroyed. Courts hold that the rule on destruction applies even when the part of the structure that actually serves as the easement is left unharmed. This, they feel, promotes the most efficient re-use of the formerly servient estate.

b. No. Ann, as the servient owner, is under no obligation to maintain either the easement or the building supporting it. The physical dilapidation of Ann's building is without her fault. The rule that applies is the rule regarding an involuntary destruction of the building. In a sense, destruction through neglect requires application of the rule devised for involuntary destructions (such as brought about by fire) because the destruction is brought about without the (legal) fault of the servient owner. The servient owner has neglected no duty owed to the dominant owner.

c. Yes, in most jurisdictions. In most jurisdictions, the servient estate owner's intentional destruction of the servient estate due to economic obsolescence does not terminate an easement. However, one jurisdiction—Massachusetts—has ruled that easements are extinguished by such action.

[D] Recapitulation

An easement terminates when the easement owner's right to enforce it ends. There are seventeen doctrines by which easements are terminated. The termination doctrines discussed in this Student Guide are:

1. Purpose for which an easement was created is accomplished or becomes impossible of accomplishment: Courts presume that the parties intend an easement to terminate when its purpose is accomplished or ceases to be accomplishable.

2. Merger: Since no one can have an easement in her own land, legal theory compels the termination of an easement when the dominant and servient estates unite in a single owner.

3. Abandonment: Abandonment occurs when an easement owner ceases to use her easement with the intent of relinquishing her right of use. Neither non-use nor intent separately amounts to an abandonment.

4. Misuse which cannot be prevented by an injunction: Using an easement for unauthorized purposes, or to an unauthorized extent, is enjoinable. When the authorized and unauthorized uses cannot be separated, courts terminate the easement to remove it as a cloud on title.

5. Voluntary or involuntary destruction of the dominant or servient estate: Voluntary destruction of either the dominant or the servient estate terminates an easement. Voluntary destruction of the dominant estate also terminates an easement. Voluntary destruction of the servient estate does not terminate an easement, in most jurisdictions. In at least one jurisdiction, voluntary destruction of the servient estate is allowed to terminate an easement.

CHAPTER

TWO

REAL COVENANTS AND EQUITABLE SERVITUDES

§ 2.01 INTRODUCTION

Real covenants derive their name from the fact that part of their conceptual roots lie in the ancient law of promises respecting land that were expressed in deeds. Land is real property; promises expressed in deeds are covenants (as are all promises contained in sealed documents). Hence the name real covenants.

Equitable servitudes derive their name from the fact that they originated in the English High Court of Chancery, which draws its jurisprudence as much from the civil law tradition as from the common law. The English High Court of Chancery is known as the court of equity; the civil law tradition refers to specific rights to use land that one neither owns nor possesses as servitudes. Hence the name equitable servitudes.

As this implies, the term servitude—the term that is today used to refer collectively to easements, real covenants and equitable servitudes—derives from the civil, not the common, law. The traditional civil law, not the traditional common law, contained a unitary term for the various present, nonpossessory rights to land.

In the common law tradition, real covenants and equitable servitudes are distinct servitudes. They evolved during the industrial revolution in response to the need to expand the common law of servitudes beyond the limitations imposed by the law of easements. (The limitations of easement law are discussed in § 3.02, below.) The English law courts began the modern development of real covenants in the late-eighteenth century. The English equity courts began the development of equitable servitudes in the mid-nineteenth century. Due to their rather contemporaneous development, real covenants and equitable servitudes have much in common, so much in common that many scholars say they ought to be melded into one concept.

Whether the differences between real covenants and equitable servitudes ought to be dropped, and the two concepts conflated into one, is something that may well be the focus of your own thought or classroom discussion.

For our purposes what is important is that the current law does distinguish between real covenants and equitable servitudes and you must come to terms with their differences. Yet, their similarities are so strong, that it seems best to study them together, highlighting at every point their similarities as well as their differences.

However, before turning to the study of real covenants and equitable servitudes, some preliminary concepts and basic distinctions must be developed. The concepts and distinctions involve a number of sets of terms: real covenant and equitable servitude; covenant and running covenant; appurtenant and in gross; servient and dominant; affirmative and negative; burden and benefit.

REAL COVENANT and EQUITABLE SERVITUDE: Real covenants and equitable servitudes are similar in that they both are promissory obligations respecting land-use that are enforceable not only between the original parties but also by and against the original parties' successors in interest merely because they have succeeded to the original parties' property. However, real covenants originated in the late-eighteenth century English law courts; equitable servitudes originated in the mid-nineteenth century English equity courts. Due to their different origins, real covenants and equitable servitudes are distinct property interests. The primary distinctions are:

a. The requirements for the creation of real covenants and equitable servitudes are not entirely the same. The traditional elements for the creation of a real covenant are: intent, privity, and touch and concern. The traditional elements for the creation of an equitable servitude are: intent, notice, and touch and concern. These elements are discussed in §§ 2.02–2.06, below.

b. The doctrines that terminate real covenants and equitable servitudes are not entirely the same. Some termination doctrines, such as abandonment, terminate both real covenants and equitable servitudes. Other termination doctrines, such as acquiescence, unclean hands, and relative hardship, terminate only equitable servitudes and the equitable enforcement of real covenants. See § 2.07, below.

c. The remedies for breach of real covenants and equitable servitudes are not entirely the same. Real covenants are enforceable in both law and equity; equitable servitudes are enforceable in equity only. Functionally, this means that real covenants may be enforced by both damages (a legal remedy) and injunction (an equitable remedy); equitable servitudes may be enforced by injunction only. See § 3.05 below.

See §§ 3.04 and 3.05 below, for further discussion of the distinction between real covenants and equitable servitudes.

RUNNING COVENANT: Because of the great similarity between the law of real covenants and the law of equitable servitudes, it is useful to have some term that refers to them collectively. Traditionally, that term is "running covenants," which is itself a contraction of the phrase "covenants that run with the land." Real covenants and equitable servitudes run with the land in the metaphorical sense that they pass with the land from owner to owner. For brevity's sake, we will use the term "running covenants" when saying something that applies equally to real covenants and equitable servitudes. Of course, we will use the separate designations—real covenants or equitable servitudes—when saying something that applies to only one or the other of them.

COVENANT and RUNNING COVENANT: The study of running covenants is not a general study of the law of covenants. In modern usage, a covenant is a promise concerning real property. A running covenant is a promise concerning real property that may be enforced by or against transferees of the property owned by the original parties. Stated in other words, an incident of all covenants is that they are enforceable between the original parties. Running covenants have the additional incident of being enforceable by or against the original parties' successors in interest merely because they have succeeded to the original parties' property.

Accordingly, the study of running covenants is a study of the criteria necessary for a covenant to gain or lose the attribute of enforcement by or against remote parties. It is a study of the criteria by which it is determined that a promise respecting real property is personal (in gross) or appurtenant.

Q45: A and B enter into a covenant by which A promises to use her land for residential purposes only.

    a.   A dispute arises over whether this agreement is enforceable between A and B. Does the resolution of this dispute involve the law of running covenants?

        A: No. This is part of the general law of covenants. It does not involve enforcement by or against parties that are remote from the original agreement.

    b.   A sells her parcel to C. A dispute arises over whether this agreement is enforceable between B and C. Does the resolution of this dispute involve the law of running covenants?

        A: Yes. Now one of the parties is a remote party. The issue now involves aspects of the law of running covenants.

    c.   Would someone interested in whether the agreement is enforceable between B and C also be interested in whether the agreement was enforceable between A and B?

        A: Yes. This is because covenants that are not enforceable by or against the original parties are almost always—but not invariably—not enforceable by or against remote parties. One way to determine that a covenant is not enforceable by or against a remote party is to determine that it is not enforceable at all.

APPURTENANT and IN GROSS; SERVIENT and DOMINANT: The terms "appurtenant" and "in gross," and the terms "servient" and "dominant" have the same meaning when used in reference to running covenants as when used in reference to easements. As with easements, an appurtenant covenant is thought of as annexed to some real estate and passes with it from owner to owner. A covenant in gross is thought of as the personal right of an individual irrespective of her ownership of any particular parcel of land. And, land that is subject to a running covenant is servient land; land that has the benefit of a running covenant annexed to it is dominant land. (See § 1.01, above, for the definition of, and questions on, these terms when used in regard to easements.)

AFFIRMATIVE RUNNING COVENANT and NEGATIVE RUNNING COVENANT: The terms affirmative and negative have related but significantly different meanings when used in reference to running covenants than they do when used in reference to easements. Affirmative and negative, when used in reference to easements, always refer to the character of the rights of the easement owner. They indicate whether the easement owner has rights to actively use the servient land, or merely restrain the fee owner from using it. Affirmative and negative, when used in reference to running covenants, always refer to the duties of the fee owner.

An affirmative running covenant prescribes some act that the servient fee owner must do in relation to her land; a negative running covenant prescribes some act that the servient land owner cannot perform on her land. An agreement that A will provide steam heat from her building to a building on B's adjacent parcel is an example of an affirmative running covenant. A covenant that A will not build more that one single-family dwelling on her land is an example of a negative running covenant. (See § 1.01, above, for the definition of, and questions on, "affirmative" and "negative" when used in regard to easements.)

BURDEN and BENEFIT: The metaphorical phrase "running covenants" may be the traditional collective designation for real covenants and equitable servitudes, but it is often misleading to think of a covenant as running with the land. A covenant, like any promissory obligation, imposes a duty on the covenantor and gives a right to the covenantee. A covenant, like any promissory obligation, may therefore be said to have a burden side and a benefit side. Consider, for example, a covenant that A will supply B's property with heat. There is one covenant; A has the burden of performing it; B has the benefit of demanding its performance. The legal concept of burden and benefit has nothing to do with the economic desirability of the performance of the promise. If A promises B that A will break B's legs should a particular loan not be repaid, A is the promisor and has the burden of performing the promise. B is the promisee and has the benefit of the performance of the promise.

Analytically, then, it is really the burden and/or the benefit of a covenant that may or may not run; it is the burden and/or the benefit of a covenant that is appurtenant or in gross. In many jurisdictions, there is no necessary linkage between the running of the burden and the benefit. That one side of a covenant is appurtenant or in gross does not necessarily determine whether the other side is.

In other words, a covenant may be said to run (to be appurtenant) only as a composite, short-hand way of saying that both its benefit and burden run. A covenant may be said not to run (to be in gross) only as composite, short-hand way of saying that both its benefit and burden do not run. But to illustrate the importance of these observations, what answers do you have to the questions: how do you describe a covenant whose burden runs and whose benefit does not run; how do you describe a covenant whose benefit runs and whose burden does not run? And just because one side of a covenant runs, how do you know whether the other side does?

In sum, it is the burden or the benefit of a covenant that may or may not run; it is the burden or the benefit of a covenant that might pass to a covenantor's or covenantee's successor in interest. With regard to any particular covenant, it may be that neither the burden nor the benefit runs. (A covenant that A will paint B's portrait as a mural in B's house is such a covenant.) Or, it may be that the burden runs but not the benefit. (When A, an oil refining company, sells B a site for a gasoline service station, a covenant that B will purchase from A all the gasoline products used in her service station is such a covenant.) Or, it may be that the benefit runs but not the burden. (When A sells a bowling alley to B, a covenant that A will not engage in the bowling alley business within a five-mile radius is such a covenant.) Or, it may be that both the benefit and the burden run. (When A and B are neighbors, a covenant that A will not use her property for commercial purposes is such a covenant.)

This point need not have been raised in the discussion of easements because the burden of easements are always appurtenant, i.e., always run with the land. An easement must always have a servient estate. Describing an easement as appurtenant or in gross necessarily has reference only to describing whether or not its benefit runs with some other parcel of land. Accordingly, describing an easement as appurtenant is a short-hand way of describing whether or not its benefit runs with some other parcel of land.

Certainly, the notion that the running of a covenant focuses on the running of the covenant's burden and benefit is a simple idea. Nonetheless, it is an idea that is not easily absorbed. The Questions that follow are designed to aid you in distinguishing between the burden and benefit of running covenants.

Q46: A and B enter into a covenant by which A promises not to sell her land without B's approval.

    a.   Who has the burden of this covenant?

        A: A has the burden of the promise. A is the promisor and is under a duty to perform the promise.

    b.   Who has the benefit of this covenant?

        A: B has the benefit of the promise. B is the promisee and has the privilege to enforce the promise.

Q47: A and B enter into a covenant by which A promises not to sell her land without B's approval. The covenant specifies that B and whoever succeeds to her land will be able to enforce the covenant, but that the covenant can be enforced only so long as A owns her land.

    a.   Do the parties intend the burden of this covenant to be appurtenant or in gross?

        A: The parties intend the burden of the covenant to be in gross. A has the burden of the covenant. The covenant specifies that it can be enforced only so long as A owns the land. Therefore, the covenant burden does not pass to A's successor in interest. It does not run with the land.

    b.   Do the parties intend the benefit of this covenant to be appurtenant or in gross?

        A: The parties intend the benefit of the covenant to be appurtenant. B has the benefit of the covenant. The covenant specifies that it can be enforced by B or her successors in interest to the land. The covenant benefit runs with B's land.

    c.   Do the parties intend this to be a personal covenant, a running covenant, a covenant with a running benefit, or a covenant with a running burden?

        A: The parties intend this to be a covenant with a running benefit. The parties intend the covenant's burden to be personal.

    d.   Rediscuss parts (a), (b) and (c) on the assumption that the covenant specified that only B could enforce the covenant, but that the covenant could be enforced against A and whoever succeeded to her land.

        A: Now the parties intend the covenant's burden to be appurtenant, and the covenant's benefit to be in gross. The parties intend this to be a covenant with a running burden and a personal benefit.

    e.   Rediscuss parts (a), (b) and (c) on the assumption that the parties intended that only B could enforce the covenant, and the covenant could be enforced only so long as A owned the land.

        A: Now the parties intend both the covenant's burden and benefit to be in gross. The parties intend this to be a personal covenant.

f.   Rediscuss parts (a), (b) and (c) on the assumption that the covenant specified that B and whoever succeeded to B's land could enforce the covenant against A and whoever succeeded to A's land.

A: Now the parties intend both the covenant's burden and benefit to be appurtenant. The parties intend this to be a running covenant.

§ 2.02 EXPRESS INTENT: THE PARTIES' EXPRESS INTENT TO CREATE A RUNNING COVENANT

[A]   Definitions

EXPRESS RUNNING COVENANT: An express running covenant is a running covenant created by documents that satisfy the requirements of the Statute of Frauds. Because formal documents are required for the creation of express running covenants, they are also known as formal running covenants.

COMMON SCHEME: A common scheme is a uniform or unified plan of development imposed through running covenants by a landowner on her subdivided land.

[B]   Discussion and Questions

As stated in § 2.01, above, our focus is not on the creation of covenants, but only on the creation of the attribute of enforcement by or against remote parties. Nonetheless, two principles of property law that apply to the creation of covenants underlie the analysis of problems in the creation of running covenants.

The first is the principle that interests in real property must be created in writing. The second is that no interest in real property may be created in favor of a stranger to the transaction. Both these principles should be familiar from our study of easements. See §§ 1.02[B][3] and 1.03[B], above. These principles do not necessarily determine the outcome of controversies in the creation of running covenants. But they are vital to understand the issues raised, their analysis and resolution.

For example, in all jurisdictions, covenants may be created through the same forms by which all property interests are expressly created, i.e., by deeds and wills. But many jurisdictions also find grounds to relax the writing requirement. Many jurisdictions enforce implied covenants. Despite the writing requirement, many jurisdictions enforce covenants created by parol, the circumstances surrounding a transaction, and writings that are formally deficient to create express property interests.

Consequently, the parties' intent not only to create a covenant, but their intent to create a covenant with the attribute of enforcement by or against remote parties, frequently may be found through construction of a formal document. However, at times, the parties' intent not only to create a covenant, but to create a running covenant, may be found in the absence of such a document. When the former occurs, we think of the parties' intent to create a running covenant as express. When the latter occurs, we think of the parties' intent to create a running covenant as implied. (Because the difference between an express and an implied running covenant really turns upon the presence or absence of formal documents, some commentators speak of formal and informal, rather than express and implied, covenants.)

Thus, the principle requiring property interests to be embodied in formal writings is not necessarily determinative of disputes over the creation of covenants and running covenants. But the principle vitally influences the dispute. An awareness of the principle, and an understanding whether you are dealing with an argument over the creation of an express, or an implied, covenant or running covenant, is the first step toward understanding the issues raised, their analysis and resolution.

This section studies the express creation of running covenants; the following section discusses their implied creation.

To understand the most frequent issues that arise with regard to expressions of intent to create a running covenant, consider the following: A, owning a large tract of land, grants part of it to B. The deed conveying the land to B contains a clause that states:

The grantee covenants that the real property conveyed herein will be used for residential purposes only. The content of the restriction contained in this deed is certainly express. But just as certainly it is ambiguous with regard to a number of salient terms: is the burden of the restriction appurtenant or in gross; is the benefit of the restriction appurtenant or in gross; if the benefit of the restriction is appurtenant, to what land is it annexed?

There are, of course, ways of drafting covenants so that the answers to the above questions are not left to construction. If, for example, the covenant in B's deed had an additional sentence saying "[t]his covenant is to run with the land conveyed herein for the benefit of the adjacent real property now owned by the grantor," the intent to create a covenant with an burden appurtenant to the granted land, and a benefit appurtenant to the grantor's retained adjacent land, would be clear enough. If A contemplates carving a number of parcels from the same tract, she might record a declaration of covenants along with a plat of the land affected by it. Then she could incorporate the covenants into the deeds she issues by reference to the plat.

Q48: O owns a tract of land which she subdivides into 2 lots. O records a plat of the subdivision, which she calls Green Acres. O sells lot 1 to A. The deed to A includes clauses stating:

The grantee covenants that the real property herein conveyed will be used for single-family residential purposes only. . .. All covenants in this deed are appurtenant to the land platted by O as the Green Acres subdivision.

O then sells lot 2 to B. There are no covenants in B's deed.

   a.   A decides to build an apartment complex on her land. Can O or B prevent her?

      A: O cannot, and B can, enjoin A's construction. The benefit of the express covenant unambiguously runs to the land B purchased from O. Whoever owns that land may enforce A's covenant.

   b.   B decides to build an apartment complex on her land. Can O or A prevent her?

      A: Neither O nor A can enjoin B's construction. There is no covenant restricting B's use of her land. B is limited only by such general limitations as the law of nuisance.

Q49: O owns a parcel of land which she subdivides into 2 lots. O records a plat of the subdivision, which she names Green Acres. O sells lot 1 to A. The deed to A includes clauses stating:

The grantee covenants that the real property herein conveyed will be used for single-family residential purposes only. The grantor covenants that the real property she retains in the Green Acres subdivision will be used for single-family residential purposes only. . .. All covenants in this deed are appurtenant to the land platted by O as the Green Acres subdivision.

O then conveys lot 2 to B. There are no covenants in B's deed, but B has been told of the covenant in A's deed.

   a.   A decides to build an apartment complex on her land. Can O or B prevent her?

      A: Same as the answer to Q48(a), <u>above</u>.

   b.   B decides to build an apartment complex on her land. Can O or A prevent her?

      A: O cannot, and A can, enjoin B's construction. When O conveyed lot 1 to A, O agreed to a covenant burdening the land she retained (lot 2) and benefiting the land she sold (lot 1). When B purchased lot 2, she took it subject to the pre-existing burden. The question mentions that B was told of the covenant in A's deed to remove any problem with the notice requirement imposed by the law of equitable servitudes and the Recording Statutes. See § 2.04, <u>below</u>.

Q50: O owns a tract of land, which she subdivides into 2 lots. O records a plat of the subdivision along with a Declaration of Covenants. The Declaration includes clauses stating:

The land herein platted is restricted to single-family residential use only. . ... The covenants in this declaration are to run with the land herein platted.

O conveys lot 1 to A and, then, lot 2 to B. There are no covenants in either A's or B's deed, but the deeds incorporate O's plat by reference.

If B were to decide to build an apartment complex on her lots, A could prevent her. Why is this case like Q49(b), <u>above</u>, and not like Q48(b), <u>above</u>?

> **A:** When a landowner conveys land subject to a Declaration of Covenants, she is presumed to intend to restrict the land she conveys and the land she retains so that the resulting neighborhood has mutually enforceable obligations. Thus, a Declaration of Covenants is construed, by judicial presumption, to be the equivalent of the two reciprocal covenants in Q49 and not the single covenant in Q48.

Q51: O owns a tract of land which she subdivides into 3 lots. O records a plat of the subdivision, which she calls Green Acres. O sells lot 1 to A. The deed to A includes clauses stating:

The grantee covenants that the real property herein conveyed will be used for single-family residential purposes only. . ... All covenants in this deed are appurtenant to the land platted as the Green Acres subdivision.

O then conveys lot 2 to B. The deed to B includes the same clauses that were in A's deed. O then conveys lot 3 to C. The deed to C contains no covenants.

a. If B were to decide to build an apartment complex on her lot, allowing A to enjoin her construction would require a departure from, or relaxation of, the principle against creating property interests in favor of a stranger to the transaction. Allowing C to enjoin B's construction would not. Why?

> **A:** When B entered into her covenant, the land C eventually purchased was still owned by O, a party to the transaction. In contrast, the land owned by A had already passed from O's ownership and, thus, was no longer owned by a party to the transaction. Vis-a-vis B, C is a subsequent purchaser from O and takes O's land subject to the running covenants that O entered into while she held it. Vis-a-vis B, A is a prior purchaser. The covenant in B's deed was entered into by O when she no longer held A's land.

b. If the covenants in A's and B's deed were the covenants presented in Q49(b), <u>above</u>, and Q50, <u>above</u>, allowing A to enjoin B's construction would not require a departure from, or a relaxation of, the principle against creating property interests in favor of a stranger to the transaction. Why?

> **A:** In Q49(b) and Q50, O entered into a covenant burdening her retained land when she conveyed lot 1 to A. In these Questions, A received the benefit of a covenant burdening B's land while it was still owned by O, a party to the transaction. In these questions, B took land that O had already burdened. In contrast, in part (a) of this Question O had not expressly burdened her land when B took part of it.

Q52: O owns a tract of land, which she subdivides into 10 lots. O records a plat of the subdivision along with a Declaration of Covenants. The Declaration includes clauses stating:

The land herein platted is restricted to single-family residential use only. . ... The covenants in this declaration are to run with the land herein platted.

a. O sells all 10 lots to A. A decides to build an apartment complex on them. Can O enjoin her construction?

> **A:** O cannot enjoin A's construction. The benefit of A's covenant is appurtenant to the 10 lots. A owns all 10 lots. No one but A has standing to complain about a violation.

b. O sells lot 1 to A and, then, lots 2-10 to B. Since A can prevent B from building an apartment complex on her lots, how can B secure the right to build an apartment complex?

A: B can obtain a release from A of A's right to restrict B's property. A is the only person with standing to object to B's activity, unless it violates the general law. If A gives up her right, B's land is free of all restriction.

c.   Rediscuss part (a) on the assumption that the Declaration said "The burden of the covenants in this declaration are to run with the land herein platted, but the benefit of the covenants are in gross."

A: Now O can enjoin A's construction. The benefit of A's covenant is personal to O, not appurtenant to land O no longer owns. O has standing to object to A's violation of her covenant.

Despite the variety of methods by which the parties may fully document their intent regarding the running of a covenant's burden and benefit, the incomplete expression of the parties' intent on these matters is a frequent occurrence. Sometimes the incomplete expression of their intent is due to oversight. Both parties are more concerned with the immediate fact that the land is to be restricted than with the more remote and subtle issue of whether the covenant is appurtenant and, if so, for the benefit of what other land. Often the explanation for the ambiguity is that the covenant was created as part of a land development scheme in which the landowner contemplated dividing her property into a number of smaller parcels. Ambiguous draftsmanship results from the landowner attempting, on the one hand, to restrict the land she sells for the purpose of inducing further sales while, on the other hand, not locking herself into a particular development scheme in case her present plan proves unmarketable, or in case a change in the plan presents a greater opportunity for profit.

But whatever the explanation, cases regularly arise which require construction of an express covenant to determine (1) whether or not it is intended to run with the covenantor's and/or the covenantee's land; and (2) the land to which the benefit is intended to be appurtenant.

In resolving controversies concerning these issues, courts presume that covenants are intended to be in gross. A fortiori, they presume that there is no land to which the benefit is appurtenant. These presumptions reflect the time when running covenants were regarded as undesirable clogs on title. No jurisdiction seems to have openly reversed this presumption. Nonetheless, the modern view that many running covenants are socially desirable is effectuated through a liberality in inferring from the facts that the burden and/or benefit run, and that there is specific land to which the benefit is annexed.

As is usual in controversies involving documentary construction, the courts determine whether their constructional preferences are overcome by considering both the words of the dispositive document and the circumstances surrounding the transaction. The classic words indicating an intent that the burden or the benefit of the covenant is appurtenant are that the covenantor covenants "for himself, his heirs, successors and assigns" and with the covenantee "his heirs, successors and assigns." Any words that indicate the appropriate intent will do, however.

Indeed, not only will any appropriate words do, but there is a distinct trend for courts to infer the intent that the burden or benefit of a covenant run merely from the subject matter of the covenant. Covenants which judges think normally are intended to run with the covenantor's or the covenantee's land may be construed as doing so.

Q53: O owns a house on a double size lot. O conveys the half of the lot that her house is not on to A. The deed to A contains a clause stating that the "grantee, for herself, her heirs and assigns covenants to use the real property herein conveyed for residential purposes only."

a.   Is the burden of the covenant personal to A?

A: No. The burden is appurtenant to the land A purchased from O. There is hundreds of years of precedent interpreting the phrase "heirs and assigns" in this context as expressing the intent to make the burden (or the benefit, if that was involved) run with the land conveyed (or the land retained, if that was involved).

b.   Is the benefit of the covenant personal to O?

A: The benefit of the covenant is probably personal to O. The text of the clause is silent regarding whether the benefit is personal or appurtenant. The presumption is that covenants are personal. However, residential restrictions are a type of covenant that usually are intended to run with neighboring land. Nonetheless, the fact that O lives on the retained lot probably would support the inference that she intended the covenant to be enforceable solely by her in order to preserve the neighborhood's residential characteristics as long as she lived there.

Whichever way you come out, the essential point is that you see the ambiguity regarding whether the benefit is appurtenant or in gross.

Q54: O, a real estate developer, owns a large tract of land which she subdivides into 100 lots. O then sells lot 1 to A. The deed to A contains a covenant that the "grantee, her heirs and assigns will use the property for residential purposes only."

a.   Is the benefit of this covenant personal to O?

A: The covenant is probably appurtenant to the retained lots. Although covenants are presumed to be personal, the subject matter of the covenant and the surrounding circumstances—the fact that O is developing a subdivision—support the inference that the covenant is for the benefit of future landowners. O's subsequent behavior, such as inserting or omitting the covenant in subsequent deeds, would be accepted in most jurisdictions in order to determine her intent at the time of her deed to A.

b.   If O had, before selling lot 1, recorded a plat of the subdivision and advertised it as a "high class residential community," would the benefit of the covenant be personal to O?

A: These additional facts help clarify the ambiguity concerning whether the benefit of the covenant is personal or in gross. They clarify that O intends to build a residential subdivision. One means of that is to allow the vendees a means to enforce the residential restrictions. That can be done only if the benefit of the covenant is appurtenant to their lots.

Q55: O, a church with strong prohibitionist tenets, owns a tract of land surrounding its house of worship. O subdivides part of the land on which its church does not stand into 25 lots and, then, sells lot 1 to A. The deed to A contains a covenant that the "grantee, her heirs and assigns will not allow liquor or other intoxicating beverages to be sold on the premises."

Is the benefit of this covenant personal to O?

A: Yes, the covenant is personal to O. O's desire to prevent the sale of intoxicating liquors is not so widely shared by the general community that by itself it would be considered as intended to run with the land retained by O. Probably, O desires to prevent the sale of intoxicating liquor as long as its church is in the vicinity. The covenant is not meant to benefit subsequent landowners.

Q56: O, after residing for many years on an oversized lot, is retiring and moving to another state. O is very friendly with her neighbors and loves the neighborhood. Concerned that her lot is large enough to construct a multi-unit building, when she sells her house and lot to A, she inserts in the deed a covenant that says "the grantee, for herself, her heirs and assigns covenants to use the real property herein conveyed for single-family residential purposes only. The benefit of this covenant is appurtenant to all real property within a 300 foot radius of the real property herein conveyed, publicly owned streets excepted."

Is the benefit of the covenant appurtenant to the land within a 300 foot radius of the land O conveyed to A?

A: In most jurisdictions the benefit of the covenant would not be appurtenant to the neighboring land. The parties clearly intend the benefit to be appurtenant to the neighboring land. But their intent violates the principle against burdening land to benefit persons not parties to the transaction. Most states relax this principle only in the presence of a "common scheme" (a concept which will be discussed below). In a few states, however, the principle is abrogated entirely and the intent of the parties would be respected. In these states, the benefit would run in favor of the neighboring land.

When the benefit of the covenant is intended to run, the classic ways of clearly specifying the benefited land are either to describe the land in the deed, or to incorporate a description by reference to a recorded plat. (See the examples of an unambiguous covenant given above.) But, again, any words from which the intent can be inferred will do.

With regard to the surrounding circumstances that influence a determination of whether a covenant is in gross or appurtenant, and, if appurtenant, the land to which the benefit runs, a frequently influential factor is whether the grantor owns other land and the relation between the land granted and the land retained. When the grantor owns adjacent land, or land nearby which will be economically benefited or burdened by the covenant, courts frequently infer an intent that the covenant is appurtenant to that land. This is especially so when the retained land will be benefited or burdened in ways different from the community in general.

Courts also are influenced by whether the covenant at bar is part of a "common scheme" of development. (A common scheme is also known as a general plan or building plan.) Running covenants are of frequent use in the development of subdivisions. Courts hold that a common scheme of covenants embracing a larger tract or subdivision is persuasive evidence indicating that a covenant in a particular deed is intended to run and that its benefit is intended to be appurtenant to the land encompassed by the common plan.

The requirements of a common scheme are a landowner who: (1) divided her land and conveyed all or part of it to separate owners; (2) had a general scheme of covenants that she intended to, and did, apply to the land as she conveyed it away; and (3) had formulated and settled upon that scheme at the time she conveyed the land against which enforcement of the covenant is sought.

That a common owner once held land that is now separately owned usually presents no difficulty. That the common owner intended to subject that land to a common scheme of covenants as she conveyed it away is far more controversial. Factors that influence the determination of whether land that was commonly owned was sold subject to a common scheme of covenants are whether:

(1)   the land was platted or mapped together;

(2)   the plat or map was brought to the attention of the transferees;

(3)   there was advertising, sales literature or sales talk that treated the land as a unit;

(4)   there was substantial uniformity in the covenants actually inserted in the various deeds;

(5)   the tract was developed in conformity with the purported common scheme;

(6)   the purported scheme gave an average reciprocity of socio-economic benefit to the various parcels.

In considering these and other factors, courts weigh and balance them for the inferences they support about the intent of the parties. No single factor is determinative. The covenants to which the separate parcels are subject, for example, need not be identical; indeed, not all lots must be subject to covenants at all. Differences in the topography of land, or the variation of uses in a planned community may counsel differences in covenants. Thus differences or absence of covenants, when interpreted against the background of all the surrounding circumstances may support, rather than undercut, the existence of a common scheme of development. What the courts are seeking to determine is whether there was a scheme of neighborhood development that the grantees had notice of and relied upon in making their purchases and in determining the price they would pay. Once this is established, courts say that departures from the scheme are important only if they prevent effectuation of the scheme's purpose.

The issue of whether the common owner had formulated and settled upon the common scheme at the time she conveyed the parcel against which enforcement of the covenant is sought is also frequently in controversy. All too often, development plans change with shifting market opportunities. Shifts in plans may occur after the initial sales from a large tract have begun, or before the sales are complete. If a landowner were to embody her development scheme in a single declaration of covenants, and append it to a map of the affected land, the existence of the scheme and the time that the scheme was settled upon would not be an issue. Unfortunately, frequently the very existence of a common scheme is supported solely by a series of deeds to contiguous land, casual remarks and advertising. From these sources it is frequently difficult to determine not only whether a common scheme existed, but also, when it was formulated.

Thus, in order for the common plan concept to form the basis of a determination that the covenant to which some land is subject was entered into for the benefit of other land, courts must determine that the scheme was settled upon before the land subject to the covenant was sold. In undertaking this difficult determination, courts consider prior and contemporaneous acts of the common grantor and various interested parties. But, more controversially, courts also consider subsequent acts of the common grantor and other interested parties. Subsequent behavior, they feel, is probative of the parties' state of mind at an earlier date. Thus, for example, that the common grantor inserted identical covenants in the deed conveying the land against which enforcement of the covenant is sought and in all subsequent conveyances of land from the same subdivision, is persuasive evidence that the common grantor had settled upon a common scheme before conveyance of the land at bar.

This discussion of the courts' consideration of the transaction's surrounding circumstances must be understood as having three caveats. The first caveat is that the common plan requirement serves two functions. It not only provides evidence concerning the intent of the grantor but also the intent of the grantee. The existence of a common plan, by providing notice to the grantee that her grantor is imposing the covenant for the benefit of neighboring land, provides evidence of the grantee's affirmation of that intent. Consequently, there is general agreement among the courts that the grantee must have notice of the grantor's common plan. Unfortunately, the courts vary substantially regarding the ease with which the grantee is found to have obtained this notice.

The second caveat is that at least two jurisdictions, California and Arizona, refuse to consider extrinsic evidence in determining the intent of the parties. These jurisdictions extend the principle that real property interests can be created only in a sufficient writing to mean that the complete agreement must be in the dispositive document. That document, they say, is the final expression of the parties' understanding; that document must express whether the parties intended the burdens and benefits of their covenants to run, and whether the benefits are to run to some land and not other. Unless future purchasers can determine the answers to these questions from reading deeds in their direct chain of title or in a recorded declaration of covenants, land titles would be insufferably difficult to determine, making the transfer of land more cumbersome.

The third caveat is that many of the jurisdictions that allow extrinsic evidence in determining the parties' intent draw a distinction between oral and other forms of parol evidence. Many of the jurisdictions that consider extrinsic evidence will allow introduction of anything that is probative. Many others, however, exclude oral evidence. They limit their consideration to informal writings and those aspects of the surrounding circumstances, such as the relation of one lot to another, that give the determination of whether a running covenant exists and, if so, for whose benefit, a more permanent basis than slippery memory.

[In Q57–61, below, assume that the covenant clearly imposes the restriction; clearly says the burden runs with the land conveyed; but says nothing about whether the benefit runs or the land to which it runs.]

Q57: O owns fifty acres of land. Ten years ago she sold a one acre lot subject to a covenant restricting it to residential use. Two years later she sold another one acre lot subject to the same covenant. The second lot was located some distance from the first lot sold. Three years later she sold three more one acre lots subject to the same covenant. These last three lots were adjacent to one another but located some distance from the first two lots sold.

    a.   Is there a common scheme?

A: There is no common plan. A finding of a common plan requires a finding that the grantor determined to treat the lots sold as a unit. There is no evidence of that here, other than the fact that the same covenant was inserted in every deed, which is a significant factor. If carried on long enough, it could amount to sufficient evidence upon which to predicate finding a common plan.

However, in this context, the sales seem to be casual, and not in pursuit of a determined plan. O has sold only 5 of 50 acres, and there is no evidence of the overall determination that certain land, and not other land, is part of the plan.

b. Assume that before selling the first lot, O had a surveyor draw up a map of the 50 acres showing them divided into 50 one acre lots. Assume that she had shown the map to prospective purchasers; and that she had occasionally advertised the lots as homesites. Is there a common scheme?

A: There is a common plan, except in jurisdictions that follow the California position. The additional evidence provides a basis for the inference lacking in part (a), that inference being that the grantor had determined to treat the land as a unit and the grantees had notice of it.

In California the courts would refuse to hold that a common plan existed because it is entirely based upon informal (parol) evidence, not formal documents in the grantees' chain of title.

c. Assume that before selling the first lot, O had a surveyor draw up a map of the 50 acres showing them divided into 50 one acre lots and that this map had been recorded as the Green Acres subdivision. Is there a common scheme?

A: In most jurisdictions, there probably is a common plan. The existence of a recorded map and O's subsequent uniform treatment of the lots may be sufficient to support a finding that O intended, from the outset, to treat the lots as a unit. That the map, singling out this land as a subdivision, was recorded (and therefore, discoverable by the grantees) may be sufficient to put them on notice—even the early grantees—that the covenant in their deed was for the benefit of the mapped land.

d. Assume that before selling the first lot, O had a surveyor draw up a map of the 50 acres showing them divided into 50 one acre lots, but that O had never shown the map to the grantees. Is there a common scheme?

A: This case is too close to call. The map, plus O's subsequent behavior may be enough to indicate O's intention. But do the grantees have notice of it? Possibly the later grantee's do, but how would the early grantees be appraised that their covenant ran to potentially 50 other landowners and not just to O? At least some courts would find that the covenant did not run to the neighboring land because the early grantees had insufficient notice of it. Other courts might find, especially after the initial sale, that there was sufficient evidence. See, for example, the majority and minority positions in Steinmann v. Silverman, 200 N.E.2d 192 (N.Y. 1964).

e. In all jurisdictions, would the advertisements be admissible as evidence? Would the unrecorded map? Could the lot purchasers testify that O had shown them the map? Could O testify about whether she intended the benefit of the covenants to be appurtenant or in gross?

A: A few courts, such as California, would not permit any evidence not drawn from formal documents placed in the parties' chain of title. Most other jurisdictions would admit all the parol evidence that was not purely oral. These courts consider the surrounding circumstances, but only those that have a quasi-permanent existence and, thus, are continually available. Some courts admit all parol evidence, even parol evidence that is wholly oral.

Consequently, the map and the advertisements would be admissible in all jurisdictions except those following the California approach. Some, but not all of these jurisdictions, also would admit the oral remarks, i.e., the grantees' testimony that the map was shown to them, and O's testimony concerning her intent.

Q58: O owns fifty acres. Five years ago, she subdivided and platted it into fifty lots. O also recorded the plat. Over the course of the next few years, O sold all the lots. The deeds to 45 of the lots contained residential use restrictions. For totally unexplained reasons, 5 lots were sold free of all restrictions.

   a.   Is there a common scheme?

   A: There is a common plan. A common scheme does not require absolute uniformity. Even unexplained deviations from a plan do not bar a court from holding that the common grantor intended to establish a neighborhood scheme of mutually enforceable covenants, and that the grantees had notice of this intent. When there are deviations, however, the court will inquire into whether the plan is capable of effectuation. In this case, 45 identically restricted lots out of 50 is usually accepted as sufficient to support the inference that all parties knew that a common scheme was being established; 5 deviations out of 50 is usually accepted as insufficient to prevent the creation of a residential neighborhood.

   b.   Assume that the 5 unrestricted lots were developed for residential use. What would the relevance of that fact be, and would a court admit evidence of it?

   A: The fact that the unrestricted lots were in fact developed for residential use is relevant to determining a) whether the plan can be effectuated despite the deviations; and b) the understanding of the grantees as to whether there was a common scheme (through considering their subsequent behavior). The evidence is parol, but it is not oral. This evidence is rather permanent, even though not embodied in formal documents, and would be admissible in most jurisdictions.

Q59: Y, who purchased a lot subject to a covenant restricting it to single-family residential use, wishes to build an apartment complex. Her neighbor, X, has sued to enjoin Y's construction. Whether or not X has standing to sue depends upon whether Y's covenant was inserted in her deed as part of a common scheme. Was there a common scheme, if all the evidence before the court is:

   a.   X's and Y's lots are part of a tract that was owned by O. O subdivided it into 30 lots. 5 of the deeds from O contained no use restrictions; 10 of the deeds contain covenants restricting the lots to residential use; 15 of the deeds contain covenants restricting the lots to single-family residential use.

   A: There is no common plan. The evidence suggests no pattern or reason for the lack of uniformity among the covenants.

   b.   In addition to the evidence in part (a), there is evidence that railroad tracks border O's tract on one side. The 5 unrestricted lots are adjacent to the tracks; the 10 lots restricted to residential use are adjacent to the 5 unrestricted lots; the 15 lots restricted to single-family residential use are adjacent to the 10 residentially restricted lots.

   A: There is a common plan. The additional facts establish a rationale for the diverse covenants. The grantor was creating a neighborhood in which the unrestricted lots buffered the residential lots from the tracks, and the residential lots buffered the single-family lots from the unrestricted lots.

Q60: O owned land along Epson Drive. When the general area had already established a reputation as a high-grade residential neighborhood, O subdivided her land into 90 lots. Over the years she sold them all. In only 50 of the 90 deeds, O inserted covenants restricting the lot to single-family residential use. Yet, all her vendees constructed only single-family residences on their property.

Now A has purchased one of the lots restricted to single-family residential use. She wishes to convert the structure to commercial use. She has secured a release from O; and claims that the neighbors cannot enjoin her construction because of the absence of a common plan. Is A correct?

A: There is no common scheme. The lots are not uniformly restricted, and the absence of uniformity is totally unexplained. It certainly seems that the inclusion of covenants in some of the deeds was casual. Normally, the absence of covenants in so many deeds would make the plan, if there were one, incapable of effectuation. Most courts would rule this way.

Nonetheless, in the leading case of Sanborn v. McLean, 206 N.W. 496 (Mich. 1925), the court held that there was sufficient evidence to support the finding of a common scheme. (Indeed, in the Sanborn case, the defendant was one of the lot owners who did not have a covenant in his deed, and the case concerned whether the court would imply one. See § 2.03, below, for a discussion of implied covenants.) This holding demonstrates how favorably some courts look upon the creation of running covenants in residential situations. Perhaps this holding is also a lesson about the power of the factor, in determining that there is a common plan, of what the actual development of the subdivision has been. A, who had a covenant in her deed and knew the character of the locale, certainly had notice of this.

Q61: O owns thirty acres of land, which she subdivides into 15 lots. In selling the land, O inserts a covenant restricting the land to single-family residential use in only 3 of the deeds. A, whose deed has a single-family residential restriction in it, wishes to build an apartment complex on her lot. When the neighbors sue to enjoin A's construction, A defends on the ground that there is no common plan. The neighbors respond that there is a common plan because a) all fifteen lots were developed for single-family residential use, and b) before A purchased her lot, O sent her a letter informing A that O was establishing a "high-grade single-family residential neighborhood."

Is A or her neighbors correct?

A: There is no common plan. In her letter to A, O may have said that she was pursuing one. But inserting the covenant in 3 out of 15 deeds seems too few to indicate that O actually followed through.

Nonetheless, in Womack v. Dean, 266 S.W.2d 500 (Tex. App. 1954) the court found that there was sufficient evidence of a common plan to allow the neighbors to enforce the covenant against A. The court focused on A's receipt of O's letter and that the entire subdivision was developed in conformity with the alleged plan. This case shows the importance to some courts of the factors of a) the expectations of the defendant, and b) the actual development of the locale.

Still, it is suggested that a proper analysis would conclude that there was no common plan, but that A was nonetheless liable on a third-party beneficiary theory. The ultimate question, after all, is whether the neighbors are the intended beneficiaries of A's covenant. The common plan is a technique for making that determination, but should not be thought of as the only one. (This suggestion was not made in the answer to Q60, above, because in that question there was no evidence, such as the letter from O to A, that supported the inference that the covenant in A's deed was intended to be appurtenant to any other property.)

Without a doubt, the common scheme concept is perplexing. Nonetheless, it must be mastered because of its importance. The common scheme concept is important because it is frequently central to the enforcement of covenants in subdivisions. Moreover, the common scheme is central to the enforcement of express covenants in two different types of subdivision cases. In both types of cases the subdivider has a scheme of covenants at the time the ambiguous covenant is inserted in the grantee's deed. Certainly, that she inserts similar covenants in deeds conveying the land she still retains indicates that the ambiguous covenant was for the benefit or burden of that land. The common plan would be important if that was its only use.

However, many courts have used the existence of a common plan to establish that the ambiguous covenant was for the benefit of land that is part of the subdivision but which was sold prior to the conveyance of the land against which enforcement of the covenant is sought. Allowing the benefit of the promise to run to prior purchasers violates the principle that no interest may be created for the benefit of a stranger to the transaction. A few courts, usually in dicta, have said that they no longer adhere to the rule against third party beneficiaries to land transactions. Most, however, still generally recognize the principle. Yet many courts allow what is in effect a third party beneficiary contract in the presence of a common plan. The existence of a common plan, by limiting the extent to which the principle barring third party beneficiaries of real property agreements is relaxed, makes the relaxation palatable. (The common scheme concept is important also because of its application in a third type of subdivision case involving the creation of implied covenants. See § 2.03[B][2][a], below.)

Q62: O owns two lots on the west side of Temple Drive, lots 1 and 2. O also owns another lot, lot 3, on the east side of Temple Drive directly opposite lot 2. O resides on lot 3. Three years ago, O sold lot 1 to A. Two years ago, O sold lot 2 to B. Last year, O sold lot 3 to C. This year, B started to build a commercial structure on her property.

 a. Can A or C enjoin B's construction.

  A: There is no covenant restricting B's lot. Consequently, neither A nor C can enjoin B's construction, unless it violates such general law obligations as the law of nuisance.

 b. Assume that B's deed contained a clause stating that the "grantee, for herself, her heirs and assigns covenants to use the property herein conveyed for residential purposes only." Can C enjoin B's construction? Can A?

  A: Neither A nor C can enjoin B's construction. B's covenant is ambiguous as to whether it is personal or appurtenant. That O inserted it only in B's deed bars the inference that it was meant to be appurtenant any land. Probably, O wanted to keep B's land residential so long as O lived across the street.

 c. If all three deeds contained a covenant restricting their use to residential purposes, what effect would it have on C's cause of action? On A's?

  A: In most jurisdictions both A and C can enjoin B's construction. That O placed the covenant in all three deeds supports the inference that she had a common scheme for the development of the lots, and intended the benefit of the covenants to be mutually enforceable.

  In a few jurisdictions, such as California and Arizona, neither A nor C could enjoin B's construction. These jurisdictions refuse to allow the grantor's subsequent behavior to supply the evidence necessary to create a common scheme. That there is a common scheme must be made manifest to the first purchaser, and clearly defined in her deed. See R&R Realty v. Weinstein, 422 P.2d 148 (Ariz. 1967). The principle that real property interests, particularly those that restrict the free use of land, must be expressed in a formal writing is taken to the extreme of holding that the deed to B (or some other formal document in her chain of title) is the conclusive evidence of the parties' agreement.

  Moreover, this strict enforcement of the principle is applied in determining whether the benefit of a covenant is appurtenant to land retained by the grantor. See Werner v. Graham, 183 P. 945 (Cal. 1919) ("It is. . . difficult to see how there can be any valid creation of what is practically a servitude without some designation or description of what is an essential factor, namely, the dominant tenement."); Citizens for Covenant Compliance v. Anderson, 906 P.2d 1314 (Cal. 1996) (covenants contained in a recorded declaration of covenants satisfy the Werner requirement). Thus, without some clear indication that the benefit of B's covenant was to run in favor of O's retained land, C, to whom O's retained land passed, has no standing to enforce the promise.

 d. If the deeds to A and B, but not the deed to C, contained a covenant restricting their use to residential purposes, what effect would it have on C's cause of action? What effect would it have on A's?

A: C and A would probably not be able to enjoin B's construction. That O placed the covenants in the deeds she issued while she lived in the neighborhood, and did not do so when she moved away, supports the inference that the covenants were not part of a common scheme to develop a restricted neighborhood, but rather, for her personal benefit.

For further reading on the Express Creation of Running Covenants, see 2 ALP §§ 9.2–9.3, 9.29–9.30; Restatement (Third) §§ 2.1–2.7; Annot., Who May Enforce Restrictive Covenant or Agreement as to Use of Real Property, 51 A.L.R.3d 556 (1973).

[C] Review Problems

PROBLEM 19

Olivia Owner subdivided and platted a tract she owned into 115 lots. She recorded the plat of the tract. Over the next five years, 17 lots were sold, none of them subject to covenants. Then Olivia conveyed a lot to Andy Andrews subject to a covenant that the "grantee, for himself, his heirs and assigns covenants to use the real property herein granted for residential purposes only." Over the next ten years, Olivia sold the rest of the lots. All of the deeds contained covenants identical to the one in Andy's deed.

Andy now plans to use his lot for commercial purposes.

a. May an owner of one of the restricted lots enjoin his construction?

b. What additional argument against enforcement of the covenant by his neighbors could Andy make if his lot were surrounded by the unrestricted lots?

ANALYSIS

a.   The fact that the first 17 lots were sold without restrictions is not determinative of the controversy. Olivia may not have had a common scheme when sales commenced. But that fact is no more than circumstantial evidence on the relevant question: did Olivia have the requisite plan at the time she conveyed Andy his lot, and did Andy have sufficient notice of it?

Courts that follow the California position would not permit an owner of a restricted lot to enjoin Andy's construction plans. No formal documents, to which Andy takes subject, clearly express the intent that the benefit of his covenant runs to their land.

Other courts might allow the restricted landowners to enjoin Andy's construction. Most courts consider more types of evidence than the California courts. In particular, they consider Olivia's subsequent acts for the light they shed on whether she had formulated her plan at the time she conveyed Andy's lot. All courts would find that including the covenant in the subsequent conveyances strongly supports the conclusion that Olivia had formulated her common scheme before conveying Andy's land.

The debatable issue, in these jurisdictions, is whether Andy had sufficient notice. Some courts would hold that he did. There was a covenant in his deed, and his land was part of a recorded subdivision. Other courts, such as the New York courts, might not find that Andy had the requisite notice. These courts hold that the covenantee must have "definite and clear" notice of his grantor's plan. These courts might, for example, distinguish between the notice given to 1) the first grantee of land in a recorded subdivision whose deed has restrictive covenants in it, and 2) the seventeenth grantee of land in a recorded subdivision whose deed is the first to have restrictive covenants in it.

b.   Andy might argue that, at least with regard to his lot, the common scheme was impossible to effectuate. Whenever there are deviations from the common scheme, courts are interested in whether they prevent the benefit of the plan from being realized. If so, then there is no mutuality of benefit from the obligations. Most cases, however, require that the benefits of the common plan be entirely subverted. Andy should consider that argument. But the facts given do not support the more extensive claim as clearly as they support the claim that he cannot realize the mutuality of benefit that forms the basis for construing the covenants as running to his neighbors.

PROBLEM 20

Olivia Owner subdivided a tract she owned into 25 lots. All of the lots were sold subject to a covenant that they would be used for residential purposes; that any construction would be set-back from the lot lines; and that any construction would have a minimum value. However, the set-backs varied. Ten lots were subject to 20 foot set-backs; ten lots were subject to 30 foot set-backs; five lots were subject to 40 foot set-backs. The minimum value covenant also varied. Eight lots were subject to a $60,000 minimum; eight lots were subject to a $70,000; and nine lots were subject to an $80,000 minimum.

Andy Andrews purchased the fifteenth lot sold. His deed says that any construction must be set-back 30 feet, and cost no less that $80,000. Nonetheless, Andy is constructing a house set-back only five feet and costing only $50,000. Andy has secured a release from Olivia of any rights Olivia may have to enjoin his construction.

Can any of the lot purchasers enjoin Andy's construction?

ANALYSIS

Most courts would rule that none of the lot purchasers could enjoin Andy's construction. Part of the common scheme's blackletter doctrine is that there is uniformity among the restrictions. Diversity is tolerated when it is explained by the topography or other factors. Diversity is also tolerated when the departures from the scheme are minor and do not prevent the scheme's effectuation. In this Problem, however, there is an absence of uniformity. Olivia seems to have wanted some set-back and minimum value restriction, but seems to have been unable to make up her mind as to what they should be.

Nonetheless, in terms of policy this result may not be warranted. As stated above, diversity is tolerated when departures from the common scheme do not prevent the scheme's effectuation. De minimis variation is inconsequential. In terms of this policy, a distinction might be drawn between the set-back and the minimum value restriction.

The set-back restriction's lack of uniformity probably destroys the utility of any set-back. Set-backs are beneficial to a community only when they provide a uniform line of sight. However, the minimum value restriction's lack of uniformity may not destroy its utility. Variation between a $60,000 and $80,000 house may not be that apparent.

Consequently, there may be an argument that the variation in the minimum value requirement does not prevent the effectuation of the common scheme, which was to provide some floor for the quality of construction and economic characteristic of the residents of the neighborhood.

Assuming there is a common scheme regarding the minimum value restriction, one can imagine two resolutions. One is that the neighbors can enforce whatever restriction is in Andy's deed. Another is that Andy is subject to the most minimum restriction contained in a deed from Olivia. The first resolution has the benefit of enforcing the burden to which Andy agreed. The second resolution has the benefit of fairness. It equitably compels Andy to invest no more in his construction than is required to maintain the actual scheme.

PROBLEM 21

Olivia Owner owned 26 acres of land known as Sunset Point. Over a period of eight years, Olivia disposed of all this property through seven separate conveyances. Although Olivia never filed a subdivision map or any declaration of covenants applicable to Sunset Point, she inserted in the 1st, 2nd, 4th, and 6th deeds a clause which read:

IT IS UNDERSTOOD AND AGREED that this conveyance is made by the Grantor and accepted by the Grantee pursuant to a plan of the Grantor to maintain the present residential rural nature of this property and that the same is for the direct benefit of the property known as Sunset Point of which this granted property is a part. ACCORDINGLY, said land is granted subject to the following covenants and restrictions, which covenants and restrictions shall run with the land in favor of the land known as Sunset Point. . ..

Ten restrictive covenants followed this clause. Among the covenants was one limiting development of the property to single-family detached dwellings for residential use.

Neither the above quoted clause nor any restrictive covenants were inserted in the 3rd, 5th and 7th deeds.

Freddie Field was the sixth conveyee. After holding the land for some time, she announced plans to erect multi-unit condominium townhomes on her parcel.

Freddie's land is subject to an express restrictive covenant and her plans violate it.

a. Is there a common plan?

b. Assume there is a common plan. May the owner of the 4th lot conveyed enjoin Freddie's construction based upon it?

c. Assume there is no common plan. May the owner of the 4th lot conveyed enjoin Freddie's construction based upon Freddie's express third-party beneficiary promise?

d. Assume the common plan and third-party beneficiary theories fail. May the owner of the 7th lot, who has no restrictions in her deed, enjoin Freddie's construction?

ANALYSIS

a.   This is a close case. In favor of a determination that there is a common plan is the fact that the grantor expressly states that there is one. This both indicates the grantor's intent and provides notice to the grantees. Countervailing this consideration is the fact that the grantor placed the covenant in only 4 of 7 deeds. Thus, there is the argument that the grantor had a common scheme but did not sufficiently follow through with it.

b.   On the assumption that there is a common scheme, in most jurisdictions the owner of the 4th lot sold has a clear case to enjoin Freddie's construction as an intended beneficiary of her covenant. However, the owner of the 4th lot sold could not sue successfully in jurisdictions that follow the California position. California decided, in Werner v. Graham, 183 P. 945 (Cal. 1919), that for a prior purchaser to sue a subsequent purchaser, the prior purchaser's deed must show not only "that the parcel conveyed [to the prior purchaser is] subject to restrictions in accordance with the plan for the benefit of all the other parcels," but also "that all other parcels [are] subject to such restrictions for its benefit." Thus, even though the deeds from Olivia that contain the covenant clearly state that the benefit of the covenant is appurtenant and specifies the land to which it is to run, no mutually enforceable running covenants were created because the deeds did not expressly state that Olivia's retained land was reciprocally burdened for the benefit of the land conveyed. Even though the reciprocal promise to burden the grantor's retained land could be inferred from the fact that it was inserted in a sufficient number of deeds, it was not expressed in those deeds. California requires all burdens to be express.

c.   In most jurisdictions, the owner of the 4th lot conveyed could not enjoin Freddie's construction based upon a third-party beneficiary promise, no matter how clearly expressed. In a few jurisdictions, such as New York, New Jersey, and Oregon, the parties' intent would be respected.

d.   The owner of the 7th lot conveyed can enjoin Freddie's construction plans—even in jurisdictions following the California approach. The owner of the 7th lot conveyed owns land that Olivia still held when she conveyed land to Freddie. Therefore, allowing the benefit of Freddie's covenant to attach to that land requires no relaxation of the principle against creating interests in real property in favor of a stranger to the transaction. All that is required is an expression of intent that the benefit of the covenant run to the grantor's retained land. That intent is stated expressly in Freddie's deed.

PROBLEM 22

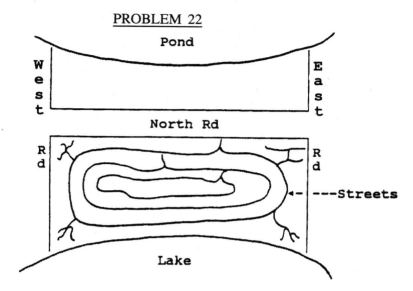

Twenty years ago, Sammie Subdivider subdivided and platted a large tract of land she owned that was bordered on the south by Lake Wyndota, on the east by East Road, on the north by Jackson Pond, and on the west by West Road.

The tract was bisected by North Road, which runs in an east-west direction, cutting it into two uneven sectors. The northern section comprises 20%, and the southern sector comprises 80%, of the tract. The northern sector is a low lying area which is marshy due to its proximity to Jackson Pond. Sammie thought it unsuitable for building and worthless. The southern sector rises to a small hill and then gracefully descends to Lake Wyndota. Lake Wyndota was renown for its swimming, boating and fishing. Sammie thought it was an excellent site for vacation homes. North Road was a beautiful country road that, due to the lack of development in the area, had not attracted much traffic.

Consequently, when Sammie platted the tract, the plat showed the southern sector divided into lots. All the streets for the lots funneled into North Road. There was no ingress or egress through any other road. The northern sector was not divided into lots.

For the next eighteen years, Sammie sold lots from the southern sector. Most, but not all, of her deeds included a clause that read:

The grantee, for herself, her heirs and assigns covenants to use the property herein conveyed for single-family residential purposes only.

Two years ago, Sammie sold the entire northern sector to Dan Developer. The deed to Dan included the clause:

The grantee, for himself, his heirs and assigns covenants to use the property herein conveyed for residential purposes only, with no construction higher than thirty feet from ground level, or an overall density greater than 10 units an acre.

After this conveyance, Sammie continued selling lots from the southern sector until last year when she sold all the southern sector's remaining unsold lots to Bette Builder. All the deeds conveying individual lots, and the deed to Bette, contained the previously quoted single-family residential restriction.

Now, Dan has announced plans to construct a garish amusement park on the land north of North road. He has secured a release from Sammie.

a. May a lot owner who purchased her lot prior to the Sammie's sale of the northern sector enjoin Dan's construction as an intended beneficiary of the covenant in Dan's deed?

b. May a lot owner who purchased her lot after Sammie's sale of the northern sector enjoin Dan's construction as an intended beneficiary of the covenant in Dan's deed?

ANALYSIS

a.   A prior purchaser may enjoin Dan's construction only if she was an intended beneficiary of Dan's covenant. That conclusion can be predicated only upon the finding that the northern sector and the southern sector comprised one common scheme of development. The required conclusion cannot be predicated upon an express third-party beneficiary promise because there was none.

In jurisdictions that follow the California position, concluding that there was a common scheme embracing both sectors would be of no avail. There is no formal document in which the common scheme is fully set out. Rather, the common scheme must be inferred from the series of conveyances. Thus in these jurisdictions, the prior purchasers clearly could not enjoin Dan's construction.

In most jurisdictions, however, the finding of a common scheme embracing the southern and northern sectors would result in the prior purchasers being able to enjoin Dan's construction. But whether there is a single common scheme embracing both sectors is a close question. This is especially so since the burden is on the neighbors to prove what Sammie's intent was, and that Dan had sufficient notice of it.

The argument in favor of the southern and northern sectors forming one common scheme is that the land was platted together. The difference in the covenants can be explained away by the marshy conditions of the northern sector. The argument against the existence of a unified scheme is that Sammie thought it impossible to build on the northern sector when she formulated her plans. Thus, when it was built upon, it represented a new plan that could not embrace the land south of North Road that already had been sold.

b.   The ability of a lot purchaser who purchased after Sammie's sale of the northern sector to enjoin Dan's construction depends upon whether or not there is a common scheme. If there is a common scheme the subsequent purchasers have standing to sue; if there is not a common scheme, they do not have standing. The discussion of whether there is a common scheme would be the same as in part (a).

There may be a tendency to think the subsequent purchasers would have standing to sue regardless of the presence of a common scheme. After all, the subsequent purchasers take land that Sammie owned at the time Dan entered into his covenant. Their standing to sue does not raise the problem of extending the benefit of Dan's covenant to land owned by a stranger to the transaction, a problem that the common scheme concept helps overcome.

Nonetheless, subsequent purchasers have no standing to enjoin Dan's construction unless they are the intended beneficiaries of Dan's covenant. At times, as in Problem 21, above, the intent that the covenant run to land retained by the grantor is expressed. At other times, as when the grantor owns adjacent land which is not subdivided, the circumstances support the inference that the adjacent land is the intended beneficiary. In both these cases, a common scheme is not necessary for subsequent purchasers of the grantor's retained land to have standing to sue.

In this Problem, however, it is not clear that Sammie intended Dan's covenant to run in favor of the land she still owned in the southern sector (let alone the land she had sold previously). The existence or nonexistence of a common scheme embracing the northern and southern sectors would indicate whether or not Sammie and Dan intended Dan's covenant to be personal to Sammie or appurtenant to her nearby retained land.

PROBLEM 23

Denise's	Plat 2
Bob's	Plat 1 ** ** * * ** * *

* = Plat 1 lots
    sold to Bob

Olivia Owner owned a square shaped 40 acre tract. Fifteen years ago, Olivia recorded a plat subdividing the southeast quarter into 60 lots. Recorded with the plat was a Declaration of Covenants that included a clause stating: "The premises are conveyed for residence purposes only and no structure other than one single private residence shall be erected, placed or permitted on the premises conveyed."

Ten years ago, Olivia recorded a plat subdividing the northeast quarter into 30 lots. A Declaration of Covenants was also recorded. That declaration was substantially similar to the one previously recorded.

Five years ago, Olivia conveyed Bob Builder all of the southwest quarter and ten unsold lots from the southeast quarter. Olivia's deed contained restrictive covenants that were substantially similar to the declarations recorded against the eastern half of her original tract. The above quoted clause was among the covenants included in the deed.

Last year, Olivia conveyed Denise Developer all of the northwest quarter. The deed contained no restrictive covenants, and Denise built low-rise apartment houses on it.

This year Bob announced plans to construct low-rise apartment houses on the land he purchased from Olivia. He has secured a release from Olivia of any rights she has to enjoin his construction.

May someone who purchased a lot in the southeast quarter enjoin Bob's construction plans regarding

(a) the 10 lots that were originally part of the southeast quarter; and

(b) the southwest quarter?

ANALYSIS

a. An owner of a lot in the southeast quarter has a clear right to enjoin Bob's construction plans regarding the 10 lots that were originally part of the southeast quarter. The lots in that section were sold subject to a recorded plat and declaration of covenants. This created a common scheme, embracing the southeast section. The traditional interpretation of such a declaration is that the burdens imposed on the lots run in favor of the other reciprocally burdened lots.

b. The benefit of covenants may run among subdivisions carved from a larger parcel in the same manner that they run among individual lots carved from a subdivision. The central issue is the parties' intent. The intent to have the benefit of covenants run between subdivisions is rarer. It is less likely to be presumed by the courts, and is harder to prove. But in a clear case, the requisite intent may be established. With this in mind, these facts present a debatable case.

The argument against finding a common scheme encompassing the southeast and the southwest sections would focus on the fact that there was no plat that included both tracts. The argument would focus also on the fact that when the northwest quarter was sold it was not subject to any restrictions. This supports the inference that Olivia extracted the covenant from Bob in order to protect her investment in the land she still retained should it be important to her to maintain the entire area as a single-family residential development.

The argument supporting the finding of a common scheme encompassing the southeast and southwest tracts would minimize the importance of the sale of the northwest quarter free from restrictions by saying that the existence of a common scheme among the remaining tracts is not necessarily refuted by admitting that the scheme did not embrace all four sections. It would focus on the fact that three of the four sections were sold subject to substantially similar covenants.

In addition, the argument supporting the finding of a common scheme encompassing the three other sections would emphasize the fact that a number of restricted lots from the southeast section were included in the sale of the southwest section to Bob. The inclusion of these lots supports an inference that Olivia saw the four sections as a unified development.

This is a close case. It is reasonable to conclude that there is insufficient evidence of a common plan. Yet, the court that decided the case upon which this Problem is based, Fey v. Swick, 454 A.2d 551 (Pa. Super. 1982), ruled that there was a common scheme embracing the three restricted sections. That court found the inclusion of the lots from the southeast section in the sale to Bob to be a very persuasive factor.

[D]   Recapitulation

1. An express running covenant is a running covenant created by documents that satisfy the Statute of Frauds.

2. Two types of controversies frequently arise in disputes over express running covenants: did the parties intend the covenant to run; and if so, to what land is the benefit appurtenant?

3. Express covenants do not run unless the parties intend them to run. Covenant benefits are appurtenant only to the land to which the parties intend to annex it. Courts construe ambiguous expressions of the parties' intent regarding the running of covenants by considering the words in the document, the transaction's surrounding circumstances and the judiciary's constructional preferences. In construing the parties' intent, courts also will consider whether the subject matter of the disputed covenant usually is intended to run.

4. The classic way the parties express the intent for a covenant to run is for the covenantor to covenant "for himself, his heirs and assigns," and the covenantee to covenant "for himself, his heirs and assigns."

5. A common scheme is a uniform or unified plan of development imposed through running covenants by a landowner on her subdivided land. The requirements for a common scheme are a landowner who (1) divides her land and conveys all, or part, of it to separate owners; (2) has a general scheme of covenants that she intends to, and does, apply to the land as she conveys it away; and (3) formulates and settles upon that scheme at the time she conveys the land against which enforcement of the covenant is sought.

    In determining whether and when a common scheme was formulated, many courts consider acts of the common grantor that were undertaken subsequent to the conveyance being construed. Most courts allow the common plan to emerge from the common grantor's conveyances, taken as a group, whether they were issued before or after the conveyance being construed. A few jurisdictions, however, not only limit their consideration to the common grantor's prior acts, but also require the entire common scheme to be set out in the conveyance being construed, or in its chain of title.

6. Common schemes are important in construing express running covenants because in most—but not all—jurisdictions:

    a. common schemes are among the surrounding circumstances considered in determining whether a covenant runs, and if so, the land to which the benefit is appurtenant; and

    b. common schemes support the relaxation of the ancient rule against granting an interest to a stranger to the transaction. In a subdivision, all who purchase prior to the conveyance being construed are strangers to the transaction because the common grantor no longer owns their land at the time the conveyance is issued. In a subdivision, therefore, all prior purchasers are strangers to the transaction between the common grantor and a subsequent grantee. Yet, in a subdivision, in the presence of a common scheme, many jurisdictions allow prior purchasers to be third-party beneficiaries of a subsequent grantee's covenant.

§ 2.03   IMPLIED INTENT: THE PARTIES' IMPLIED INTENT TO CREATE A RUNNING COVENANT

[A]   Definitions

IMPLIED RUNNING COVENANT: An implied running covenant is a running covenant that is not sufficiently expressed in documents satisfying the requirements of the Statute of Frauds. Implied running covenants are said to arise by "operation of law." Because formal documents are not required for the creation of implied running covenants, they are also known as informal running covenants.

ESTOPPEL: Estoppel is the doctrine by which a party's own act or representation prevents her from denying the validity of the other party's claim.

COMMON SCHEME: See the definition of common scheme in § 2.02[A], above.

IMPLIED RECIPROCAL NEGATIVE SERVITUDES: Implied reciprocal negative servitudes is the doctrine by which, in a subdivision, a common scheme of running covenants burdening the grantees' land supports the implication of identical running covenants burdening grantor's retained land.

[B]   Discussion and Questions

Justice Cardozo once described the area of implied running covenants as a "battlefield" of the law. Conflict among fundamental principles of real property law has led courts and commentators to take a variety of positions on the enforcement of running covenants that are not expressed in sufficiently formal documents.

On the one hand, it is said that enforcing claims to land that are not created by formal documents on the public record interferes with title security, title research, and land marketability. Enforcing implied covenants also removes from the decision to create an encumbrance on title the extra awareness and thoughtfulness that comes from taking the time to embody it in a formal document. And, countenancing informal covenants invites attempts to establish fraudulent claims. In short, recognizing implied covenants diminishes certainty of title and all the benefits that flow from it.

On the other hand, principles of morality and fair dealing are said to argue for enforcing implied running covenants. Land is often transferred subject to commitments and expectations to which good conscience demands adherence. Consider, for example, a developer who divides her land into 100 lots; advertises them as quality homesites; tells prospective purchasers that she will restrict the lots to single-family residential uses; puts that restriction into deeds to the first 75 lots sold; and then, when opportunity for greater profit arises, sells the remaining lots for apartment or commercial development. In addition, given the frequency with which insufficiently documented commitments and expectations arise in the land development and subdivision context, the integrity of many neighborhoods depends upon the enforcement of implied covenants. Implied covenants, therefore, often protect efficient and socially desirable land utilization; they often protect settled expectations. In sum, informal running covenants frequently interdict fraudulent behavior, and protect land value, marketability and utilization.

Implied running covenants involve a clash of basic jurisprudential concerns. On the one hand, the Statute of Frauds prohibits enforcing property interests that are not evidenced by a sufficient writing. On the other hand, exceptions to, and circumvention of, the Statute have "ar[isen] out of the fact that the law was unable to give relief in many instances where fair dealing and good conscience demanded that relief should be given." Johnson v. Mt. Baker Park Presbyterian Church, 194 P. 536 (Wash. 1920). The outcome of the clash of principles is that courts have taken differing positions on the application of the Statute of Frauds to running covenants.

[1] Estoppel

The first area of disagreement involves the application of traditional exceptions to the Statute: the doctrines of part performance and estoppel. Courts agree that the part performance doctrine, limited as it is by its requirement that the covenantee's performance be explainable solely by the alleged informal agreement, has little application to running covenants. The covenantee's performance, usually paying for the land and taking possession, is ascribable to many inducements other than an informal covenant relating to use of the land conveyed to the grantee or retained by the grantor.

Estoppel, however, is another matter. Traditionally the doctrine of estoppel in pais (or equitable estoppel) required a fraudulent misrepresentation and justifiable, detrimental reliance upon that misrepresentation. Fraudulent misrepresentation involved misrepresentation of an existing fact or, at most, present intention. It did not include changing one's mind or simple breach of promise. Some courts continue to confine estoppel to such situations.

But other courts, paralleling the development of the doctrine of promissory estoppel in contract law, have expanded the doctrine of estoppel applicable to interests in land to include "those cases in which it would be substantially unfair to allow a party to deny what he has previously induced another to believe and take action on. . .." The test, in these jurisdictions, is "whether in all the circumstances of the case conscience and duty to honest dealing should deny one the right to repudiate the consequences of his representations or conduct." PMZ Oil Co. v. Lucroy, 449 So.2d 210 (Miss. 1984). Simple breach of a promise that the promisee justifiably and detrimentally relied upon fits within the ambit of this expanded concept of estoppel. We will call the expanded doctrine "promissory estoppel" to distinguish it from the traditional doctrine.

According to its critics, the expanded doctrine of estoppel threatens (1) to undercut the Statute of Frauds entirely; (2) to vest in the courts vast discretionary power to reallocate land ownership rights; and (3) to make title to real estate largely dependent upon the uncertain recollection and testimony of interested witnesses.

These criticisms of promissory estoppel are, of course, just an enlargement upon the tendencies inherent in traditional estoppel doctrine. Accordingly, at least one court has adopted a third position. The California Supreme Court has said, in dicta, that estoppel has "no application" to running covenants. Riley v. Bear Creek Planning Committee, 551 P.2d 1213, 1222 (Cal. 1976). (Ironically, the California court has been at the forefront, and among the most liberal, in the development and application of promissory estoppel to property interests outside the running covenant context. In any event, as the facts in Riley did not involve fraudulent misrepresentations, one wonders whether the Court meant to deny application of the traditional doctrine to running covenants.)

Q63: O, owning 10 acres of land, subdivided and platted it into 40 lots. The deeds to the first five lots sold contained covenants restricting the lots conveyed to residential uses. In negotiating the sales, O asserted that she would sell her remaining land subject to the same restrictions. When the grantees of the first five lots learned that O was selling her remaining land for commercial use, they sued to enjoin the sale.

a.   Do the lot purchasers have a good claim based upon the traditional doctrine of equitable estoppel?

   A: The lot purchasers do not have a good claim under the traditional doctrine of estoppel. Estoppel requires an actionable misrepresentation that causes justifiable and detrimental reliance. In the traditional doctrine, the actionable misrepresentation must be fraudulent. It must involve a misrepresentation of fact or present intention. Fraud generally cannot be founded on representations that are promissory in nature, unless made with no intention to perform. Under the given facts, there is no direct evidence that O had no intent to perform at the time she made her statement. It is unlikely that a court would conclude that O made the assertion with no intent to perform.

b.   Do the lot purchasers have a good claimed based upon the modern doctrine of promissory estoppel?

A: The lot purchasers have a good claim under the modern doctrine of estoppel. Like the traditional doctrine, modern estoppel doctrine requires an actionable misrepresentation that causes justifiable and detrimental reliance. But under the modern doctrine, actionable misrepresentation may involve failures to perform acts that the misrepresenter fully intended to perform at the time she spoke. Modern promissory estoppel covers failures to perform undertakings that in good conscience and equity ought to be performed.

c. Would your answer to either part (a) or (b) change if none of the 5 lot purchasers' deeds contained residential use restrictions?

A: The answer to part (b) should change. Although the misrepresentation is the same, the lot purchasers could not have justifiably relied upon it. O is beginning to sell 10 acres of land and each lot purchaser knows that O has not even restricted her (the lot purchaser's) lot. Moreover, by the time of the second conveyance, and certainly by the fifth, the public record would show that none of the prior lots were restricted.

It would also be arguable that there was insufficient detrimental reliance. Certainly the lot purchasers may have purchased and taken possession in reliance upon O's promise. But since their lots are not restricted, they are not confined to residential use and, accordingly, are not as harmed as they would be if the neighboring land is developed for commercial uses. They can redevelop their property.

Q64: O, owning 3 acres of land which she used as a trailer park, sold one acre to A. In negotiating the sale, A insisted as a condition of the sale that O permanently discontinue using her retained land as a trailer park. O not only agreed, but also removed the trailers before the sale closed. Two years later, O began using her remaining two acres as a trailer park. A sued to enjoin O's activity.

a. Does A have a good claim under the traditional doctrine of equitable estoppel?

A: Under the traditional doctrine of estoppel, this is a close case. But a thoughtful application of the doctrine would conclude that O is estopped. O has done something more than make a promise that she did not perform. O removed the trailers and then reintroduced them. If the reintroduction were quick enough, that might support a conclusion that O intended from the outset to reintroduce them and not perform her commitment. But more significantly, O's removal of the trailers is an affirmative action and A may have relied upon that action as much as on the naked promise. Affirmative action that misleads is one of those situations that sits on the fringes of types of behavior that traditionally was deemed fraudulent.

b. Does A have a good claim under the modern doctrine of promissory estoppel?

A: A has a good claim under promissory estoppel doctrine based solely on the unperformed promise, let alone the affirmative action.

Q65: O, owning 20 acres of land, subdivided and platted the northern 10 acres into 15 lots. O recorded the plat, along with a Declaration of Covenants restricting the platted land to single-family residential use. In marketing the lots, O distributed brochures describing the subdivision's locale as ". . .beautifully rural and. . . being developed to remain that way. . .. An unspoiled section of country in which to live and raise families, now and in the future. . .. Prime homesites. . ." O also showed prospective vendees an unrecorded map on which both the northern and southern halves were divided into streets and lots. In addition, there were billboards, saying "HOMESITES FOR SALE," located on both the northern and southern sections.

After the 15 lots were sold, O announced plans to develop an industrial park on the southern 10 acres. Lot purchasers in the northern sector sued to enjoin her plans claiming that O is estopped to deny that the southern sector is restricted to residential use. O defends the suit, pointing out that she never said the southern section was restricted; that the recorded covenants expressly applied to the northern section only; and that the unrecorded map contained no restrictions.

In other words, O is defending on the ground that she has not made a representation that the southern section is restricted to residential use. Has she?

A: This is a close case. The lot purchasers, i.e., the parties attempting to establish the implied covenant, have the burden of persuasion. They must present a "clear and convincing" case. With that in mind, the advertising brochure and the placement of billboards are not particularly helpful to the lot purchasers' case. They will be read as referring only to the lots then offered for sale. (If those lots were not expressly restricted, the brochure and the billboard might be sufficient to represent that they would be.)

The map, however, is another matter. It clearly conveys the message that there is a plan to develop the southern section in conformity with the northern section. The map by itself probably would not be enough to make out a clear representation. But all three pieces of evidence together may well add up to more than the sum of the parts; and the lot purchasers may have sufficient evidence to state a case of implied representation.

Whatever the result, this question alerts you to the fact that estoppels are based upon representations; and that representations may arise from any form of communication.

[2] The circumstances surrounding the transaction

The second area of conflict over implied running covenants concerns the propriety of inferring running covenants from, in the words of the Restatement (First) § 527, "the circumstances under which a conveyance of land. . . is made." See also Restatement (Third) § 2.11 (implying servitudes based on "[t]he circumstances surrounding the conveyance of another interest in land"). The fact patterns that are in dispute in this area of conflict most frequently involve (a) common schemes and (b) suits between grantees of the original promisor.

[a] Common schemes

The concept of a common scheme, which plays an important role in the construction of ambiguous express covenants, plays a role in the implication of covenants. We saw in § 2.02[B], above, that when a developer subdivides and conveys land, the existence of a common scheme of covenants aids the determination of whether the covenants are intended to run, and if so, the land to which their benefit is annexed. But the common scheme can do something more extensive. The existence of a common scheme can also support the inference that the parties intended the land retained by the grantor to be restricted for the benefit of the land conveyed.

Consider the following: O subdivides and plats a tract of land into 100 lots. She records the plat. Although the plat contains no restrictions, O conveys the first 75 lots by reference to the plat (for purposes of description), and she includes in each deed a covenant that "the grantee agrees to use the land herein conveyed for residential purposes only." Our previous discussion of the common plan allowed us to construe the express covenant, to determine that it was intended to run and be for the benefit of the other 99 lots in the subdivision. Here we discuss whether we can imply, due to the common scheme, a reciprocal covenant that "the grantor agrees that the land she retains in the subdivision shall be used for residential purposes only."

Note that when there is a common scheme, the common grantor frequently has made some other representations, through comments or advertising, that the entire subdivision will be restricted. If so, then an estoppel may have arisen. But there are situations where the common grantor has not made any representations other than those that may be implied from the acts that establish a common scheme of development for the land she has conveyed. Or sufficient time has passed so that the other evidence is lost; or the representations may be oral and the court may not allow the consideration of oral evidence; or the court may adhere to the traditional limitations on estoppel. Then, the creation of an implied reciprocal covenant must rest solely on the existence of the common scheme.

When, in these circumstances, a reciprocal covenant is implied, the land embraced within the common scheme that the developer has not yet conveyed is subject to the common scheme's covenants. Similarly, land embraced within the common scheme, that the developer through neglect or guile has conveyed without restrictions to a party who is or should be aware of the common scheme, is subject to the same covenants. As one early case said, although some land within a subdivision may not have been expressly burdened by a covenant

> if the general plan has been maintained from its inception, if it has been understood, accepted, relied on and acted upon by all in interest, it is binding and enforceable on all inter se. . ..

Allen v. City of Detroit, 133 N.W. 317, 319 (Mich. 1911). And as another early case explained

> If the owner of two or more lots, so situated as to bear the relation, sells one with restrictions of benefit to the land retained, the servitude becomes mutual, and. . . the owner of the lot or lots retained can do nothing forbidden to the owner of the lot sold. . . [The implied covenants] originate[] for mutual benefit. . .. They arise. . . out of a benefit accorded land retained, by restrictions upon neighboring land sold by a common owner. . ..

Sanborn v. McLean, 206 N.W. 496 (Mich. 1925). This is known as the doctrine of implied reciprocal negative servitudes.

Q66: O subdivided and platted a tract of land into 100 lots. In the first 90 lots sold, she inserted a covenant restricting the property conveyed to residential use. When O's vendees learned that O was contemplating selling the 91st lot without restrictions to someone who planed to use it for commercial purposes, they sued to enjoin O from making the sale.

    a.   Is there a common scheme?

        A: There is a common scheme.

    b.   Assuming there is a common scheme, may the owners of the first 90 lots sold enjoin O's contemplated sale based upon it?

        A: In some jurisdictions, no; and in other jurisdictions, yes. Some jurisdictions do not imply running covenants from common schemes. They relax the requirements for the Statute of Frauds only when the facts fit without the traditional exceptions of part performance and estoppel. Other jurisdictions do imply running covenants from common schemes. They think that a common scheme functions like an estoppel—the existence of a common scheme functions as part of the inducement to make the purchase and is relied upon by vendees. Moreover, purchasers are willing to pay a higher price due to their expectation of a uniform provision of restrictions.

Q67: O owned land along Epson Drive. When the general area had already established a reputation as a high-grade residential neighborhood, O subdivided her land into 90 lots. Over the years she sold them all. In only 50 of the 90 deeds, O inserted covenants restricting the lot to single-family residential use. Yet, all O's vendees constructed only single-family residences on their property.

Now A has purchased one of the lots that was not restricted to single-family residential use. She wishes to convert the structure to commercial use. The jurisdiction where Epson Drive is located does imply running covenants from the existence of a common scheme. Nevertheless, A claims that none of her neighbors, even those whose lots are restricted to single-family residential use, can enjoin her plans because there is no common scheme.

Is A correct?

        A: This is the same question as Q60, § 2.02[B], above, re-written so that the question involves whether a common scheme exists for the purpose of implying a running covenant, not for the purpose of construing the benefit of an express covenant.

        As stated in response to the former question, most courts would rule that there is no common scheme.

        The lots are not uniformly restricted; and the absence of uniformity is totally unexplained. It certainly seems that the inclusion of covenants in some deeds was casual. Normally, the absence of covenants in so many deeds would make the plan, if there were one, incapable of effectuation.

Nonetheless, in the leading case of Sanborn v. McLean, 206 N.W. 496 (Mich. 1925), the court held that there was sufficient evidence to support the finding of a common scheme. The court implied a covenant restricting the defendant's lot. This holding demonstrates how favorably some courts look upon the creation of running covenants in residential situations. Perhaps this holding is also a lesson about the power of the factor, in determining whether there is a common plan, of what the actual development of the subdivision has been. After all, at least 50, and perhaps more, of the neighbors were induced into purchasing, paid a price, and developed expectations that their area was a high-grade residential neighborhood. A, who had no covenant in her deed, but knew the character of the locale, certainly had notice of this.

This question is repeated to illustrate the connection between common schemes as studied in § 2.02, above, and in this section, and to show how favorably at least one jurisdiction looks upon implied covenants based upon common schemes. Most courts, however, would not be as generous and would require greater uniformity before finding a common plan—whether the case involved construing the benefit of an express covenant or implying a covenant.

[b] Suits between grantees of the original promisor

Suppose O conveys a parcel of land to A by a deed containing a covenant restricting it to residential use. A then subdivides the land into two lots and conveys one to B and one to C without reimposing the residential use restriction. If C violates the covenant, may B enjoin her? If the benefit of A's covenant was meant to be personal to O, certainly not. But suppose that the parcel conveyed to A was 10 acres in area; that it was but one of five large parcels carved from O's 50 acre tract; and that O had inserted the residential use restriction into all her conveyances. In other words, the covenant was part of a common scheme for the subdivision. Then all of C's neighbors, other than B, clearly could enjoin C's violation. Should B have standing to sue?

It is not irrational to think that the circumstances surrounding the grant from O to A (in this case the conveyance of a large tract and the existence of a common scheme of mutually enforceable covenants restricting the subdivision) supports an inference that the parties anticipated further subdivision and intended the benefit of A's covenant to run to the purchasers of the resubdivided land. But legal theory interferes with the effectuation of this intent. To effectuate this intent involves creating an interest in which both the burden and benefit attach to the same land. A, the original promisor, would have the right, as owner of one part of her land, to restrict her use of another part. It would be like having an easement in one's own land; and it is as conceptually impossible.

Thus there is a conflict between practical reality and legal theory. Practical reality counsels that

it would be absurd to hold that a grantee could not restrain a violation on the part of his immediate neighbor, who derived title from the same [original promisor], although he could enjoin precisely the same act on the part of the owner of a parcel, more remotely located, obtained from a different [original promisor]. . . .

Silverman v. Uhrlaub, 102 N.Y.S 299 (App. Div. 1907). But according to legal theory

[t]o say that [the original promisor] could assert against himself a covenant in favor of a part of his land against another part, to all of which at the same time he held title, would indeed be anomalous. . . .

Rehard v. Rini, 128 N.E.2d 451 (Ohio. App. 1954).

In response, the Restatement (First) has suggested the doctrine of implied running covenants as a path between the Scylla of practical reality, and the Charybdis of legal theory. The circumstances surrounding the transaction between the original promisor and her grantees, Restatement (First) § 527 com. (c) says, may support the implication of a new covenant identical to the covenant in the original promisor's deed. The argument is that because original promisor's grantees expected the existing restrictions to be mutually binding, the necessary running covenants may be implied into the deeds between the original promisor and her grantees.

These are the most frequent situations in which the "circumstances of a transaction" are said to support the inference of a covenant. Courts, however, differ over whether they will infer covenants from these "circumstances." Some courts entirely refuse to, taking the position that the Statute of Frauds bars informal or implied covenants, except when the facts raise an estoppel.

Other courts do imply covenants from these circumstances, or from some of them. However, their rationales differ substantially. With regard to implying running covenants from the existence of a common scheme, for example, some courts argue that what they are doing is within, or a development of, the estoppel concept. Other courts say that they really are construing the written documents which evidence the common scheme, and thus, the writing requirement has been satisfied. Still other courts describe implying covenants from common schemes as a sui generis exception to the Statute, countenanced by years of precedent. Finally some courts freely indulge the inferences that arise from the existence of a common scheme on the grounds that the Statute of Frauds does not apply to running covenants. Running covenants, they say, are contract rights, not property interests. Running covenants, accordingly, are not within the Statute's requirement that property interests be embodied in a sufficient writing. (These jurisdictions seem to overlook the fact that another part of the Statute requires all contracts that cannot be performed within a year to be in writing.)

With regard to implying running covenants between the grantees of the original promisor, a few courts have in the past refused to do so because it is repugnant to legal theory. In most, if not all, recent cases courts have been willing to consider suits between the original promisor's grantees. Some courts give no explanation for their actions. Others say that they are enforcing the intent of the original parties. A few courts have accepted the first and third Restatements' theory for so doing.

Because the intent of the original parties frequently is found in an express covenant, these courts tend to think that their decisions do not conflict with the Statute of Frauds. Massachusetts, for example, takes a strong position on the Statute and refuses to enforce implied covenants absent an estoppel. Massachusetts, therefore, will not imply running covenants from the existence of a common scheme. Yet Massachusetts will consider enforcing a covenant in a suit between the grantees of the original promisor. Compare Sprague v. Kimball, 100 N.E. 622 (Mass. 1913), reaff'd in Houghton v. Rizzo, 281 N.E.2d 577 (Mass. 1972), with Ward v. Prudential Ins. Co. of America, 13 N.E.2d 411 (Mass. 1935). If Massachusetts adopted the first and third Restatements' view of the fact pattern, that is, saw itself as implying a new covenant into the deeds between the original promisor and her grantees, it then could not allow the original promisor's grantees standing to sue to each other.

Q68: O owned a 500 foot by 125 foot parcel of land in a generally residential area of the city. It was the only land she owned in the vicinity. O conveyed the tract to A by a deed that contained a residential use restriction. The deed also stated that the restriction was imposed "for the benefit of subsequent grantees of any part of the parcel conveyed, and in case of breach thereof an owner of any part of the parcel hereby may enforce the same by appropriate proceedings." A then subdivided the tract into 20 lots and sold them. The deeds A issued contained no restrictions.

Now one of A's grantees has begun developing a commercial use on her lot. When A's other grantees learned of this, they sued to enjoin her activity.

a.   Can they?

A: In most jurisdictions A's other grantees have a good claim. A entered into a covenant restricting the land she was conveyed, and expressly naming her grantees as beneficiaries. The issue is whether effectuation of this intent is conceptually possible. Some jurisdictions would find a conceptual impediment, reasoning that the burden and benefit of a promise cannot inure to the same land. Many other jurisdictions would not rule that way. In general they elude the conceptual difficulty by not discussing it. Commentators, however, have suggested that the original promisor's grantees have standing to sue on the basis of an implied covenant. The circumstances surrounding the transaction between the original promisor and her grantees, they say, might support the implication of a covenant, identical to the original promisor's original covenant, into the deeds between the original promisor and her grantees. The theory is that the circumstances of the transaction support the inference that the original promisor and her grantees intended such a covenant. The original promisor and her grantees did not insert the covenant in their deeds because they thought the prior covenant sufficient to accomplish their purpose.

The covenant in A's deed, expressly stating that her grantees are its beneficiaries, certainly would be a circumstance sufficient to support the required inference.

b. Reconsider part (a) on the assumption that O's deed did not state to whom the benefit of the restriction ran. (I.e., the deed did not contain the language inside the quotation marks).

 A: Assuming that the jurisdiction finds that the concept of the suit is conceptually possible, this is a close case. Without the express designation of A's grantees as beneficiaries, do the "circumstances" support the inference that they are? Factors that courts find weigh in favor of drawing the inference are that a) O owns no other land in the vicinity and the subject matter of the covenant is one that frequently is intended to run with some land; b) the size of the parcel conveyed by O is such that the parties understood that it would be further subdivided in the normal course of events; and c) the character of the general locale. Factors that would weigh against the inference are that a) the deed from O did not expressly name A's grantees as beneficiaries; and b) A and her grantees could have reinserted the covenants.

c. Reconsider part (a) on the assumption that O's deed did not state to whom the benefit of the restriction ran; and that before conveying the property to A, O had subdivided it into 15 lots and had sold 5 of them subject to residential use only restrictions.

 A: The change in the facts adds a factor that usually is considered as weighing heavily in favor of allowing A's grantees to sue. O's actions show that she contemplated a common scheme for the development and protection of a residential neighborhood. The viability of that scheme is substantially diminished if suits between A's grantees are not allowed. Thus, when the sale to the original promisor is of a parcel normally large enough to require further subdivision and sale to multiple owners, subdivision and restricted sales prior to the conveyance to the original promisor strongly support the inference that the original covenant was intended and understood as created for the benefit of the original promisor's grantees.

 Note that the grantees of the five lots that O sold before selling to A may have standing to sue due to the existence of a common plan. But they are not the complainants. A's grantees are the complainants; the issue is whether there is a covenant of which they are the beneficiaries.

[3] The <u>Restatement (Third)</u> and implied running covenants

In general, the <u>Restatement (Third)</u> adopts the doctrines that have been discussed this section for implying running covenants. In addition, due to the <u>Restatement (Third)</u>'s integration of servitude law, the <u>Restatement (Third)</u> also approves two new doctrines for implying running covenants. The <u>Restatement (Third)</u> extends to running covenants two doctrines that traditional common law confined to easement law— the doctrines of implication by necessity and by prior use. These doctrines are discussed in § 1.03[B], <u>above</u>.

[4] Conclusion

The law of implied running covenants is a "battlefield." The courts and commentators have adopted a variety of positions and a variety of rationales for similar positions. There is also the ever present problem of divergent application of supposedly similar positions and rationales. Finally, small differences in the facts at bar lead to large differences in result. These differences, then, can easily be overlooked, and a decision reached for one reason can be misapprehended as resting on another—one that is quite different. Accordingly, this discussion ends with a Question focused on distinguishing between express and implied running covenants, and between the different types of implied running covenants.

Q69: In each of the following, A claims that there is a covenant restricting B's lot to residential use, and that B is violating it. The question is: Is A's claim based upon an express or an implied covenant?

Assume as general background to the specific facts given that O owned a tract of land which she subdivided and platted into two lots. O sold one lot to A, and then sold the other lot to B. Additionally:

a. A's deed contains a covenant stating "[t]he grantee covenants, for herself, her heirs and assigns, that the real property herein conveyed will not be used for other than residential purposes; the grantor covenants, for herself, her heirs and assigns, that the real property she owns immediately adjacent to the real property herein conveyed will not be used for other than residential purposes." B's deed contains no covenant restricting her lot's use.

A: A's claim is based on an express covenant. O expressly covenanted to restrict the use of her retained land. B took subject to O's express commitment. (Whether or not A's suit would be successful depends upon whether B took with notice, see § 2.04, below, not whether the land was subject to an express covenant.)

b. A's deed contains a covenant stating "[t]he grantee covenants that the real property herein conveyed will not be used for other than residential purposes." B's deed contains an identical covenant.

A: Many courts would say that A's claim is based on an express covenant. B expressly covenanted to restrict the use of the lot granted to her. Any issue that might arise regarding A's standing to sue involves construing B's covenant to determine whether the benefit of it ran to A's land. § 2.02, above, discussed how courts approach construing B's covenant. In that section, it was said that if A could sue, it would be because in the presence of a common scheme courts relax their stricture against allowing rights to be created in favor of strangers to the transaction.

Nevertheless, other courts would say that A's claim is based on an implied covenant. Some jurisdictions explain allowing prior purchasers (such as A) to sue subsequent purchasers (such as B) as based upon an implied reciprocal servitude. These courts say that A has standing to sue because the presence of a common scheme supports the inference that when A was conveyed her land, O and A intended to restrict O's retained land as well. Accordingly, A is the beneficiary of O's implied covenant; and B took subject to it. Under this theory, A's claim is based upon an implied covenant.

In other words, some courts prefer to explain allowing A to sue based upon a relaxation of the strictures against third-party beneficiary rights. Other courts prefer to explain allowing A to sue based upon a relaxation of the Statute of Frauds. Under either approach, the existence of a common scheme is crucial to A's rights.

c. A's deed contains the same covenant given in part (b). B's deed, however, contains no covenant. Nonetheless, before A purchased, O orally promised to restrict the use of her retained land to residential purposes.

A: A's right is based upon an implied covenant. O's covenant is express in the sense that it was unambiguously stated. However, express covenants are covenants that are embodied in formal documents, i.e., writings sufficient to comply with the Statute of Frauds. O's covenant is, therefore, an implied or informal commitment.

d. A's and B's deeds contain no covenants restricting the use of their land. However, before offering the lots for sale, O distributed brochures in which the lots were described as "restricted to residential development."

A: A's claim is based upon an implied covenant. O's covenant is evidenced by a writing, i.e., the brochure. But that writing is not sufficient to satisfy the Statute of Frauds. Any restriction, therefore, is based upon an implied or informal undertaking.

e. The deed by which O was conveyed the tract that she eventually subdivided and sold to A and B contains a covenant that "the grantee, for herself, her heirs and assigns, agrees that the real property herein conveyed will be used for residential purposes only."

A: This is a case of resubdivision of already burdened land. Most commentators argue that A's claim is based on an implied covenant. A's claim, they say, is best thought of as deriving from a new covenant, identical to the covenant in the deed to O, inferred from the circumstances surrounding the transaction between A and O. The crucial circumstance is, of course, the covenant in O's deed.

Nonetheless, many of the courts that allow suits between grantees of the original promisor seem to do so on the theory that they are enforcing O's express covenant. A jurisdiction such as Massachusetts, which recognizes implied running covenants only on the grounds of traditional estoppel only, still enforces an original promisor's covenant between her grantees.

f. Before conveying any land, O recorded the plat of her subdivision along with a declaration of covenants. The deeds to A and B incorporated the plat and its covenants by reference.

A: A's claim is based on an express covenant. The recorded plat satisfies the Statute of Frauds. It was incorporated into the deeds, and is as much a part of them as if it was reprinted in them.

g. Before conveying any land, O drew up a map of her subdivision along with a declaration of covenants. O never recorded these documents, but she showed them to prospective purchasers, including A and B. The deeds to A and B referred to the unrecorded plat, but only for its description of the land conveyed.

A: A's claim is based on an implied covenant. The unrecorded Declaration of Covenants does not satisfy the Statute of Frauds' writing requirement and was not incorporated into the deeds. Any covenant, accordingly, is not derived from sufficiently formal documents to satisfy the Statute; if it exists, it must be based on an informal or implied covenant.

For further reading on the Implied Creation of Running Covenants, see 9 Powell §§ 60.02–60.03; CSW §§ 8.14, 8.23, 8.32; Restatement (First) §§ 522, 524–5, 527, 541; Restatement (Third) §§ 2.9–2.11, 2.13–2.14; J. Calamari & J. Perillo, The Law of Contracts 696-7, 735–8 (2d ed. 1977).

[C] Review Problems

PROBLEM 24

Shady Acres (The Map)

10 acres sub-divided on Map and included in First Filing→

←15 acres not sub-divided on Map and not included in the First Filing

25 acres subdivided on Map but not included in the First Filing

Sammie Subdivider owned a 50 acre rectangular tract, oriented in a north-south and east-west direction, with its east-west axis as the longer edge. When she decided to develop it, Sammie mapped the entire tract, showing the western 35 acres divided into streets and one-half acre lots. The map, entitled "Shady Acres Subdivision," was never recorded. Instead, Sammie recorded a plat, entitled "Shady Acres Subdivision, First Filing," that covered only the westernmost 10 acres, showing it divided into streets and one-half acre lots.

The map, however, was hung in Sammie's sales office. Sammie made clear that at present she was offering lots in the westernmost 10 acres only. But in response to questions, she said that all the lots depicted on the map were one-half acre in area.

In every deed Sammie issued conveying lots in the westernmost 10 acres, Sammie inserted a covenant subjecting the land conveyed to a density requirement of one-half acre per dwelling.

As sales of lots to the westernmost 10 acres closed out, Sammie realized that economic conditions—specifically her inability to contract for utility services and financing—prevented selling the rest of the tract in one-half acre lots. Accordingly, she recorded a plat of the rest of the tract, entitled "Shady Acres Subdivision, Second Filing" showing the remaining 40 acres divided into streets and one-quarter acre lots.

When the owners of lots in the "First Filing" learned of Sammie's intent to sell the remaining land in one-quarter acre lots, they sued to enjoin her plans. They base their rights on the doctrine of estoppel.

a. Discuss the merits of the lot purchasers' claim with regard to the 25 acres depicted in the map as divided into one-half acre lots but not covered by the "First Filing."

b. Discuss the merits of their claim with regard to the easternmost 15 acres shown on the map as not divided into lots.

ANALYSIS

a. The lot purchasers' claim depends upon the law of estoppel. In a jurisdiction that adheres to the traditional doctrine of equitable estoppel, they probably do not have a good claim. In a jurisdiction that adheres to the modern doctrine of promissory estoppel, their claim has a far greater chance of success.

Courts that adhere to the traditional, strict doctrine and courts that adhere to the modern, liberal doctrine might differ over a number of issues. They might disagree over whether the map was sufficient to hold that Sammie made a representation that the 25 acres not covered by the First Filing but depicted on the map as divided into one-half acre lots were to be restricted to one-half acre minimum size. Assuming there was a representation, the courts might disagree over whether the lot purchasers justifiably relied upon it. The public land records, after all, clearly showed that the land was not restricted. Fairly fundamental views of the conduct of market negotiations, and of morality and self-reliance in the market place, would guide the various courts' concept of representation and justifiable reliance.

But the central reason for the different outcome is that traditional estoppel doctrine requires a fraudulent misrepresentation while promissory estoppel does not. Assuming there was a representation, Sammie will argue that it was not a misrepresentation of her present intention. Sammie can point to the change in economic conditions to support the inference that she changed her mind regarding the size of the lots. The thrust of this argument is that she did not commit fraud—she did not misrepresent a present fact since she never said the lots were restricted; and she did not misrepresent her present intention regarding their size. At most, she is guilty of breach of promise. For that reason she did not commit an actionable misrepresentation within the scope of the traditional doctrine.

For the very same reason, however, she might have engaged in an actionable misrepresentation within the scope of the modern doctrine. In liberal jurisdictions, the clarity of her representation, the justifiability of the reliance upon it, and the reason for her change of mind would all be weighed carefully and considered to determine whether in good conscience she should be allowed to develop the lots in less than one-half acre minimums.

b. In all jurisdictions the lot purchasers have a dubious claim. To prevail they would have to establish that the map implicitly promised that the easternmost 15 acres would not be subdivided at all. This seems an unreasonable reading of the map. Most commonly, the map would be read as reserving that land for future development. Thus no representation was made regarding the eastern 15 acres' development. Another way of expressing the same conclusion would be to say that even if there were a representation, the lot purchasers did not justifiably rely on it.

PROBLEM 25

proposed site for townhomes→ and woodland

←the lot purchasers' 15 acres

Oscar Owner, owning a 100 acre rectangularly shaped tract, subdivided and platted the most southeastern 15 acres. He recorded the plat with a Declaration of Covenants restricting the platted land to development for single-family detached dwellings on no less than one-half acre lots. In marketing the lots, Oscar told prospective purchasers that he intended to develop the entire tract for single-family homes with one-half acre minimum lots, and that he would impose appropriate restrictions on any land he developed or placed on the market.

After the lots in the 15 acre tract were sold, Oscar discovered that soil conditions in the extreme northwestern corner made it impractical to develop single-family homes there. Accordingly, Oscar announced plans to develop townhomes on the 10 acres in the northwest corner. The overall density of townhomes would be 10 to the acre. A "green belt" of wooded land would buffer the remainder of the tract from the townhomes.

Upon learning of Oscar's plans, the purchasers of lots in the southeast corner brought suit to enjoin Oscar's construction. They claim that Oscar is estopped from developing the northwest corner according to his present plans.

You are retained by Oscar. Application of estoppel to running covenants is a matter of first impression in the jurisdiction. What arguments will you make on Oscar's behalf?

ANALYSIS

One argument is that the court should go no further than adopting the traditional doctrine of estoppel that requires a fraudulent misrepresentation. Oscar's statements were not fraudulent; they involved neither a misrepresentation of fact nor of present intention.

Another argument is that even if the court adopts the modern less stringent standard of promissory estoppel, Oscar should prevail. There are a variety of reasons for this:

(1) Even under a promissory estoppel theory there was no actionable misrepresentation. Oscar's misrepresentation was not only not intentional, it was not negligent (unless as owner of the land he should have known the soil conditions of the entire tract at the time he offered the southeast corner for sale). Innocent misrepresentations are not actionable. Estoppel, even under the modern standard, is not a strict liability concept.

(2) There was no detrimental reliance. More facts might have to be developed, but the land planned for townhome development is rather distant from the land that the complainants purchased. Moreover, there is a "green belt" buffer. It is said that estoppels are found to protect expenditures made in reliance

upon the misrepresentation. One wonders whether the lot purchasers will suffer any decline in the economic or amenity value of their lots.

(3) In general, promissory estoppel is found when in all the circumstances of the case "it would be substantially unfair to allow a party to deny what he has previously induced another to believe and take action on." Even if there was some actionable misrepresentation that produced reasonable, detrimental reliance, it was slight compared to the impact on Oscar. The land is useless for single-family development. Given the reasonableness of Oscar's behavior, and the insubstantiality of its detrimental impact on the complainants, it would not be accurate to say that it is "substantially unfair" to allow him to develop townhomes on 10 acres on the northwest corner of his 100 acre tract.

There is a final argument that is suggested with some hesitation: the lot purchasers did not reasonably rely on Oscar's representations. If a court was not too liberal, it might accept this proposition. After all, Oscar was in the initial phase of developing a 100 acre tract. Fashions in land development are subject to change. Prospective purchasers should be aware of that. These particular lot purchasers also knew or should have known that the remaining 85 acres were unrestricted. To some extent, then, the lot purchasers took their chances, regardless of the plans that their vendor might share with them.

PROBLEM 26

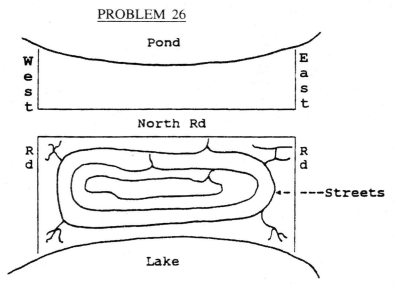

Twenty years ago, Sammie Subdivider subdivided and platted a large tract of land she owned that was bordered on the south by Lake Wyndota, on the east by East Road, on the north by Jackson Pond, and on the west by West Road.

The tract was bisected by North Road, which runs in an east-west direction, cutting it into two uneven sectors. The northern section comprises 20%, and the southern sector comprises 80%, of the tract. The northern sector is a low lying area which is marshy due to its proximity to Jackson Pond. Sammie thought it unsuitable for building and worthless. The southern sector rises to a small hill and then gracefully descends to Lake Wyndota. Lake Wyndota was renown for its swimming, boating and fishing. Sammie thought it was an excellent site for vacation homes. North Road was a beautiful country road that, due to the lack of development in the area, had not attracted much traffic.

Consequently, when Sammie platted the tract, the plat showed the southern sector divided into lots. All the streets for the lots funneled into North Road. There was no ingress or egress through any other road. The northern sector was not divided into lots.

For the next eighteen years, Sammie sold lots from the southern sector. Most, but not all, of her deeds included a clause that read:

The grantee, for herself, her heirs and assigns covenants to use the property herein conveyed for single-family residential purposes only.

Two years ago, Sammie sold the entire northern sector to Dan Developer who was well acquainted with land development in the area and the contents of the deeds to Sammie's subdivision in particular. The deed conveying the northern sector to Dan contained no restrictions.

After this conveyance, Sammie continued selling lots from the southern sector until last year when she sold all the southern sector's unsold lots to Bette Builder. All the deeds conveying individual lots, and the deed to Bette, contained the previously quoted single-family residential restriction.

Now, Dan has announced plans to construct a garish amusement park on the land north of North road.

a. Is there a common scheme embracing the northern and the southern sections?

b. Assuming there is a common scheme, may a lot purchaser in the southern section sue to enjoin Dan's construction?

ANALYSIS

a.   This is the same Problem as Problem 22, § 2.02[C], above, redrafted so that the issue is not the construction of an express covenant but the inference of an implied one. The overall lesson of the Problem is that the same fact pattern may require determining whether a common scheme exists for the purpose of construction (when there is an express covenant) or implication (when there is no express covenant). As stated in the previous discussion of the facts, whether there is a single common scheme embracing both sectors is a close question. This is especially so since the burden is on the neighbors to prove what Sammie's intent was, and that Dan had sufficient notice of it.

The argument in favor of the southern and northern sectors forming one common scheme is that the land was platted together. The difference in the covenants can be explained away by the marshy conditions of the northern sector. The argument against the existence of a unified scheme is that Sammie thought it impossible to build on the northern sector when she formulated her plans. Thus, when it was built upon, it represented a new plan that could not embrace the land south of the North Road that already had been sold.

This discussion is, by and large, the same as when the issue was the construction of the express covenant. The only difference, in fact, is that Olivia's deed to Dan contained a covenant in Problem 22, but not here. Is this difference significant for the purpose of determining whether there is a common scheme embracing the northern and southern sections? This question is one way of raising the more general issue of whether or not the standards for finding a common scheme should be the same for the construction of covenants as for their implication.

There is no case law discussion of this point. No case even hints that facts that might be a common scheme for the purposes of covenant construction might not be a common scheme for purposes of covenant implication. And commentators, in discussing common schemes, cite cases involving either issue interchangeably.

Nonetheless, the difference between covenant construction and covenant implication is sure to arise in one's mind and potentially affects the outcome of the case. Arguments that the two issues ought to be treated differently are that the implication of a covenant is more likely to surprise a landowner, and be more onerous, than the extension of the ambit of enforcement of a covenant that she clearly agreed to. On the other hand, as California has pointed out in refusing to construe covenants based upon common schemes, the extension of the ambit of a covenant increases the burden of a servitude. It increases the number of people whose acquiescence must be secured before embarking on a use that violates the express restriction. It is especially onerous when the common scheme is the basis for holding that the covenant is not personal to the grantor but runs to several neighbors.

b.   The conclusion that there is a common scheme embracing both the northern and southern sections does not, by itself, determine the southern lot purchasers' suit in their favor. Some jurisdictions hold that the existence of a common scheme is insufficient to satisfy or set aside the Statute of Frauds' writing requirement. In these jurisdictions, no covenant may be implied except when the facts arise to an estoppel. In these jurisdictions, the southern lot purchasers' suit would fail, despite the presence of a common plan embracing both sectors of Sammie's development.

Other jurisdictions, however, hold that the existence of a common scheme is sufficient to satisfy or set aside the Statute's requirements. Still other jurisdictions hold that the Statute's requirements do not apply to equitable servitudes since they are contractual, not property, interests. In these jurisdictions, the existence of a common scheme embracing both sections would determine the matter in the southern lot purchasers' favor.

PROBLEM 27

Fifty years ago, Oscar Owner purchased a residential two-flat on a double size lot in the city. It was the only land he owned in the vicinity. Twenty years later, he conveyed half of the lot, the half on which the two-flat did not stand, to Andy Andrews. Oscar's deed to Andy restricted the property conveyed to residential use. Andy built a residential two-flat on the parcel. Five years later, Oscar sold the other half of the lot. In that deed, he also inserted a residential use restriction.

Last year Andy converted his two-flat building into a condominium and sold the ground floor unit to Bette Benton and the second floor unit to Charles Chew. The deeds to Bette and Charles contained no restrictions. When Bette began renovating her unit into a clothing boutique, Charles sued to enjoin her construction relying on the restriction in the deed from Oscar to Andy.

The jurisdiction does, in appropriate cases, allow suits between the grantees of an original covenantor. Is this an appropriate case?

ANALYSIS

Most courts probably would hold that this is not an appropriate case. A court that finds no conceptual impediment to allowing suits between grantees of an original promisor usually says that it will allow the suit only if the original parties intended their covenant to inure to the covenantor's grantees. In this case, the original parties probably had no such intent.

In reaching that conclusion, most courts would emphasize as a factor the fact that O's sales involved small lots. When such a small parcel is involved, courts usually conclude that the parties did not contemplate a further subdivision of the granted land. This would be particularly true when interpreting a 30 year old deed. Condominium development, which probably is the only way this land could be subdivided further, was nearly unheard of at the time O conveyed the lot to A. Not contemplating a further subdivision, O and A did not contemplate allowing the covenantor's grantees to sue.

Nevertheless, some courts seem willing to emphasize as a factor the fact that O's deeds evidence a common scheme. The purpose of the common scheme was to allow suits between O's successors in interest in order to preserve the residential character of this (small) subdivision. To effectuate this purpose, modern developments must be kept up with. That A's resubdivision would not have been directly contemplated 30 years ago is not determinative.

This is a close case. However, it is important to note that if one adopts the first and third Restatements' approach, both of the above analyses are somewhat misconceived.

Both analyses focus on the intent of the original parties. According to the Restatements, the appropriate question is what is the inferred intent of the original promisor and her grantees. Not the original deed between the original promisor and promisee, but the later deeds between the original promisor and her grantees are the determinative documents. That the original deed contained a restrictive covenant is one of the circumstances of the transaction between the original promisor and her grantees. That the original promisee and the original promisor did not contemplate the resubdivision is irrelevant. What is relevant is whether the original promisor and her grantees contemplated the resubdivision. Clearly they did, since they are the ones resubdividing or contracting after resubdivision. Thus the only question that remains is whether, given all the circumstances, they implicitly inserted restrictions in their deed.

There is, in other words, a conflict in focus between the approach of the courts and the approach of the Restatements. The courts, claiming to be construing the express original covenant, focus on the correct interpretation of the original deed. The Restatements, claiming to infer the intent of a later transaction, focus on the correct interpretation of a later deed.

<u>PROBLEM 28</u>

```
                                                              |-Bl.Horse
     *    *        *              **  |*Filing 6 *|           |  Tpk.
     Filing 2     *  Filing 4         |-----------|           |
                                      | Filing 3 *|           |
 * =    Filing 7   OR's remaining     | *    *    |           ---the 3 acres
 platted    *      unplatted land     | *  |------>|          |   Denise plans
 land OR       *                      | * Denise's|          |   to sell with
 had not                              |   30 acre |          |   the 5 acres
 sold       *   *            *        | ----------|          |
 prior    Filing 1      Filing 5      |  parcel   |          ---the 5 acres
 to its       *      *    *    *   *  |           |          |   sold free of
 sale to                                                     |   covenants
 Denise                                 10 acres
                                    platted by Denise
```

Thirty years ago, Owner Realty Co. (OR) acquired a rectangular 200 acre tract known as Shady Acres. Over the next 29 years, OR recorded 7 plats subdividing different portions of the tract. The plats were entitled Shady Acres, First Filing; Shady Acres, Second Filing; etc. Each plat was recorded with a declaration of covenants applicable to the land depicted in the plat. All the declarations were substantially similar. A covenant restricting the land to residential use was among those invariably included. By last year, over 200 lots had been sold, and Shady Acres had become a desirable and exclusive residential community.

Despite Shady Acres' success, OR still had an inventory of land there. Almost 15% of the platted lots remained unsold; almost 25% of the tract had not yet been subdivided. Among the unsold land was a contiguous 30 acre parcel in the southeast corner.

Last year, OR sold the 30 acre parcel to Denise Developer. The deed conveying the land to Denise specified that 5 acres fronting on Black Horse Turnpike were sold "free of any and all restrictions." The deed also specified that the other 25 acres were sold subject to restrictions. The restrictions listed in the deed were substantially similar to those found in the Shady Acres' seven recorded plat declarations. It included a covenant restricting the land to residential use.

Denise immediately subdivided and platted 10 of the 25 restricted acres. From then until now, she sold a number of the platted lots. All the deeds conveying the lots contained use restrictions identical to those in the deed that conveyed the 30 acre tract from OR to Denise.

For a while no sales were made from the unrestricted 5 acres primarily, Denise learned, because the parcel was too small for commercial development.This year, Denise found a potential purchaser for the 5 unrestricted acres. That purchaser, however, required 8 contiguous acres for the manufacturing plant it contemplated constructing. Denise, therefore, secured a release from OR of any restrictions applicable to 3 acres of land adjacent to the 5 acres that had been sold free of restrictions. The 3 acres were part of the 15 acres that Denise had not yet subdivided.

When residents of Shady Acres learned of Denise's planned transaction, and the use intended by the potential purchaser, they sued for a declaratory judgment establishing their right to bar the commercial use contemplated by Denise's potential vendee.

a. Are the lot owners in Filings 1-7, whose land was sold by OR prior to its conveyance to Denise, entitled to a declaration barring commercial use of 1) all 8 acres; or (2) the 3 acres expressly restricted by the OR-Denise deed?

b. Are the lot owners in the 30 acre tract, whose land was sold by Denise prior to her securing the release from OR, entitled to a declaration barring commercial use of (1) all 8 acres; or (2) the 3 acres expressly restricted by the OR-Denise deed?

(Matthew Bender & Co., Inc.)

ANALYSIS

a. (1) The ability of lot owners whose land was sold by OR prior to its conveyance to Denise to bar commercial use of all 8 acres entirely depends upon the existence of a common scheme embracing the entire 200 acre tract. In jurisdictions that do not set aside the requirements of the Statute of Frauds merely due to a common scheme, the answer is no.

In jurisdictions that will imply running covenants based solely on a common scheme, the answer is less clear. Most jurisdictions would not find a common scheme embracing the entire 200 acre tract. The central argument against finding a common scheme is that OR carefully documented its work to limit each filing to an independent subdivision. The various declarations expressly were made applicable to the land then being subdivided. There is no evidence that the various plats ever showed more than the land then being subdivided.

OR also could argue that a ruling that its piecemeal development of part of this large tract binds it to a particular development of the rest of the tract would have devastating implications for the land development industry. Acquisition of large tracts, and their sequential development over time, would be threatened by an uneconomic constraint against responding flexibly to changes in the market place. In other words, public policy should require "clear and convincing" evidence to support a finding that there is a common scheme encompassing land that is not platted together.

The argument in favor of finding a common scheme would focus on the similarity of the declarations between all the various filings and the similarity in the name. The identical filings give objective manifestation to the view that OR is sequentially implementing a common scheme of development. Also, Shady Acres has become a residential community, investments have been made and expectations reasonably have been raised by the singular, consistent and uniform development of the entire tract. For nearly thirty years, the residential character of the locale's development has induced sales. Public policy argues in favor of protecting established residential neighborhoods. One can imagine that such a continuous sale of restricted lots would be held to be a common scheme. The series of plats is like a series of individual deeds, only on a larger scale.

This is a close case, particularly as courts are more hesitant to find common schemes encompassing separately platted land than they are to find common schemes encompassing separately deeded land.

a. (2) The ability of lot owners whose land was sold by OR prior to its conveyance to Denise to bar commercial use of the 3 acres that was expressly restricted by the covenant in the OR-Denise also depends entirely on the existence of a common scheme. Thus, in the few jurisdictions that follow the California position and refuse to construe the benefit of an express covenant the answer is no. In all other jurisdictions this is a close case. The answer to whether the complainant lot owners have standing to sue as beneficiaries of the express covenant would depend upon the same analysis just undertaken in part (a)(1) to determine if there was a common scheme embracing the entire 200 acre tract. These lot owners, after all, are strangers to the transaction. They are not expressly named as beneficiaries. Therefore, even in jurisdictions that allow suits by pure third party beneficiary complainants, it would require a common scheme to demonstrate that they are the intended beneficiaries. See § 2.02[B], above.

b. (1) The lot owners whose land was sold by Denise prior to her securing the release from OR have no right to bar the commercial use of any of the 8 acres. Even if there is a common scheme embracing the entire tract supporting the implication of covenants binding the 8 acres, OR and Denise expressly released 5 of those acres from their burden as far as they (OR and Denise) were legally able. At the time of the release, either OR or Denise owned the land that the complainant lot owners later purchased. The complainant lot owners' land, accordingly, no longer had as an appurtenance the benefit of the implied covenants burdening the 5 acres.

b. (2) The right of lot owners whose land was sold by Denise prior to her securing the release from OR to bar commercial use of the sale of the 3 acres originally restricted by the OR-Denise deed turns entirely upon whether or not they are the beneficiaries of Denise's covenant to restrict 25 acres of her land to residential development. This is a close case.

Arguments against finding that Denise's vendees are beneficiaries of the covenant in her deed would focus on the vast amount of land OR still owned in the tract. At the time of the sale, 15% of the platted lots were unsold, and 25% of the tract was unsubdivided. This means that OR had an inventory of around 10 acres of lots and 50 acres of raw land in the vicinity. After the sale to Denise, OR had 10 acres of lots and 20 acres of raw land. The inference to draw from these facts is that OR imposed the covenant for its benefit. At most, the covenant was imposed for the benefit of the land OR still retained.

Arguments in favor of finding that Denise's grantees are beneficiaries of the covenant in her deed would focus on a number of facts. One fact would be the amount of restricted residential development in the vicinity. The inference from these facts is that the covenant was not personal to OR, but intended to be part of its common scheme of development of the tract into a high grade residential community. All residents who owned lots originally purchased from OR would then be beneficiaries of Denise's covenant; they could enjoin her sale. As a practical matter, then, it would be absurd to allow distant lot owners to enjoin Denise's plans but not to allow adjacent lot owners who purchased from Denise (the original promisor).

Another factor would be the quantity of the land and the nature of the covenant involved. Twenty-five acres of residentially restricted land clearly required further subdivision. OR and Denise, therefore, must have anticipated resubdivision. The purpose of the covenant was to guarantee development of a protected residential community. This purpose is especially likely given that the 25 acres are part of a larger protected residential community. Therefore, OR and Denise must have intended Denise's grantees—the people with the most interest in the restrictions' enforcement—to have standing to enforce the restrictions as the most efficient way to effectuate their purpose.

A final fact favoring a ruling in favor of those who own lots sold by Denise before she secured the release of the 3 acres is that she inserted identical covenants in her deeds conveying the lots. Under the first and third Restatements' theory, the focus is on the circumstances surrounding the transaction between the original promisor and her grantees. The question is whether it is reasonable to infer that these parties, not the original parties, thought the original covenant an implicit part of their agreement. One could argue that by expressly reinserting the original covenants into her deeds, Denise was demonstrating her understanding that it was meant to be, and was part of, her agreement with her grantees. Finding the covenant in their deeds also raised the grantees' expectation that the original covenant was intended to be part of their later agreement with Denise.

In other words, the argument is not that Denise's insertion of the restrictions raised implied reciprocal covenants burdening her retained land (the 15 unsubdivided acres). That argument is subject to all the difficulties discussed in part (a)(1) of implying servitudes beyond the confines of land that is platted together. Rather, it is that the insertion of the restrictions, in a context framed by the presence of the covenant in the OR-Denise deed (which does bind the unsubdivided land), supports implying a servitude beyond the confines of the land that Denise platted together. Denise's common plan, and her original promise, have a synergy and support a conclusion that neither part alone may be sufficient to support.

[D]   Recapitulation

1. An implied running covenant is a running covenant that is not sufficiently expressed in documents satisfying the requirements of the Statute of Frauds. Implied running covenants are said to arise by "operation of law."

2. There are two branches of the law of implied running covenants. Running covenants may be implied on the basis of (a) an estoppel or (b) "the circumstances surrounding the conveyance of another interest in land." Restatement (Third) § 2.11. See also Restatement (First) § 527.

3. All courts imply running covenants on the basis of an estoppel. An estoppel is established when one party to a transaction makes a misrepresentation upon which the other party justifiably and detrimentally relies. However, courts differ in their notion of misrepresentation.

   a. Some courts adhere to the traditional doctrine of estoppel which requires a fraudulent misrepresentation. A fraudulent misrepresentation involves a misrepresentation of existing fact or present intention.

   b. Other courts adhere to the modern doctrine of promissory estoppel, which allows a simple breach of promise to qualify as a misrepresentation when "in all the circumstances of the case conscience and duty to honest dealing should deny one the right to repudiate the consequences of his representations or conduct." PMZ Oil Co. v. Lucroy, 449 So.2d 210 (Miss. 1984).

4. Many courts imply running covenants on the basis of the circumstances under which a conveyance of land is made. Other courts, relying of the Statute of Frauds, refuse to imply running covenants on this basis.

5. The most frequent circumstances surrounding a land transaction that justifies implying a running covenant involve a) common schemes and b) suits between grantees of the original promisor.

   a. Common schemes were described in § 2.02, above, as part of the discussion of their role in construing ambiguous express covenants. But common schemes also serve as a basis upon which courts support the implication of running covenants. In a subdivision, a common scheme of running covenants burdening the grantees' land supports the implication of identical running covenants burdening the grantor's retained land. This is known as the doctrine of implied reciprocal negative servitudes.

   b. Suits between grantees of the original promisor involve implied covenants because legal theory prevents the burden and benefit of a covenant from attaching to the same land. When land burdened by a running covenant is subdivided, legal theory prevents the grantees of the original promisor from having the benefit of any covenant in the original promisor's deed. In response, Restatement (First) § 527 com. (c) suggests that the covenant in the original promisor's deed may be a sufficient circumstance surrounding the transaction between the original promisor and her grantees to support implying a new covenant into the deed between the original promisor and her grantees. The new covenant is, of course, identical to the covenant in the original promisor's deed, only it runs between the parcels that comprise her subdivision.

§ 2.04 NOTICE

In the traditional common law, priority among property interests generally was determined by the maxim "first in time, first in right." In the law courts, this rule was absolute. Property interests were enforceable against subsequent purchasers regardless of whether they had notice of the preexisting claim. Equity, however, recognized an exception. Equitable property interests were not enforceable against subsequent purchasers who acquired their interest for value and without notice of the preexisting claim.

These principles were carried over into the law of running covenants. Accordingly, real covenants were enforceable against remote parties regardless of notice; equitable servitudes were not enforceable against remote parties who purchased for value without notice. Hence, the blackletter learning that notice is not an element for the running of real covenants, but is an element for the running of equitable servitudes.

This blackletter learning is wrong in two respects. First, regardless of notice, equitable servitudes were always enforceable against donees of property burdened by an equitable servitude, i.e., subsequent takers who did not pay value. Second, real covenants are no longer enforceable against subsequent purchasers who acquire their interest for value and without notice of the preexisting claim. This is because modern American recording statutes, by and large, have made the equitable rule the rule at law too.

Most American recording statutes impose notice as a requirement for the enforcement of all property interests against purchasers for value, and sometimes against all purchasers. The reason for the difference with England is that England traditionally maintained no public record of land transactions. In general, in America, notice is an element for the running of real covenants as well as equitable servitudes.

Potentially, there are residual differences in the role of notice in the running of real covenants and equitable servitudes due to cases that fall outside the notice requirement imposed by recording statutes. We will not go into them because they turn upon an understanding of the recording statutes, but be assured that these differences are more theoretical than real possibilities. No actual case has arisen which was outside the ambit of the recording acts. See Note, Covenants Running With the Land: Viable Doctrine or Common-Law Relic?, 7 Hofstra L. Rev. 137, 177 n.218 (1978); Newman and Losey, Covenants Running With the Land and Equitable Servitudes: Two Concepts or One?, 21 Hastings L.J. 1319, 1342 (1970) (giving example of a fact pattern in which the enforcement of a real covenant and an equitable servitude would differ due to notice.)

In sum, in contemporary law, notice is an important element for the running of real covenants as well as equitable servitudes. The notice requirement for running covenants grows out of, and is entirely dependent upon, the recording statutes. Therefore, discussion of the notice requirement for running covenants is beyond the scope of this Student Guide.

Consequently, this section will do no more than note the notice requirement. In this Student Guide we will always assume that a subsequent purchaser has sufficient notice under the recording statutes to be subject to enforcement of a running covenant. But at some point you might be interested in reading Hagan v. Sabal Palms, Inc., 186 So.2d 302 (Fla. App 1966), for extensive discussion of the recording acts and notice in the context of running covenants, and in reading Sanborn v. McLean, 206 N.W. 496 (Mich. 1925), for an example of a controversial application of the notice requirement. (See Q67, § 2.03, above, which is based on the Sanborn case.)

For further reading on the Notice requirement, see CSW § 8.28; 2 ALP § 9.25.

§ 2.05 PRIVITY

[A] Definitions

PRIVITY: Privity is the relationship that must exist between the covenantor and the covenantee, and between them and their successors in interest for a covenant affecting land-use to run.

HORIZONTAL PRIVITY: Horizontal privity is the relationship required between the covenantor and the covenantee for a covenant affecting land-use to run.

VERTICAL PRIVITY: Vertical privity is the relationship required between the covenantor and her successors, and between the covenantee and her successors, for a covenant affecting land-use to run.

MUTUAL PRIVITY: Mutual privity is a type of horizontal privity. It is the relationship that exists between a covenantor and covenantee who already have or who, because of the transaction of which the covenant is a part, will have related interests in the same land. The relationship between an easement owner and the servient landowner is an example of this type of horizontal privity.

INSTANTANEOUS PRIVITY: Instantaneous privity also is a type of horizontal privity. It is the relationship that exists between a covenantor and covenantee whose covenant is a part of a transaction involving the transfer of an interest in land between themselves. The relationship between the grantor and grantee of a fee simple estate is an example of this type of horizontal privity.

COMPLETE ASSIGNMENT and PARTIAL ASSIGNMENT: A complete assignment occurs when a property owner transfers her entire ownership interest to another. A complete assignment involves the outright sale of the property. A partial assignment occurs when a property owner transfers less than her entire ownership interest to another. A partial assignment involves the property owner carving a lesser ownership interest out of her estate. A lease granted by a fee simple owner is an example of a partial assignment.

AFFIRMATIVE RUNNING COVENANT and NEGATIVE RUNNING COVENANT: See the definitions of affirmative and negative running covenants in § 2.01[A], above.

[B] Discussion and Questions

Privity is a relatively straightforward topic. Yet it is one that generates a large amount of confusing analysis in the courts. One source of the confusion is a failure to distinguish between the two distinct branches of privity—horizontal and vertical. Another source of the confusion is a failure to realize that the courts vary in their views on what horizontal privity is and when, if at all, it is necessary for a covenant to run. (Courts are in general agreement regarding what vertical privity is and when it is necessary for a covenant to run.)

Accordingly, the overview of privity that follows not only separately considers horizontal and vertical privity, but also separately considers the concept of privity and the necessity of privity. The concept of privity means its definition, its notion. The necessity of privity means its role, the effect of its presence or absence. The concept of horizontal privity and its necessity will be discussed first. Then the concept of vertical privity and its necessity will be considered. Finally, a few miscellaneous topics associated with the privity requirement will be examined.

As with the presentation of previous topics, the Restatement (Third)'s treatment of privity will be mixed into the discussion. An exception is made for vertical privity. The Restatement (Third)'s suggested reform of vertical privity is sufficiently novel and complex to warrant separate analysis immediately following presentation of the traditional law.

[1] The concept of horizontal privity

As stated above, horizontal privity is the relationship that must subsist between the covenantor and covenantee for a court to allow a covenant respecting the use of land to run. American courts adhere to two different concepts of horizontal privity: mutual and instantaneous.

Mutual privity exists between a covenantor and covenantee who already have, or who because of the transaction of which the covenant is a part will have, related interests in the same land. In modern practice, the relationships that satisfy this concept of privity are limited to the relationship between landlords and tenants, and the dominant and servient owners of easements. Mutual privity is also known as a) substituted privity because it substitutes for the tenurial privity that is required in England, and b) Massachusetts privity after the first jurisdiction to enunciate it.

Instantaneous privity exists between a covenantor and covenantee whose covenant is a part of a transaction involving the transfer of an interest in land between themselves. Modern relationships that satisfy this concept of privity include not only the relationships encompassed by mutual privity, but also grantors and grantees of fee interests. Instantaneous privity is also known as successive privity.

Obviously, mutual privity is the stricter of the two concepts of horizontal privity. Most states have no decision that definitively chooses between mutual and instantaneous privity. Nonetheless, a substantial majority of jurisdictions indicate, in dicta, that instantaneous privity is the preferable concept of horizontal privity. All commentators describe instantaneous privity as the majority rule.

Q70: O, owning two adjacent lots, sells one of them to A. The deed of conveyance contains a covenant restricting the land conveyed to residential purposes.

    a.   Is there mutual privity?

        A: No. The transaction between O and A did not concern a property interest, such as an easement or leasehold, in which they had related interests; nor did it create such an interest.

    b.   Is there instantaneous privity?

        A: Yes. The transaction between 0 and A involved the transfer of an interest in property between themselves.

Q71: A and B own adjacent lots. They reach an agreement, which they formalize in a document that meets the requirements of the Statute of Frauds, restricting their lots to residential use.

    a.   Is there mutual privity?

        A: No. There is no mutual privity, for the reason expressed in the answer to Q70(a), <u>above</u>.

    b.   Is there instantaneous privity?

        A: No. The covenant was not part of a transaction between A and B that involved the transfer of a property interest.

Q72: O, owning two adjacent lots, sells one of them to A, reserving an appurtenant easement of way over it. The deed of conveyance contains a covenant that A will keep the easement in repair.

    a.   Is there mutual privity?

        A: Yes. The transaction resulted in O and A having related interests in the same land. O has an easement and A a fee interest in the same land.

    b.   Is there instantaneous privity?

        A: Yes. The transaction involved the transfer of a property interest, an easement, between O and A.

Q73: A and B own adjacent lots. A has an appurtenant right of way over B's lot. A and B reach an agreement, which they formalize in a document that meets the requirements of the Statute of Frauds, that A will use the easement only during daylight hours.

    a.   Is there mutual privity?

        A: Yes. The covenant concerns the shared interest that A and B have in the same land.

    b.   Is there instantaneous privity?

        A: Yes. Analytically, there is no instantaneous privity between A and B because the transaction did not involve the transfer of a property interest. However, all jurisdictions that adhere to instantaneous privity recognize mutual privity for the purpose of determining whether a covenant may run. One might say that there is instantaneous privity because it encompasses mutual privity also.

[2] The necessity of horizontal privity

All courts, commentators, and both <u>Restatement</u>s agree that horizontal privity has no function in determining whether the benefit or the burden of a covenant runs in equity. In other words, horizontal privity is not required for the running of equitable servitudes. Functionally, this means that covenants created without horizontal privity may be enforced by or against remote parties by injunction.

The law regarding suits at law is more complex. Some courts hold that horizontal privity is necessary for covenants to run at law. In these jurisdictions, horizontal privity is required for the running of real covenants. Functionally, this means that damages are not obtainable by or against remote parties for the breach of covenants created without horizontal privity.

Other courts, and the <u>Restatement (First)</u>, adopt the position that horizontal privity is necessary for the burden of a covenant to run at law, but that horizontal privity is unnecessary for the benefit to run. In these jurisdictions, the burden of a covenant may be enforced against a remote party only if the covenant's original parties were in horizontal privity; but the benefit of a covenant may be enforced by a remote party regardless of the existence of horizontal privity.

Still other courts, most commentators, and <u>Restatement (Third)</u> § 2.4 adopt the position that horizontal privity is not necessary for either the burden or the benefit of a covenant to run at law. Since horizontal privity never was required in suits in equity, this position abolishes the horizontal privity requirement.

History and differences over public policy underlie the differing positions on the concept and necessity of horizontal privity. The horizontal privity requirement was first applied to litigation between fee owners over running covenants affecting land-use in late-eighteenth century England. At that time, the law courts viewed them as undesirable encumbrances on title. Accordingly, the law courts imposed a number of requirements designed to limit their proliferation. The requirements were taken over from the far older and more developed law of running covenants between landlord and tenant. A narrow concept of horizontal privity was one of them.

Indeed, the English law courts confined horizontal privity to the landlord-tenant relationship, and held that it was necessary for the burden of a covenant to run at law. Thus, in England, the burden of covenants affecting land-use could not, and still do not, run at law between fee owners. The mid-nineteenth century intervention of equity, commencing with Tulk v. Moxhay, 41 E.R. 1143 (Ch. 1848), to enforce running covenants between fee owners without regard to the existence of horizontal privity represented a liberalization of the law of running covenants—a liberalization predicated on the recognition that in the emerging urban-industrial society running covenants affecting land use were often desirable encumbrances.

All American jurisdictions have liberalized the English position somewhat. Jurisdictions that require mutual privity in suits at law for the running of both the benefit and the burden of a covenant have liberalized the English position the least. These jurisdictions still regard running covenants between fee owners, at least in actions for damages, as generally undesirable.

Jurisdictions that have abolished the requirement of horizontal privity have liberalized the English position the most. These jurisdictions (as well as the Restatement (Third) and commentators that agree with them) regard the horizontal privity requirement as an irrational means to limit the running of covenants affecting land-use. These jurisdictions and authorities think that there is no acceptable reason to require horizontal privity in suits at law when it is not required in suits in equity. They condemn the mutual privity requirement as too restrictive. They condemn the relaxed instantaneous privity requirement as exalting form over substance. Transactions, they observe, can always be arranged to satisfy the requirements of instantaneous privity. See, for example, Problem 31, § 2.05[C], below. Requiring instantaneous privity, therefore, only serves as a trap for the unwary.

Despite the cogency of this position, most jurisdictions require some form of horizontal privity for the running of covenant burdens. Many require some form of horizontal privity for the running of covenant benefits, too.

[Q74-77, below, are based on the assumption that A and B own adjacent lots; that they sign an agreement in which B, for valuable consideration, covenants to restrict her lot to residential uses; that the transaction creates neither mutual nor instantaneous privity; and that C and D know about A's and B's agreement.]

Q74: B commences a commercial use of her property.

    a.   Can A enjoin B's activity?

        A: Yes. A and B are the original parties and B is bound by her promise made directly to A. The rules regarding running covenants are irrelevant because this situation involves the original parties.

    b.   Can A receive damages from B?

        A: Yes. The reason is the same as that given to part (a).

Q75: A sells her lot to C. B commences a commercial use of her property.

    a.   Can C enjoin B's activity?

        A: Yes. Horizontal privity is not required in equity. C, who is a remote party, may be awarded an injunction despite the absence of horizontal privity.

    b.   Can C receive damages from B?

        A: In some jurisdictions, and under both Restatements, C can receive damages from B; in other jurisdictions she cannot. Horizontal privity is not required for the benefit of a covenant to run at law in some jurisdictions and under the Restatements. In other jurisdictions, some form of horizontal privity is required—either mutual or instantaneous.

Q76: B sells her lot to D. D commences a commercial use of her property.

a.   Can A, who still owns her lot, enjoin D's activity?

A: Yes. Horizontal privity is not required in equity, even when the running of the burden of a covenant is involved.

b.   Can A, who still owns her lot, receive damages from D?

A: In some jurisdictions, and under the Restatement (Third), A can receive damages from D; in other jurisdictions she cannot. Horizontal privity is not required for the burden of a covenant to run at law in some jurisdictions and under the Restatement (Third). In other jurisdictions, and under the Restatement (First) some form of horizontal privity is required— either mutual or instantaneous. The difference between this answer and the answer to Q75(b), above, involving the running of the benefit of a covenant is that more jurisdictions require horizontal privity for the running of a burden at law than for the running of a benefit at law. C's action for damages in Q75(b) would be allowed in more jurisdictions than A's action for damages in this Question.

Q77: A sells her lot to C. B sells her lot to D. D commences a commercial use of her property?

a.   Can C enjoin D's activity?

A: Yes. Since horizontal privity is not required for a suit in equity, it does not matter that both the burden and the benefit of the covenant were transferred, i.e., that the suit is brought by a remote party against a remote party.

b.   Can C receive damages from D?

A: In some jurisdictions, and under the Restatement (Third), C can receive damages from D; in other jurisdictions, she cannot. This suit involves a suit by a remote party against a remote party. The suit will be allowed only in jurisdictions that have abolished the horizontal privity requirement at law. Some jurisdictions, and the Restatement (Third), have abolished it; most jurisdictions have not. (And recall that under the Restatement (First) C could not have received damages from D because the Restatement (First) required horizontal privity for a covenant burden to run at law.)

[3]   The concept of vertical privity

Vertical privity concerns the relationship that must subsist between the original parties and their successors for a court to allow a covenant to run. The relationship that courts look for is succession to the covenantor's or the covenantee's ownership interest. But the succession required for the running of a burden and for the running of a benefit differ. For a benefit to run, courts require succession to the covenantee's possessory interest. For a burden to run, courts require succession to the covenantor's entire ownership interest. In other words, for a burden to run, the vertical privity requirement is satisfied only if the successor received an assignment of the covenantor's entire estate, and not a new and lesser estate carved out of it.

To illustrate: When the original parties are fee owners, a lessee for years is not in vertical privity if she has succeeded to the burdened land; the lessee for years is in vertical privity if she has succeeded to the benefited land. And, when the original parties are fee owners, someone who succeeds to the burdened or the benefited land through adverse possession is not in vertical privity with regard to either the burden or the benefit of a covenant. An adverse possessor has created a new title, and has neither succeeded to the title of one of the original parties, nor to their possessory interest.

Q78: O, owning two adjacent lots, sells one of them to A. The deed of conveyance contains a covenant restricting the land conveyed to residential use, and stating that the covenant is to run with the land conveyed and the adjacent land that O retains. O sells her remaining lot to B. A sells her lot to C. C uses the property commercially. The jurisdiction does not require horizontal privity.

a.   Is B in vertical privity with O?

> **A:** Yes. B has succeeded to O's entire ownership interest.

b. Is C in vertical privity with A?

> **A:** Yes. C has succeeded to A's entire ownership interest.

c. Is B in vertical privity with C?

> **A:** No. Vertical privity concerns the relationship of the covenantor and her successors; and the relationship of the covenantee and her successors. B and C are in privity of estate because they satisfy the jurisdiction's horizontal and vertical privity requirements.

Q79: O, owning two adjacent lots, sells one of them to A. The deed of conveyance contains a covenant restricting the land conveyed to residential use, and stating that the covenant is to run with the land conveyed and the adjacent land that O retains. O leases her remaining lot to B for 10 years. A leases her lot to C for 10 years. C uses the property commercially. The jurisdiction does not require horizontal privity.

a. Is B in vertical privity with O?

> **A:** Yes. For the running of the benefit of a covenant, vertical privity is satisfied if the remote party succeeds to the covenantee's possessory interest.

b. Is C in vertical privity with A?

> **A:** No. For the running of the burden of a covenant, vertical privity is satisfied only if the remote party succeeds to the entire estate of the covenantor.

[4] The necessity of vertical privity

Vertical privity is required for the burden of a covenant to run at law. It is a misnomer, therefore, to describe the burden of a real covenant as running with the land. The burden of real covenants run with the original covenantor's estate. Vertical privity also is required for the benefit of a covenant to run at law. (But recall that it is the relaxed standard. Courts permit the holder of the covenantee's possessory interest to enforce the benefit of a real covenant on the theory that the benefit of a covenant was intended to follow the possessory interest in the benefited land.)

Vertical privity is not required for a covenant to run in equity. Equitable servitudes run with the land to whoever has succeeded to the actual possession of the land. Whoever is in actual possession, even a licensee (who has no possessory interest) or an adverse possessor (who did not succeed to the original parties' interest) may have the benefit or the burden of the covenant.

Q80: Same facts as Q79, above.

a. Can B enjoin C's commercial use?

> **A:** Yes. Vertical privity is not required in equity. Suits may be brought by the actual possessor of the benefited land against the actual possessor of the burdened land.

b. Can B sue C for damages?

> **A:** No. Vertical privity is required in law. The benefit of the covenant has run to B, due to the relaxed vertical privity requirement for the running of a benefit. But the burden of the covenant has not run to C, due to the rigorous vertical privity requirement that requires succession to the covenantor's entire estate. B, therefore, may not sue C for damages.

[5] The **Restatement (Third)** and vertical privity

Despite the general agreement among courts on the concept and necessity of vertical privity, the Restatement (Third) suggests an entirely new approach to the issue. Rather than focusing on such questions as whether the remote party has succeeded to the original party's entire ownership interest, or whether the suit is in law or equity, the Restatement (Third) focuses on whether the suit involves a negative or affirmative running covenant.

For negative running covenants, Restatement (Third) § 5.2 abrogates the vertical privity requirement. By this approach, all subsequent owners and possessors of land burdened or benefited by negative running covenants, even if they are lessees or adverse possessors, may sue or be sued in law or equity for breach of the covenant. For affirmative running covenants, however, the Restatement (Third) retains a modified vertical privity requirement. Most importantly, Restatement (Third) § 5.3 allows the benefits of affirmative covenants to run to lessees only when they involve "covenants to repair, maintain, or render services to the property" or when the lessees may enjoy the covenants "without diminishing their value to the lessor and without materially increasing the burden of performance on the person obligated to perform the covenant." Similarly, Restatement (Third) § 5.3 says the burdens of affirmative covenants run to lessees only when the present possessor can "more reasonably" perform the obligation than the lessor.

The Restatement (Third) admits that its new approach to the concept and necessity of vertical privity is not simpler than the traditional approach. But Restatement (Third) § 5.2 com. (b) insists that its approach is preferable because it more likely reflects the expectations of the affected parties. In addition, the Restatement (Third)'s rules are default rules that the parties may change by agreement. The traditional rules were unchangeable rules of law that were imposed regardless of the parties' intent.

Q81: Would using the Restatement (Third) approach to vertical privity change the answer to Q80, above?

A: Yes. Under the Restatement (Third), B can sue C for damages as well as an injunction. The land C has leased is subject to a negative covenant. The Restatement (Third) does not impose a vertical privity requirement on restrictive covenants. The present possessor of land burdened by a negative covenant is subject to suit in both law and equity.

Q82: Discuss the following fact patterns under traditional law and under the Restatement (Third).

a. O, owning two adjacent lots, sells one of them to A. The deed of conveyance prohibits landscaping the lot conveyed to A in a manner that casts shadows on solar panels located on O's retained land. After the conveyance, B enters A's land adversely and, after the statutory period has run, acquires the land through adverse possession. B then plants trees that cast shadows on O's solar panels. May O sue B for an injunction compelling her to remove the trees? May O sue B for damages for O's increased heating costs?

A: Under traditional law, O may sue B in equity and compel her to remove the trees; but O may not receive damages for her increased heating costs. Under the Restatement (Third), O may receive damages as well as an injunction.

B, as an adverse possessor, did not succeed to A's title. B's relation to A does not meet the traditional notion of vertical privity. Under traditional law, O can sue B in equity because equity traditionally did not require vertical privity. But under traditional law, O cannot sue at law, which does require vertical privity.

Under the Restatement (Third), O can sue B in both law and equity because the Restatement (Third) does not require vertical privity for enforcing negative covenants.

b. O, owning a condominium apartment, leases it for one year to A. The condominium declaration allows apartment owners (1) to vote at association meetings; (2) access the internet through ethernet ports in the apartments that connect to the building's high-speed gateway; and (3) have reduced-rate membership at a nearby health club. Which of these covenants may A enjoy?

A: Under traditional vertical privity doctrine, A would enjoy all three covenants. Traditional vertical privity doctrine allows the current holder of the covenanting party's possessory interest to enjoy the benefit of a running covenant. As a lessee, A holds O's possessory interest. (Anticipating this analysis, condominium statutes and declarations typically are drafted to prevent tenants from voting at association meetings.)

Under the Restatement (Third), A would not be allowed to vote at condominium meetings. She would be allowed access to the internet interface. Whether she would be allowed reduced-rate membership at the nearby health club is unclear. All three covenants are affirmative covenants. The <u>Restatement (Third)</u> allows lessees the benefit of affirmative covenants when doing so does not decrease their value to lessors or increase the burden on the parties subject to the covenant. With regard to the right to vote at association meetings, allowing A to vote would deny the right to O and reduce the value of that right to her. With regard to the right to access the internet, allowing A access to the internet interface would not deny that right to O because O already has lost access by not being in the apartment. A's access would not substantially increase interface usage in the building. With regard to the club membership, both O and A could enjoy reduced-rate membership. Compelling the club to admit extra reduced-rate members might be a material increase in cost.

c.   O, owning a condominium apartment, leases it for one year to A. The condominium declaration requires apartment owners to (1) wash their windows twice a year; and (2) pay monthly assessments. Which of these covenants must A perform?

A: Under traditional law, A must perform neither of these covenants. Under traditional vertical privity doctrine, covenant burdens do not run to lessees because lessees do not acquire the covenanting party's entire estate. Under the <u>Restatement (Third)</u>, A must perform the window washing covenant but may not be compelled to pay monthly assessments. Under the <u>Restatement (Third)</u>, the burden of an affirmative covenant runs to a lessee only when she is in a better position to perform it than the lessor. A, as possessor of the apartment, is in a better position to wash the windows. But A and O are equally well situated to pay the monthly assessments.

A: The <u>Restatement (Third)</u>'s treatment of horizontal and vertical privity is one of its more changes in current law. The decision to abolish horizontal privity reflects the trend of the courts and the view of all commentators. The <u>Restatement (Third)</u>'s reform of vertical privity, however, is more controversial. The <u>Restatement (Third)</u>'s approach may better ·match the parties' expectations, but it does so by substituting a complex and ambiguous standard for an easily applicable, if somewhat arbitrary, rule.

[6] Miscellaneous topics

Three topics associated with the privity requirement should be considered along with it: (a) the liability of the covenantor after a complete or partial assignment of her ownership interest; (b) the apportionment of covenant burdens and benefits among remote parties after subdivision of the burdened or benefited land; and (c) the circumvention of the rules on privity by providing that a covenant is enforceable by a lien.

[a] The continued liability of the covenantor after a complete or partial assignment of her ownership interest

A running covenant establishes two types of privity between the original parties, privity of contract and privity of estate. When the covenantor transfers all of her ownership interest, she is no longer in privity of estate with the covenantee. But, absent a novation, she has not divested herself of her privity of contract. The issue arises, therefore, of the continued liability of the covenantor based upon her contractual obligations.

The generally agreed effect of a complete assignment of the covenantor's ownership interest is an end to her contractual liability. Courts and commentators explain this result, in effect an implied novation, as the presumed intent of the original parties. Since covenants running with the land last for extraordinary periods of time, courts conclude that few people enter into them intending to remain liable after they have completely separated themselves from, and lost control of, the land. The beneficiary of the covenant must look entirely to the remote party who is now in privity of estate. Of course, the covenantor may not rid herself of liability at law for breaches that accrued before her assignment. And it should be noted that the parties can always draft their agreement to rebut specifically the presumption that the covenantor is no longer liable after assignment.

The effect of a transfer of part of the covenantor's ownership interest (for example, a fee owner's grant of a lease) is more complex. At law, a partial assignment—because it does not involve a transfer of the covenantor's entire ownership interest—does not put the remote party in privity of estate with the beneficiary of the promise. At law, the remote party is immune from suit. In equity, however, she is liable because vertical privity is not required for suits in equity. Consequently, the original party's liability at law continues; her liability in equity ceases. In equity, in any event, the remote party, having control of the land, would be the party against whom an effective injunction would have to operate.

Under the Restatement (Third) a different result would follow from a transfer of part of the covenantor's ownership interest. In many situations, discussed in § 2.05[B][5] above, the remote party who succeeds to part of the covenantor's ownership interest is liable at law for the covenant's breach. Nonetheless, despite the remote party's liability, the Restatement (Third) says the covenantor should remain liable for the breach, reasoning that "[t]he covenantee bargained for the liability of the holder of the greater estate." Restatement (Third) § 5.2 com. (c). Under the Restatement (Third), both the covenantor and, for example, her lessee would be subject to damage actions for the covenant's breach.

Q83: Same facts as Q79, above.

 a. Can B sue A to enjoin C's commercial use?

  A: No. A is not in possession of the land, and therefore, is not able to abate its commercial use.

 b. Can B sue A for damages?

  A: Yes. A has not transferred her entire estate. She is still in privity of estate with B, who has the present possessory interest in the benefited land. B may maintain a suit for damages based upon this privity. It is true that under the traditional approach, B could sue only A for damages. Under the Restatement (Third), B could sue C as well as A.

 c. Reconsider part (b) on the assumption that A conveyed a fee interest to C.

  A: No. Now A has transferred her entire estate. She is no longer in privity of estate with B. Courts presume that the original parties did not intend the covenantor's liability for damages to last longer than her ownership of her estate.

[b] The apportionment of covenant burdens and benefits after subdivision of the burdened or benefited land

When the burdened land is subdivided, injunctions are obtainable against any breaching successor in interest. Suits for damages are more complicated. Each breaching successor is liable for the damages caused by her breach. Each breaching successor is jointly and severally liable for all the damages if the damages are not separable. But covenants involving the payment of money are considered apportionable among the subdivided parts of the burdened land. The apportionment may be based on the proportional acreage or the proportional value of each parcel. The Restatement (Third) § 5.7 generally adopts these rules, too.

When the benefited land is subdivided, each successor to the benefited land may independently enforce covenants except, in the words of the Restatement (First) § 551, "in so far as such enforcement presents an unsolvable problem of computation or impose[s] an undue burden upon the obligor." See also Restatement (Third) § 5.7. In application, this generally means that each successor to a part of the benefited land may sue independently for her damages. She also may sue independently to enjoin the breach of negative covenants. Suits compelling performance of affirmative obligations are allowed on a case by case basis. In general independent actions to enforce affirmative covenants are allowed when the performance due the owner of part of the benefited land is separable from the performance due the owners of other parts of the benefited land; or when, though the performance is not separable, allowing suit by the owner of part of the benefited land does not materially increase the charge on the burdened land. Thus the owner of a part of the benefited land may sue independently to compel the maintenance of only that part of a border marking fence that borders her land. She can sue independently to compel the cleansing of an entire drainage ditch (assuming the entire ditch affects drainage of her land). But her suit to compel the payment of money requires joinder of all the present owners of the benefited land because multiple suits would be an undue burden on the owner of the burdened land.

Q84: Same facts as Q78, <u>above</u>, only O sells one-half of her remaining lot to B and the other half to X. A sells one-third of her property to C, another third to Y, and the other third to Z.

   a.   Can B enjoin C's commercial use?

   A: Yes. An owner of a part of the benefited land is injured by the use of any part of the burdened land in violation of the covenant. All jurisdictions and commentators agree that permitting a suit by the successor to part of the benefited land to enforce a negative covenant never raises a problem of apportioning the remedy to the sole complainant. They also agree that it does not impose any material hardship on C that she is sued by only one of a number of potential complainants. (There is some potential hardship depending on the jurisdiction's law of collateral estoppel.)

   b.   Can B sue C for her damages?

   A: Yes. B owns only part of the benefited land, but her damages are separately determinable from the damages that might be inflicted on the other owners of the benefited land. Thus B's suit involves no apportionment problems.

Q85: O owned a 6 acre tract of land adjacent to a lake. She subdivided it into 2 three acre parcels. One parcel had no beach area; the other did. O sold the parcel without the beach area to A. A's deed contained a covenant by which A agreed to pay $3000 annually to O to defray the cost of maintaining the beach. O covenanted to maintain the beach and allow A access to it. The deed said the covenants ran with A's and O's respective parcels. O then sold the beachfront parcel to B.

   a.   A subdivided her tract into 3 lots. C purchased one of them. Is C liable for all or some share of the $3000 annual charge; and if so, for how much?

   A: Yes. C is liable for an apportioned share of the $3000 annual charge. C's share would be determined by her proportional acreage, or her proportional value, depending upon the jurisdiction.

   b.   B subdivided her tract into 3 lots, each with beachfront. B sold D, E, and F one lot each. If A, who has not yet subdivided or sold any of her tract, refuses to pay the $3000 annual charge, may D sue A for all or some share of it; and if so, for how much?

   A: There is no case law on the point, but both <u>Restatements</u> and all commentators say that permitting a suit by D, who owns part of the benefited land, to compel a payment of money involves either impossible apportionment problems or significant hardship on A, who owns all the burdened land. The feeling seems to be that the annual charge is not necessarily split pro rata among the benefited owners. The annual charge is used as a fund for some purpose (maintenance of a beach in this case). Application of the fund is not subject to any general formula. (One area of beach may require more maintenance because it is subject to stronger tides than the other parts; another part may be more popular and require greater maintenance for that reason.) Thus, a suit to compel the payment of money is not like a suit for damages. In a suit for damages, the amount due each benefited lot owner is independently ascertainable; in a suit for the payment of most annual charges, the amount due each benefited lot owner is not ascertainable at all.

Q86: Same basic facts as Q85, <u>above</u>, only B subdivided her tract into 3 lots, each with beachfront. B sold D, E and F one lot each. D and E fail to maintain their respective beach areas. A, who rather than subdividing has built a resort hotel on her parcel, is damaged by D's and E's neglect of their beachfront.

   a.   May A sue D in equity to compel D to maintain all the neglected beachfront?

A: No. The beachfront is in the separate ownership of D, E and F. D controls only her section of beach. D can maintain only her section. That is all a court of equity would compel her to maintain.

b. May A sue D in law to collect all the damages caused by the neglected beachfront?

A: Yes. The damages caused by the failure to maintain D's and E's sections of beachfront are not separable. D, therefore, is jointly and severally liable for all the damages. (D may implead E and cross-claim against her.)

[c] The circumvention of the rules on privity by providing that a covenant is enforceable by a lien

A lien is an equitable property interest. Equity enforces liens through foreclosure proceedings. Foreclosure results in a money judgment. Liens, therefore, give rise to money judgments, but require neither horizontal nor vertical privity to run with the land and to be enforced by or against remote parties.

In other words, as a number of jurisdictions have held, creating a lien to secure performance of a running covenant allows the covenantee or her successors to sue for either an injunction or a money judgment regardless of the existence of privity. The sole limit on the lien's ability to supplant suits for damages, and circumvent the privity requirement at law, is the doctrine that liens can secure only those obligations that are expressed in, or reducible to, money. But according to precedent, liens may secure not only covenants that call for the payment of money (i.e., liquidated sums), liens may also secure any covenant that has a calculable, nonspeculative value. See, e.g., Application of Jeffrey Towers, Inc., 291 N.Y.S.2d 41 (Sup. Ct. 1968), in which a mortgage lien was allowed to secure a covenant to build a driveway, sewer line and apartment house, but was not allowed to secure a covenant to consent and support any applications and petitions for changes in zoning. In addition, the value of a covenant frequently is more or less equivalent to the damages caused by its breach.

Courts and commentators justify allowing lien foreclosure—which requires no privity—to supplant suits at law for damages (with its privity requirement) because a foreclosure decree, unlike a damage judgment, creates no personal liability. A foreclosure decree can be satisfied only by proceeding against the burdened land. However, in most every case, this fact is of no practical importance since value of the land should be greater than the value of the covenant.

Q87: Faced with declining municipal expenditures on street and park maintenance, a group of landowners agreed to assess themselves $200 per landowner per year to create a fund to maintain the public streets and parks in their area. They formalized their agreement in a writing that they all signed. The following year O, one of the landowners, sold her parcel to A. A, who knew of the agreement, refused to contribute to the fund. When the other parties to the agreement sued A for her contribution, A defended on the grounds that there was insufficient privity for the covenant to run.

a. Is A correct?

A: A is correct in those jurisdictions that require horizontal privity for the burden of a covenant to run at law. A is incorrect in those jurisdictions that have abolished the horizontal privity requirement.

b. Reconsider part (a) on the assumption that the document stipulated that each annual $200 payment would become a lien on the land when it fell due?

A: Now, A is incorrect. A lien is an interest in property. Liens run with the land, like any equitable property interest, without the need of horizontal or vertical privity.

In many, if not all, jurisdictions that require horizontal privity for a burden of a covenant to run at law there is sufficient privity for the covenant to run. The lien would create an equitable right obviating the need for privity. However, there would be a difference in allowing the lien to run but not the covenant. If the covenant ran, A would be personally liable. If the lien runs, a judgment may be enforced only against the land through foreclosure proceedings. This difference has more theoretical than practical importance whenever the value of the land exceeds the amount of the lien.

In sum, the rules on privity have an apparent complexity which dissolves away if the fact patterns are taken one at a time. That is what the Questions have attempted to do. The Problems that follow have the same focus. Their goal is to give a firm foundation for addressing the true major difficulty in the area: a determination of what the rules on privity ought to be.

For further reading on Privity, see CSW §§ 8.17–8.18, 8.26–8.27; 9 Powell §§ 60.04[2][c] & [3]; 2 ALP §§ 9.11, 9.15, 9.18, 9.20, 9.26, 9.31; Restatement (Third) §§ 2.4, 5.1–5.4.

[C] Review Problems

PROBLEM 29

Bette Builder and Dan Developer owned adjacent lots. When Bette and Dan learned that they were both interested in developing small office buildings on their respective lots, Bette and Dan executed a written agreement in which Bette covenanted to build a heating plant large enough to heat both buildings, and Dan covenanted to build a cooling plant large enough to cool both buildings. The covenants were expressly said to run with the adjacent lots as long as the buildings stood.

A few years after the buildings were constructed, Bette sold her lot and building to Alice Adams. Dan sold his lot and building to Bill Baker. Both Alice and Bill knew about Bette's and Dan's agreement. But when inflation in the cost of electricity proved significantly higher than inflation in the cost of natural gas, Bill decided to stop supplying Alice's building with air conditioning.

a. Is there sufficient privity for Alice to sue Bill for an injunction compelling him to supply her with air conditioning?

b. Is there sufficient privity for Alice to sue Bill for damages resulting from his failure to supply her with air conditioning?

c. Would your answer to either part (a) or part (b) change if Dan had leased his building to Bill for 30 years?

d. Would your answer to either part (a) or part (b) change if Bette had leased her building to Alice for 30 years?

ANALYSIS

a. Yes, there is sufficient privity for Alice to sue Bill for an injunction compelling him to supply her with air conditioning. The reason is that neither horizontal nor vertical privity is required in equity.

b. Whether there is sufficient privity for Alice to sue Bill for damages depends upon the jurisdiction. The problem is not with vertical privity. Alice has succeeded to the covenantee's entire estate; Bill has succeeded to the covenantor's entire estate. The problem is with horizontal privity.

Bette and Dan's agreement was not part of a transaction conveying an interest in land. Accordingly, it does not satisfy instantaneous privity. Nor did the agreement relate to an existing easement. Therefore, it does not satisfy mutual privity.

Consequently, in jurisdictions that require horizontal privity of any sort, Alice may not sue Bill at law. Damages, which are a legal remedy, are not obtainable. Under the Restatement (Third) and in jurisdictions that do not require horizontal privity, Alice may sue Bill for damages.

c. Yes, the answer to part (b) changes. That Dan leased, rather than sold, his building to Bill for 30 years means that Bill did not succeed to Dan's entire estate. For an action at law, traditional vertical privity doctrine requires that the remote party succeed to the entire estate of the covenantor (the party who is burdened by the covenant). This is the rule in all jurisdictions. Thus, rather than the result varying from jurisdiction to jurisdiction, now no jurisdiction would allow a suit for damages.

A suit for damages still would be successful, however, under the Restatement (Third) approach. Alice is suing Bill, a lessee, for breach of an affirmative covenant. The Restatement (Third) allows the burden of affirmative covenants to run to lessees when the lessee is in a better position to perform the covenant than her landlord. Since Bill is in possession of the building and the cooling plant, only he is able to perform the covenant.

d.   No, the answers to part (a) and part (b) do not change at all. In particular, the answer to part (b) does not change because even in an action at law the traditional doctrine of vertical privity requires no more than that the remote party succeed to the possessory interest of the covenantee (the party who is benefited by the covenant). Thus there is, in every jurisdiction, sufficient vertical privity for the benefit to run to Bill.

Under the Restatement (Third) the result is the same also. The Restatement (Third) allows the benefit of affirmative covenants to run to lessees when enforcement by the lessee neither diminishes their value to the lessor nor increases the burden on the covenant's obligor. Enforcement by Alice meets these criteria.

PROBLEM 30

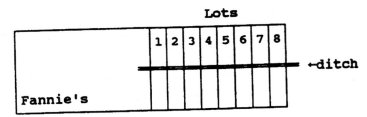

Twenty years ago, Dan Developer bought a 10 acre parcel of land adjacent to Fannie Farmer's farm. Fannie's land had a drainage easement over Dan's parcel. Drainage was accomplished by an open ditch bisecting Dan's land. In order to reduce the overall interference with his development plans, Dan offered to assume the cost of maintaining the easement if Fannie would consent to his straightening, tiling, and covering it. Fannie agreed. Fannie and Dan executed an agreement, purporting to run with their land, that Dan would straighten, tile, and cover the ditch and thereafter bear the cost of its maintenance.

Dan then subdivided the parcel into 8 lots. As Dan designed his subdivision, the ditch ran under and across all of the lots. Over the years, Dan sold all the lots.

This year Fannie noticed that the ditch was clogged and not draining her land properly. She sued all Dan's lot purchasers for an injunction compelling them to repair the ditch and for damages for the injury to that year's crops.

The lot purchasers have moved to dismiss Fannie's suit alleging an absence of horizontal privity between Fannie and Dan.

Analyze the lot purchasers' motion.

ANALYSIS

The lot purchasers' motion should fail. Some jurisdictions, and the Restatement (Third), do not require horizontal privity even in suits at law. In addition, in jurisdictions that adhere to the requirement, Fannie's and Dan's agreement is supported by both mutual and instantaneous horizontal privity.

Before executing their agreement, Fannie and Dan had related interests in a drainage easement. Fannie and Dan's agreement adjusts their relationship in that mutual interest. Their agreement satisfies the concept of mutual privity. All jurisdictions that require instantaneous privity will accept mutual privity as well. Thus, even though Fannie and Dan's agreement did not create an easement or transfer a property interest between themselves, Fannie and Dan are in horizontal privity.

PROBLEM 31

Bette Builder and Dan Developer owned adjacent lots. When Bette and Dan learned that they were both interested in developing small office buildings on their respective lots, Bette and Dan thought it cost efficient for Bette to build a heating plant large enough to heat to both buildings, and for Dan to build a cooling plant large enough to cool to both buildings. After some negotiation, the only hitch in their finalizing an agreement obligating themselves to build the respective plants and supply the required heating or cooling was a concern that the covenants would not be fully enforceable by or against their successors due to an absence of privity.

Bette and Dan know that privity is not required for a covenant to run in equity. But they are concerned that breach of their covenants will result in significant damages, which are compensable only in suits at law.

a. Bette and Dan are in a jurisdiction that requires instantaneous privity for a covenant to run at law. Can their transaction be structured so that there is instantaneous privity; and if so, how?

b. Bette and Dan are in a jurisdiction that requires mutual privity for a covenant to run at law. Can their transaction be structured so that there is mutual privity; and if so how?

c. Bette and Dan are in a jurisdiction that requires vertical privity for a covenant to run at law. Can their transaction be structured to circumvent the vertical privity requirement, and if so how?

ANALYSIS

a.   Yes. The transaction can be structured to create instantaneous privity. One way would be for Dan to convey his lot to Bette, and for Bette to reconvey the lot with the appropriate covenants. Another way that parallels the technique most popular when multiple lots are involved would be for Bette and Dan to convey their lots to X, a third party. X could reconvey Bette's lot to Bette, with the appropriate covenants; and, then, reconvey Dan's lot to Dan, reiterating the appropriate covenants.

b.   Yes. Bette could convey Dan an easement in her heating plant, and covenant that she, the servient landowner, would maintain the facilities and provide adequate heat. Dan could convey Bette an easement in his cooling plant, and covenant that he, the servient owner, would maintain the facilities and provide adequate cooling. The easements would provide the mutual privity sufficient to support the covenants relating to their use.

c.   Maybe. One way to structure the agreement so that it would bind lessees would be to require the covenantor to covenant for herself, her heirs and assigns not to grant a lease to anyone who had not directly contracted with the covenantee, her heirs and assigns to adhere to the terms of the original agreement. This agreement would be specifically enforceable. It could be recorded if it were part of a deed. Then any attempt to lease the property in violation of the covenant could be enjoined. However, there is always the possibility that a lease might be executed before one could enjoin it.

Another possibility is to create a lien to secure the performance of the covenants. Enforcement of a lien is in equity, which obviates the vertical requirement. A lien could secure the covenants here. Liens may secure not only liquidated amounts (sums expressed in money), but also any obligation that is reasonably calculable in money. Damages for the breach of most covenants are reasonably calculable in money; and this would be the case for the covenants involved in this transaction.

(The lien technique might even be used in parts (a) and (b) to obviate the need for horizontal privity. But the techniques described there have more precedent attesting to their effectiveness; and they accomplish just as much with less remedial complexity. The lien technique is theoretically more effective in cases where mutual privity is required and the covenants cannot be expressed as easements. But since jurisdictions requiring mutual privity tend to be liberal in their concept of an easement, and since many covenants receive effective enforcement through injunction, it actually is quite rare that the "covenant disguised as an easement" technique is not sufficiently effective to circumvent the mutual privity requirement.)

Finally, Bette and Dan would not have to restructure their transaction if the jurisdiction were to adopt the Restatement (Third) approach. Bette and Dan have entered into affirmative covenants to supply heat and cooling from heating and cooling plants in their respective buildings. The Restatement (Third) does not require vertical privity when original parties transfer their entire ownership interest. When the original parties transfer less than their complete ownership interest limitations do arise. Still, the Restatement (Third) allows the benefit of an affirmative covenant to run to a lessee when enforcement by the lessee neither diminishes the covenant's value to the lessor nor increases the burden on the party obligated to perform the covenant. The Restatement (Third) allows the burden of an affirmative covenant to run to a lessee when the lessee is in a better position to perform the covenant than her landlord. Should Bette or Dan lease their respective buildings, their lessees would meet these criteria.

[D]   Recapitulation

1.   Privity is the relationship that must exist between the covenantor and the covenantee, and between them and their successors in interest for a covenant affecting land-use to run. Privity has two distinct branches: horizontal privity, which is the relationship required between the covenantor and the covenantee; and vertical privity, which is the relationship required between them and their successors.

2.   Courts differ in their concept of horizontal privity. Some courts require mutual privity. Mutual privity exists between a covenantor and a covenantee who already have or who, because of the transaction of which the covenant is a part, will have related interests in the same land. Only the relationships between landlords and tenants, and the dominant and servient owners of easements, satisfy this concept of horizontal privity.

Other courts, require instantaneous privity. Instantaneous privity exists between a covenantor and covenantee whose covenant is part of a transaction involving the transfer of an interest in land between themselves. All the relationships encompassed by mutual privity and the relationship between grantors and grantees of fee interests satisfy this concept of horizontal privity. A majority of courts treat instantaneous privity as the preferable concept of horizontal privity.

3.   Horizontal privity is not required for an equitable servitude to run. Courts differ in the necessity of horizontal privity for a real covenant to run. Some courts hold that horizontal privity is not required for a real covenant to run. Other courts, and the Restatement (First), hold that horizontal privity is required for a covenant burden to run, but not for a covenant benefit. Other courts hold that horizontal privity is required for both a covenant burden and a covenant benefit to run.

4.   Restatement Third) § 2.4 abrogates the horizontal privity requirement. Under the Restatement (Third), covenants may run in both law and equity without any horizontal privity between the covenantor and covenantee.

5.   Courts agree on the concept of vertical privity. For a covenant benefit to run, the successor must succeed to the covenantee's possessory interest. For a covenant burden to run, the successor must succeed to the covenantee's entire ownership interest.

6.   Courts also agree on the necessity of vertical privity for a covenant to be enforced by or against remote parties. Vertical privity is not required for an equitable servitude to run. Vertical privity is required for the running of both the benefit and the burden of a real covenant.

7.   The Restatement (Third) abrogates the vertical privity requirement for negative covenants while retaining a modified requirement for affirmative covenants. Restatement (Third) § 5.3 allows lessees to enforce the benefit of affirmative covenants only (a) when they involve covenants to repair, maintain, or service the property, or (b) when doing so neither diminishes the covenant's value

to the lessor nor increases the burden on the party subject to the covenant. Lessees may be sued for their nonperformance of affirmative covenants only when they are in a better position to perform the covenant than the lessor.

8. After complete assignment of the servient land, a covenantor no longer is liable for breach of a running covenant. After a partial assignment, i.e., a transfer of the possessory interest, a covenantor is liable for breach of a running covenant in a suit at law, but not in a suit in equity.

9. After subdivision of the servient land, each successor to the burdened land who breaches a running covenant is liable in a suit in equity. In suits at law, each successor who breaches a real covenant is liable for the damages caused by her breach. Each breaching successor is jointly and severally liable for all the damages if the damages are not separable. Covenants requiring payment of money are apportioned according to acreage or the proportional value of each parcel.

    After subdivision of the dominant land, each successor to the benefited land may independently enforce running covenants except when there are unsolvable problems of computation or when multiple suits impose an undue burden on the obligor.

10. The rules on privity are circumventable by providing that the running covenant is enforceable by a lien. Liens may secure a running covenant whenever the covenant calls for the payment of money, and whenever the covenant has a calculable, nonspeculative value.

§ 2.06 TOUCH AND CONCERN

[A] Definitions

TOUCH AND CONCERN: Touch and concern is the relationship required between a covenant affecting land-use and a parcel of land for the covenant to run with the land. Touch and concern is a public policy limitation that overrides the parties' intent to create a running covenant; it is a public policy limitation on the type of obligation that may become a running covenant.

[B] Discussion and Questions

In all the Questions in this section, assume that (a) the parties have expressed the intent that the covenant run with any land mentioned in the Question; (b) the privity requirement is satisfied; and (c) subsequent purchasers have notice of the covenant.

The "touch and concern" requirement is the central doctrine through which the judiciary controls landowner discretion to impose running covenants. Unlike notice and privity, which determine whether covenants run by considering the circumstances surrounding their creation or transfer, the touch and concern doctrine determines which covenants run by considering their content. Through the touch and concern test, the judiciary directly addresses the type of obligation that public policy allows to be a servitude.

Unfortunately, directness does not mean clarity. Courts frequently lament that "it may be inexpedient and perhaps impossible to formulate a rigid test or definition which will be entirely satisfactory or which can be applied mechanically in all cases. . ." Neponsit Property Owner's Ass'n. v. Emigrant I. Sav. Bk., 15 N.E.2d 793, 796 (N.Y. 1938). Commentators say that touch and concern "has space and content that can be explored and felt better than it can be defined." CSW p. 471. One commentator even has suggested that no general notion of touch and concern exists by concluding "that courts will handle. . . [it] differently with respect to different types of covenants." 9 Powell § 60.04[2][a] at 60-53.

At bottom, formulating a definition of the touch and concern concept is difficult because the function it serves, and the policy it attempts to effectuate, is elusive. The concept of contracts that are void as against public policy focuses on whether a covenant ought to be enforced ab initio between the original parties. The concept of covenant termination due to changed conditions focuses on whether a covenant ought to be enforced when it no longer can accomplish its purpose. See § 2.07[B][5], below. The touch and concern concept sits between these two clearly understandable doctrines. The touch and concern requirement determines whether enforcement of a valid, effective covenant must cease merely because the land is transferred.

The difficulty of articulating a reason to void covenants solely because the current landowner is not the covenantor or the covenantee has led some commentators to suggest that there is no reason. These commentators suggest abolishing the concept. See Epstein, Notice and Freedom of Contract in the Law of Servitudes, 55 S. Cal. L. Rev. 1353 (1982); French, Toward a Modern Law of Servitudes, id. at 1261. Other commentators, however, argue the doctrine still serves a policy function and urge its retention. See Sterk, Toward and Economic Understanding of Touch and Concern, 1988 Duke L. J. 925; Reichman, Judicial Supervision of Servitudes, 7 J. Leg. Stud. 139 (1978) (policy is to allow covenants to run only when they "further implement the economic function of possessory estates," and thus, taken as a whole, "promote land utilization"); Browder, Running Covenants and Public Policy, 77 Mich. L. Rev.12 (1978) (relating the touch and concern requirement to the policies underlying the rules against restraints on alienation and perpetuities).

Joining this debate, the Restatement (Third) advocates abrogating the traditional touch and concern doctrine. Acknowledging that there should be public policy limitations on permissible servitudes, Restatement (Third) §§ 3.1–3.7 suggests replacing the vague touch and concern requirement with policy limitations that directly address the social harms that may flow from running covenants.

The Restatement (Third)'s position surely will be influential. As yet no court has embraced it. At present, courts impose some form of the touch and concern test on running covenants. Despite the difficulty of articulating a satisfactory abstract statement of the touch and concern test, courts continue to attempt to do so. Confusion, particularly when it comes to application, abounds.

We will attempt to parse the confusion by separating the discussion of the concept of the touch and concern requirement from a discussion of its necessity. Then, we will review the Restatement (Third)'s suggested reform of the area. Finally, a few miscellaneous topics related to the touch and concern requirement will be discussed. But be forewarned: little that is concrete will emerge until a feel is developed by considering the application of the general doctrine in the Questions and Problems.

[1] The concept of touch and concern

In the courts, the most frequent statement encountered describing the touch and concern test is that a covenant touches and concerns a particular parcel of land when its "performance or nonperformance will affect the quality, value, or mode of enjoyment" of the land. This statement, which the courts say is derived from Professor Bigelow's landmark article on running covenants in leases, The Content of Covenants in Leases, 12 Mich. L. Rev. 639 (1914), is totally circular. All covenants increase or decrease the rights, or value of the rights, to a particular parcel of land if courts permit them to run with that land.

A more fruitful formulation, one that is closer to Bigelow's actual suggestion and, perhaps, is what most courts mean when they speak as described above, is that a covenant which runs with the land must "affect the legal relations—the advantages and the burdens —of the parties to the covenant, as owners of particular parcels of land and not merely as members of the community in general." Neponsit Property Owner's Ass'n. v. Emigrant I. Sav. Bk., 15 N.E.2d 793, 796 (N.Y. 1938). The additional requirement, that the covenantor's or covenantee's interest in the performance of the covenant must affect her directly as the owner of the land—not merely as the named party—is the core of the concept distinguishing covenants that touch and concern land from those that do not. When a landowner is as interested in the performance or nonperformance of a covenant, or as able to perform or not perform a covenant, regardless of her status as the owner of the land, the covenant is collateral to the land and does not touch and concern it. See, e.g., Bigelow, above, pp. 645-6; 5 Restatement (First), pp. 3150-52 (whether a promise touches and concerns land requires judgment of whether the land's involvement is more than casual and incidental).

In fleshing out Bigelow's suggestion, courts and commentators have developed three somewhat divergent strands. The oldest and narrowest strand is essentially a "physical effects" test. According to this approach, a covenant touches and concerns a particular parcel of land only when it affects the "physical use or enjoyment" of the land or title to the land. Covenants touch and concern land when they control the use of the land's physical corpus or make its physical use or enjoyment more satisfactory. See, e.g., Norcross v. James, 2 N.E. 946 (Mass. 1885); Bill Wolf Pet. Corp. v. Chock Full of Pow. Gas. Corp., 333 N.Y.S.2d 472 (Sup. Ct. 1972); Clear Lake City Water Auth. v. Clear Lake Utilities, 549 S.W.2d 385, 388 (Tex. 1977); Restatement (First) §§ 537, 543.

The second strand is essentially a "common sense" test. Under this approach, the touch and concern requirement is met by covenants which laymen regard as so intimately related to land-use that they normally are entered into to promote land utilization. Covenants normally entered into for reasons other than the parties' interest in the land do not, in common understanding, touch and concern land. See, e.g., C. Clark, Real Covenants and Other Interests Which "Run With the Land" 99 (2d ed. 1947); Berger, A Policy Analysis of Promises Respecting the Use of Land, 55 Minn. L. Rev. 167, 211-12 (1970).

The third strand is essentially a pragmatic "balancing" or "reasonableness" test. This approach, which is similar to the balancing of interests technique found in many areas of law, weighs the advantages and disadvantages of covenant enforcement. All aspects of the covenant arrangement may be considered. As was said by Davidson Bros. Inc. v. D. Katz & Sons, Inc., 579 A.2d 288, 294 (N.J. 1990), one of the leading cases to adopt the reasonableness approach, the test is inherently "fact sensitive," allowing courts "to consider the enforceability of a covenant in view of the realities of today's . . . world and not in the light of out-moded theories developed in a vastly different . . . environment."

Over time, courts using the reasonableness test frequently have found certain factors important in considering the validity of running covenants. Among them are a comparison of the burden of performance on the promisor with the benefit to the promisee; the importance of the covenant to society and the parties; whether the covenant is to last for a limited or unlimited time; the covenant's impact on the land's marketability; and whether a running covenant is necessary to accomplish the parties' objectives. Fundamentally, the balancing approach attempts to invalidate running covenants whose enforcement is uncommonly inconvenient for one of the parties and unimportant for society.

Concretizing the meaning of the physical effects, common sense, and balancing approaches to the touch and concern requirement must await their application to particular covenants. Suffice it to say, at this point, that it is generally helpful to differentiate between a) those covenants that prevent or compel some act that must be either done or not done on the land and b) those covenants that may be either done or not done off of the land. The former generally are found to touch and concern the land. (But be wary of the fudge word "generally." See, e.g., Q89 and Q90, below.) The latter present mixed results. Some covenants that may be performed off the land, such as covenants that compel or restrain changes in the title to the land or provide services that affect the physical use or enjoyment of the property, generally are found to touch and concern the land. Covenants to pay money, for example, may be performed off the land. Nevertheless, covenants to pay money generally are held to touch and concern the land if the money is spent to provide services that benefit the physical use or enjoyment of the land. See Restatement (First) § 537 com. (g). Suffice it to say also that although some jurisdictions adhere to one strand of the touch and concern requirement rather than the others, most jurisdictions draw from all three approaches as the occasion warrants. They see each of the strands of the touch and concern requirement as a partial description that contributes something to the overall concept.

The Concept of Touch and Concern and Negative Covenants

Q88: O, owning two adjacent lots, conveys one of them to A. The deed to A contains a covenant restricting A's lot to residential use.

    a.   Does the covenant's burden touch and concern A's land?

        A: Yes. The covenant restrains acts that can be done only on A's land; only the current landowner may perform or not perform the covenant. The covenant substantially affects the physical use of the property; public policy favors such covenants; and laymen regard the covenant as one landowners enter into as landowners.

b. Does the covenant's benefit touch and concern O's land?

A: Yes. One might wonder how the covenant physically affects O's land. Courts and commentators respond that a residential use restriction directly and substantially affects the benefited lot owners' "quiet enjoyment." The physical surroundings, or the physical environment, of O's retained land is affected by the residential restriction burdening A's lot. Covenants that control physical characteristics of surrounding land development touch and concern the benefited land.

c. Rediscuss part (b) on the assumption that O's retained land was not immediately adjacent, but was 10 blocks (1 mile) away from the lot conveyed to A.

A: Probably not. O's retained land may be so distant that any benefit to it would be de minimis. Courts do inquire into the reality of the claimed effect on the benefited land. Courts say that the benefited land must be close enough to be affected adversely by breach of the covenant. However, there is no case in which the intent of the parties was clear and the court held that the actual benefit of a building restriction was insufficient. (The cases that usually arise involve deeds in which the expression of intent to benefit certain land is ambiguous and the distance of the allegedly benefited land aids in the construction of the covenant.)

d. Suppose O owned a 100 acre parcel, subdivided it into lots, blocks and streets, and conveyed one lot to A. The deed to A contained a covenant restricting A's lot to residential use. Later O conveyed a lot to B, subject to the same restriction in A's deed. B's lot was located 10 blocks (1 mile) away from the lot conveyed to A. Does the benefit of the covenant in A's deed touch and concern B's lot?

A: Yes. Although the distance between the lots in parts (c) and (d) are the same, in part (d) the burdened and benefited lots are part of one subdivision development. Courts accept the argument that through a "domino" effect the use of land anywhere in the same subdivision sufficiently impacts even the most distant land to touch and concern it.

Q89: O, owning two adjacent lots, conveys one of them to A. The deed to A contains a covenant that A will not use the property to engage in the retail drugstore business so long as O continues a retail drugstore use on her retained lot.

a. Does the covenant's burden touch and concern A's land?

A: In most jurisdictions the burden touches and concerns A's lot. Courts and commentators remark that the burden of covenants controlling business competition restrict the way that the burdened landowner can use her property. An anti-competition covenant can be performed or not performed only on the burdened land because it identifies specific land as the site on which certain business activities cannot be carried out.

Nonetheless, a few courts, and the Restatement (First), say that the burden of these covenants do not touch and concern land. This result can be defended in terms of the physical effects, common sense, and balancing tests. In terms of physical effects, anti-competition covenants do not restrict the physical characteristics of land-use—they control the characteristic of business activity. After all, the same building that can be used for a prohibited drugstore can be used for a permitted stationary store. Anti-competitive covenants are not like covenants that prohibit all commercial activity. General prohibitions of business activity truly affect the physical environment of the land. Thus in terms of common sense, these covenants are directed at the control of business activity, not land-use. In terms of balancing, these covenants tend to promote and protect monopolies by inhibiting competition. Inhibiting competition generally is considered undesirable.

Commentators claim that the policy of promoting competition underlies this minority position. Many commentators suggest that this policy is better effectuated by screening anti-competition covenants through the law of unreasonable restraints of trade. This, they suggest, is preferable to adopting a strict version of the physical effects concept of touch and concern to combat what is essentially an anti-trust problem.

b. Does the covenant's benefit touch and concern O's land?

> **A:** Most jurisdictions hold that the benefit of anti-competition covenants touch and concern nearby land. By reducing business competition, the value of the benefited land is increased. The covenant, accordingly, touches and concerns the land.
>
> Again, a minority of jurisdictions dissent. They point out that the benefit to the benefited land is purely financial. The land's physical environment and quiet enjoyment are not affected.

Q90: O, owning a parcel of vacant land that is restricted to residential use, sells it to A. The deed conveying the property to A contains a clause by which A agrees to hire O's construction firm as general contractor when "constructing the original dwelling or building" on the property. The agreement says that the purchase price of A's lot has been reduced due to the construction provision. Does the covenant's burden touch and concern A's land?

> **A:** Probably not. It is true that the covenant requires an act—hiring O's firm as general contractor for certain construction on A's land—that only the current landowner can do. Moreover, the covenant seems directed towards physical acts that will be done on the land. Nevertheless, the covenant does not substantially affect the physical use and enjoyment of the property. Unlike a covenant restricting the land to residential use, this covenant does not affect the general character of the land-use; it does not even affect the physical characteristics of the house that will be built. Thus the covenant does not affect some permanent aspect of the physical use of the land. Moreover, nonlawyers would understand this covenant as connected with O's business interests, not with the land. Finally, the relation between a landowner and her general contractor is one that requires the personal trust and confidence that comes from free selection. Compelling someone to use a general contractor that is not of her choice is undesirable from a policy standpoint.

Q91: O, owning a parcel of land developed with an office building, conveys it to A. The deed contains a covenant by which A agrees that as long as the building stands, it will continue to be named the "O Building." The name "O Building" is carved in the granite facade over the main entrance to the building. Renaming the building involves erasing the name.

a. Does the covenant's burden touch and concern A's land?

> **A:** No. The name of a building generally is regarded as a matter of sentiment or business, not something that substantially affects the use of the land. It is true that renaming a building is something that typically the current owner alone can do. It is also true that in this case renaming the building could well involve physical acts on the property (i.e., sandblasting the facade). But these acts, which are dependent upon present ownership, are fairly de minimis.

b. Rediscuss part (a) on the assumption that O is the historic landmark preservation commission; it has just spent $5,000,000 refurbishing the "X Building" which it considers a landmark of modern architecture; and the covenant said that as long as the building stood it would continue to be known as the "X Building."

> **A:** Yes. When a landmark structure is involved, a significant part of the quiet enjoyment of the property may well be identified with the name. Moreover, public policy strongly supports the effectuation of permanence in the enforcement of landmark preservation agreements.

Q92: O, owning a parcel of land, conveys it to A, reserving to herself the right to mine all coal and minerals. The deed contains a covenant exculpating O from liability for any injury to the surface of the land, or structures thereon, due to her mining activities.

a.   Does the covenant's burden touch and concern A's land?

A: Yes. Under the standing law A would have the right to sue for negligently inflicted injuries to her real property. Moreover, only A, as the current landowner, can sue or not sue for injury to her land. By restraining A's exercise of her right to sue, the covenant directly affects one of A's valuable legal rights. Of course, an argument can be made that exculpatory clauses are undesirable from a public policy standpoint. And, therefore, like anti-competitive covenants, on balance they ought not to be allowed to run. No jurisdiction as yet has upheld this argument.

b.   Does the covenant's benefit touch and concern O's land?

A: Yes. Under the standing law O would not have the privilege of inflicting negligent injuries on the owner of the surface. This covenant increases the rights that are part of O's title.

c.   Rediscuss part (a) on the assumption that the covenant also exculpated O from liability for personal injury to A.

A: Probably not. There has not yet been any case discussion of whether an exculpatory clause applicable to personal injury touches and concerns the land. It probably would not. A's right to sue for personal injury is something any injured individual could do. A's ability to sue does not turn upon her status as landowner. Stated another way, restraining A's ability to sue for personal injury does not remove any right from her title to the land. In addition, in terms of balancing, exculpatory clauses that apply to personal injury are even more undesirable than exculpatory clauses that apply only to property injury.

The Concept of Touch and Concern and Affirmative Covenants

Q93:   O owns a tract of riverfront land that is protected from flooding by levees along the riverbank. O sells part of the land fronting on the river to A. The deed contains a covenant requiring A to maintain the part of the levee along her riverbank.

a.   Does the covenant's burden touch and concern A's land?

A: Yes. This affirmative covenant obligates A to undertake acts on her land. They are acts that only the owner of the land can do. Moreover, the acts vitally affect the physical characteristics of her land.

It is true that in England this covenant would be said not to touch and concern the land. England strictly limits the burdens that run against fee estates; and England, some commentators suggest, has stricter limits on the issuance of mandatory injunctions. Thus, for reasons of public policy and equity jurisprudence, the burdens of affirmative covenants are not permitted to run against fee estates. Accordingly, it is clearest to say that the covenant does touch and concern the land but that additional policy considerations still prevent the covenant's burden from running. If with this understanding one says that in England the burdens of affirmative covenants do not touch and concern the land, then no harm is done.

Additionally, reflecting some of the concerns of the English judiciary, a few American jurisdictions will scrutinize affirmative covenants more closely. That a covenant is affirmative is a factor to be considered in weighing whether the covenant is sufficiently desirable to be allowed to run. See, e.g., Eagle Enterprises, Inc. v. Gross, 349 N.E.2d 816 (N.Y. 1976). But there are no facts in this case that would tip the balance against enforcing the burden of this affirmative covenant. Its enforcement is not difficult to supervise; it provides O's land with a substantial benefit; and it probably benefits A's land (the legally burdened land) as well.

b.   Does the covenant's benefit touch and concern O's land?

A: Probably. Under the reasonable assumption that if the levees on A's land are not kept in repair O's land is threatened with flooding, O's land is physically benefited from the performance of the covenant. If O's land is not affected by flooding on A's land, then the covenant's benefit would not touch and concern O's land.

c. Rediscuss part (a) on the assumption that the covenant required A to maintain the levee along O's riverbank.

A: Probably. Anyone with O's permission may enter O's land and maintain the levee there. The performance or nonperformance does not depend upon A's status as neighboring landowner. If that were all, the covenant's legal burden would not touch and concern A's land. However, if flooding on O's land affects A's land, A's land is physically benefited from the performance of the covenant. The covenant's burden, under this consideration, touches and concerns A's land. The concept is that when performance of a covenant redounds to benefit the physical use and enjoyment of the land legally burdened by the covenant, the covenant's burden touches and concerns that land. See 2 ALP pp. 381-2; Restatement (First) § 537(b) (discussing covenants to pay money).

Q94: O, owning a large tract of land, conveys part of it to A. The deed contains a covenant by which O agrees to convey a 30 foot wide strip from her retained land to the City for public street purposes (if the City will accept it). The 30 foot wide strip is immediately adjacent to the land conveyed to A and connects it to other streets.

a. Does the covenant's burden touch and concern O's land?

A: Yes. Only the current landowner is in a position to perform the covenant. O's covenant directly affects the continuation of her title to part of the land. Title is what makes physical use and enjoyment possible. Covenants that restrain or compel acts regarding title touch and concern the land itself.

b. Does the covenant's benefit touch and concern A's land?

A: Yes. Provision of access to and through public streets substantially affects the physical use and enjoyment of property.

c. Rediscuss parts (a) and (b) on the assumption that the 30 foot wide strip is not immediately adjacent to the land conveyed to A.

A: The answer to part (a) would not change. O has obligated herself to convey away title to part of her retained land. However, on the reasonable assumption that A would not have a unique right to use the nonadjacent street, the answer to part (b) would change.

Landowners have a unique right of access to, and make a unique use of, abutting streets. But landowners normally do not have that right in, or are as interested in, nonabutting streets. All members of the public have the same rights regarding nonabutting streets. The current owner of nonabutting land has no unique rights. (This answer would be different if O's dedication were part of a subdivision plan that gave A an easement of access over nonabutting streets; it would be different if A lacked any other means of access and, therefore, had an easement by necessity over the intervening land which gave a right of access to the dedicated nonabutting street.)

Q95: O, owning a large parcel of land on the suburban-rural fringe that she wishes to develop for single-family residential purposes, contracts with the Electric Co. for service. One clause of the contract provides that within one year from the execution of the agreement the Electric Co. will extend wires to O's land that are sufficient to meet the expected increase in demand. Does the covenant's benefit touch and concern O's land?

A: Yes. Electric service is vital to any physical use of land in contemporary society. Accordingly, the benefit of a covenant to supply electricity constitutes an advantage to the physical use and enjoyment of land. Texas, however, apparently limits its physical use test to acts that must be done or not done on the land. Covenants to provide basic services, such as gas, electricity and water, are considered personal covenants. See <u>Lakewood Heights v. McCuiston</u>, 226 S.W. 1109 (Tex. App. 1921); <u>Clear Lake City Water Auth. v. Clear Lake Utilities Co.</u>, 549 S.W.2d 384, 388 (Tex. 1977).

<u>The Concept of Touch and Concern and Affirmative Covenants Requiring Monetary Payments</u>

Q96: O, owning a parcel of land, conveys it to A. The deed contains a covenant by which A agrees to pay a debt that O owes to B. The purchase price of A's lot is reduced by the amount of the debt. Does the covenant's burden touch and concern A's land?

> **A:** No. In general, a covenant requiring a monetary payment has no necessary connection with any particular parcel of land. The payee need not be the current landowner to make a monetary payment; the payment need not be made on the burdened land. Only when a payment is for services that redound to the physical benefit or quiet enjoyment of the land, or in a common sense way promotes the current landowner's use and occupation of the land, do courts hold that the covenant meets the touch and concern requirement.
>
> The monetary payment required by this covenant has no connection with the land. The payment is not made for any service to the land. It is a payment of a personal debt. It is not an agreement that touches and concerns the land even though the parties reduced the land's purchase price by its amount.

Q97: O purchases a unit in a condominium. The unit is subject to a declaration of covenants. Among the covenants is one obligating the unit owners to pay assessments to maintain the common areas in the building and its surrounding lot.

> a.   Does the covenant's burden touch and concern O's unit?
>
> > **A:** Yes. The monetary payment required by this covenant provides funds that are to be expended to pay for services to the burdened land (the common areas are owned by the burden landowners) that significantly affect its physical use and quiet enjoyment. Non-lawyers regard covenants mandating assessments to pay for the maintenance of condominium common areas as related to the land; and social policy strongly supports their enforcement.
>
> b.   Rediscuss part (a) assuming that the assessments are used to fund contributions to the maintenance of public streets and parks immediately adjacent to the condominium property.
>
> > **A:** Maybe. We might have to know more about the spatial relationship between the public streets and parks and the condominium. It is possible that the spatial relationship is close enough so that the funds expended on the streets and parks strongly redound to benefit the physical atmosphere and social enjoyment of the burdened land. For an example of such a situation, see the landmark decision <u>Neponsit Prop. Owners' Assn. v. Emigrant Savings Bank</u>, 15 N.E.2d 793 (N.Y. 1938). Nonetheless, that the money is not expended for services to the actual grounds of the condominium would lead other courts to hold that the benefit to the burdened land is too insubstantial or indirect.
>
> > There is, of course, an analogy between these expenditures and the expenditure of funds to secure the bringing of essential services—such as water, gas and electricity—to the property. Yet, supporting neighboring streets and parks are not so specifically and uniquely beneficial to the burdened land; and parks are hardly as essential. Finally, a jurisdiction like Texas that holds that a covenant to supply water does not touch and concern the land would certainly not hold that maintaining public streets and parks does. See the answer to Q95, <u>above</u>.

Q98: O, owning a parcel of land, subdivided it into lots and blocks and recorded a declaration of covenants. Among the covenants was a clause requiring the lot owners to insure the structures on their lots against fire and other casualty loss. A purchased a lot in the subdivision.

a. Does the covenant's burden run with A's lot?

A: In most jurisdictions, no. It is true that only the current landowner may insure the property. To procure insurance, one must have an insurable interest, i.e., some current property interest. It is also true that insurance provides compensation for injury to the property. But the insured landowner is not obligated to spend the insurance proceeds upon the injured land. Specifically, she is not obligated to use the funds to repair or reconstruct the property. Thus a covenant obligating the landowner to procure insurance requires her to procure insurance and pay money (which are acts that do not have to be done on the land) to receive a fund that need not be spent upon services that benefit the land. Because the monetary payment (i.e., the insurance premium) does not necessarily redound to benefit the physical use or enjoyment of the land, the covenant to insure is collateral to the land.

Yet a few jurisdictions would hold that this covenant touches and concerns the land. The basis for this conclusion is the perception that in common understanding a covenant to insure provides a fund to restore or replace the property. See, e.g., C. Clark, Real Covenants and Other Interests Which "Run With the Land" 99 n.21 (2d ed. 1947).

b. Does the covenant's benefit run with the other lots in the subdivision?

A: In most jurisdictions, no. Since the funds will not necessarily be spent in reconstructing the injured property, no benefit to the neighboring land flows from the provision of the fund.

c. Rediscuss parts (a) and (b) on the assumption that the covenant requires the insurance proceeds to be used to repair or rebuild.

A: Now the covenant's burden touches and concerns A's land; and the covenant's benefit touches and concerns the neighboring land. The covenant is no longer a "bare" covenant to insure. Because the funds must be used to repair and reconstruct the injured property there is a substantial benefit to the physical use and enjoyment of the burdened land. The quiet enjoyment of the neighboring land is benefited by the increased likelihood that the lot will not remain injured and unutilized.

Q99: O, owning a large parcel of land on the suburban-rural fringe that she wishes to develop for single-family residential purposes, contracts with the Electric Co. for service. One clause in the agreement provides that O is to pay a $100,000 deposit. Another clause provides that the $100,000 deposit is refundable, in part when service is initiated and in part when usage reaches a certain level. O pays the $100,000 deposit. Does the benefit of the covenant obligating the Electric Co. to refund the $100,000 deposit touch and concern O's land?

A: No. The covenant to repay the deposit does not necessarily have to be performed on O's land. Anyone is capable of receiving and enjoying the repayment of a deposit, not just the current landowner. (Compare this to the covenant in Q95, above, where the current landowner is uniquely situated to enjoy the provision of electricity.) Concomitantly, the repayment of the money does not necessarily redound to the benefit of the land. Compare 165 B'Way Build. v. City Invest. Co., 120 F.2d 813 (2d Cir. 1941) (covenant to repay money held to touch and concern the land because the funds were to be used to repair physical damage to the land caused by the event that triggered the obligation to repay the money); and see Q98, above, on covenants to insure.

Q100: O owns a parcel of land which is mortgaged. O conveys the land to A. The deed contains a covenant by which A agrees to pay each mortgage installment as it falls due. The purchase price of A's lot is reduced by the amount of the mortgage she has assumed. Does the covenant's burden touch and concern A's land?

A: No. The covenant to pay the mortgage need not be performed on the land nor by the current landowner. It does not pay for any service that redounds to the benefit of the land. It calls solely for the payment of a personal debt of O's.

It may seem that the debt is related to the land in that the mortgage debt is secured by a lien attached to the land. Thus, paying the mortgage protects the continuation of title, something in which the current landowner is uniquely interested. But this is not so. The mortgage lien secures O's debt regardless of A's covenant to pay the mortgage installments. The obligation on the land, i.e., its liability to foreclosure if the debt is unpaid, is unaffected by A's covenant. Consequently, even without the covenant, A would be interested in paying the mortgage installments. A's covenant to pay the mortgage installment, i.e., her assumption of the mortgage, makes A personally liable for O's mortgage debt. In sum, unless the mortgage is paid off, A must take the land subject to it. The covenant does not touch and concern the land.

Q101: O, owning a parcel of land developed with an apartment complex, contracts with the A Management Co. to manage the building. The contract provides that A will receive as compensation 10% of the property's rental income. Does the covenant's burden touch and concern O's property?

    A: Probably not. This covenant calls for monetary payments for services to the land. In that it is like a covenant obligating the landowner to pay for electric service. See Q95, <u>above</u>. However, management services are not nearly so essential to the quiet enjoyment of the property as electric service. Management contracts are more commonly regarded as personal business arrangements than contracts calling for the provision of utility services. The aspect of the personal relation of trust and confidence between owner and management agent is very important. Consequently, social policy counsels that the agreement be held collateral to the land.

[2]   The necessity of touch and concern

As can be anticipated from the discussion of the touch and concern concept, some commentators argue that the touch and concern requirement should play no direct role in the determination of whether the burden or benefit of a covenant runs. The touch and concern concept may be useful, these commentators say, in construing the parties' intent regarding running when that intent is ambiguous. Covenants that normally are regarded as bound up with landownership should be presumed to run; but, a clear expression of intent regarding the running of a covenant should foreclose any judicial inquiry into whether the covenant touches and concerns the land. There is no social policy gain in second guessing the desires of the parties beyond barring covenants <u>ab initio</u> and, perhaps, terminating them when they no longer can effectuate their purpose.

No court has accepted this position. In all courts the burden of covenants may not run with the land unless it survives the touch and concern test; the same is true for the benefit of a covenant. In other words, touch and concern is necessary for either the burden or the benefit of a covenant to run.

But in all courts if the benefit of a covenant touches and concerns land it may run with that land even if the burden of the covenant is in gross. However, the courts are evenly divided on whether a covenant burden that touches and concerns land may run when the covenant benefit is in gross. The courts that refuse to allow a covenant's burden to run when its benefit is in gross reason that land should not be burdened unless land is benefited. For that reason they have adopted what will be described as a "twofold" touch and concern test. This locution, i.e., "twofold," means that a covenant's burden cannot run unless the covenant's benefit is appurtenant. But be forewarned: the locution is somewhat misleading in that the cause of the covenant's benefit being in gross may be that it does not pass the touch and concern test; but the cause also may that the parties simply did not intend the covenant's benefit to be appurtenant.

Additionally, <u>Restatement (First)</u> §§ 537 and 539 com. (k), takes the position that the burden of a real covenant cannot run unless the benefit does, but that the burden of an equitable servitude can run even if the benefit is in gross. The <u>Restatement (First)</u>, in effect, differentiates the necessity of the touch and concern requirement in law and equity. Only one jurisdiction seems to follow this view; it will not be considered further.

Q102: O, owning two adjacent lots, conveys one of them to A. The deed to A contains a covenant restricting A's lot to residential use.

a.   Does the covenant's burden run with A's land?

 A: Yes. All the elements for a covenant to run in law or equity are present.

b.   Does the covenant's benefit run with O's land?

 A: Yes. All the elements for a covenant to run in law or equity are present.

c   Rediscuss part (a) on the assumption that the deed says the covenant's benefit is personal to O and not intended to run with O's land.

 A: In some jurisdictions, no; in other jurisdictions yes. Somewhat more than half the jurisdictions have a twofold touch and concern requirement for a covenant burden to run. In these jurisdictions the covenant's burden does not run with A's land—even though it touches and concerns A's land—because the covenant's benefit does not run with O's land. The covenant's benefit does not run with O's land—even though it touches and concerns O's land—because the parties did not intend it to run. In the minority of jurisdictions that do not have a twofold touch and concern requirement, the covenant's burden runs with A's land.

d.   Rediscuss part (b) on the assumption that the deed says the covenant's burden is personal to A and not intended to run with A's land.

 A: Yes. No jurisdiction has a twofold touch and concern requirement for a covenant's benefit to run.

Q103: O, owning one lot, conveys it to A. The deed conveying the lot contains a covenant restricting it to residential use. The covenant says that it runs in favor of O and the immediately adjacent lots, which are owned by B and C.

a.   Does the covenant's benefit run with B's and C's lot?

 A: In most jurisdictions, no; in a few jurisdictions, yes. For the covenant's benefit to run with B's and C's lots, the covenant benefit must touch and concern their lots. In a straightforward sense, it does: the covenant is a use restriction that substantially controls acts that can only be done or not done on the land. Nonetheless, for B's and C's lots to enjoy the benefit of the covenant, the jurisdiction must have abolished the rule against granting a benefit to someone who is a stranger to the transaction. The jurisdiction must allow pure third-party beneficiary contracts to run between landowners. Few jurisdictions do so. See § 1.02[B][3], above. In most jurisdictions, therefore, the covenant's benefit would not run with B's and C's lot.

 In other words, even though the covenant's benefit touches and concerns B's and C's lot, a rule of policy prevents it from attaching to those lots, and thereby prevents it from running with them. Some courts might say that the covenant does not touch and concern B's and C's lot as a way of expressing the conclusion that it does not run with them. It is preferable to say that it touches and concerns the lots, but that a policy judgment, external to the touch and concern concept, prevents the covenant's benefit from running.

b.   Does the covenant's burden run with A's lot?

 A: Maybe. As explained in part (a), in most jurisdictions the covenant's benefit does not run with B's and C's lots. The covenant's benefit, therefore, is in gross. Consequently, even though the covenant's burden touches and concerns A's lot, the covenant's burden would not run in jurisdictions that (1) have not abolished the rule against granting property interests to strangers to a transaction, and (2) adhere to the twofold touch and concern requirement. The covenant's burden would run in jurisdictions that (1) have abolished the rule against third party beneficiaries; or (2) do not adhere to the twofold touch and concern requirement.

Q104: Reread the covenants in Q88(a), Q91(a) and Q91(b), above. Assume that the jurisdiction imposes a twofold touch and concern requirement. (I.e., the jurisdiction does not allow a covenant burden to run unless the covenant benefit is appurtenant.) Assume also that the burdens of these covenants touch and concern land so that they would run but for the twofold touch and concern test. Would the burdens of the covenants nonetheless not run because the covenant fails the twofold touch and concern test?

>   **A:** Both the benefit and the burden of the covenant in Q88(a) touch and concern the land. That covenant satisfies the twofold touch and concern requirement. The benefit of the covenant in Q91(a) does not touch and concern any land because it clearly benefits only O's pride. It fails the twofold touch and concern requirement. Accordingly, in a jurisdiction with a twofold touch and concern requirement, the covenant burden would not run even if it touches and concerns the building.
>
>   The analysis of the covenant in Q91(b) is fairly subtle. Analytically, it appears similar to the covenant in Q91(a). The beneficiary of the covenant is the landmark preservation commission. However, it is reasonable for a court to hold that the covenant to maintain the name of the building redounds to the benefit of the building itself. Accordingly, land is burdened for the benefit of land. In this case it is the same land that is benefited and burdened rather than two discrete pieces of land. Since the policy basis of the twofold touch and concern requirement is to prevent land from being burdened unless land is benefited, this covenant fulfills that purpose. It should, therefore, be held to pass the twofold touch and concern requirement.

[3]   The Restatement (Third) and touch and concern

Restatement (Third) § 3.1 rejects the traditional formulation of the touch and concern requirement in favor of a general rule invalidating running covenants that are "illegal or unconstitutional or violate[ ] public policy." The Restatement (Third)'s position is that running covenants generally are socially beneficial and that landowner agreements generally should be enforced. However, the Restatement (Third) also maintains that, on occasion, running covenants may harm public welfare, for example, by unduly interfering with the alienability of land or by unreasonably burdening fundamental constitutional rights.

In the Restatement (Third)'s view, the traditional touch and concern requirement does not adequately ferret out these occasions. The problem with the traditional doctrine is that it is cryptic and ambiguous: it neither articulates its underlying policy concerns nor targets them directly. Indeed, the Restatement (Third) says that over the past century courts have manipulated touch and concern doctrine to protect the public from socially undesirable running covenants. However, applying the obsolete and obscure touch and concern concept only promotes confusion and inconsistency. It is time, the Restatement (Third) says, to set aside the illusive touch and concern inquiry in favor of a test that candidly asks whether a running covenant violates public policy.

Restatement (Third) §§ 3.1–3.7 discusses the policies that courts have drawn from in invalidating running covenants. Over the past century, the Restatement (Third) says, courts have voided covenants that

>   a.   unreasonably burden constitutional rights;
>   b.   unreasonably restrain alienation of property;
>   c.   unreasonably restrain trade; or
>   d.   are arbitrary, spiteful, capricious, or unconscionable.

The above list, the Restatement (Third) says, states well known public policy limitations that apply across American law. In contrast to the traditional touch and concern requirement, these limitations reflect "widely accepted rules that directly target risks of social harm created by [running covenants]." Restatement (Third) § 3.1 com. (b).

Significantly, Restatement (Third) § 3.3 concludes that the Rule Against Perpetuities should not be used to invalidate running covenants. On the one hand, the Rule's time period applies arbitrarily to covenants arrangements. On the other hand, other public policy limitations, such as the ban on unreasonable restraints on alienation, sufficiently protect the public. Also, a consequence of the Restatement (Third)'s decision to validate all running covenants that do not infringe clear public policy is that it does not impose a "two fold" requirement, i.e., the Restatement (Third) allows covenant burdens to run even when covenant benefits are in gross.

In conclusion, it must be emphasized that the Restatement (Third)'s listing of public policy limitations on running covenants is illustrative, not exhaustive. As Restatement (Third) § 3.1 says, the public policies courts should be vigilant to vindicate "include, but are not limited to" the policies discussed in Restatement Third) §§ 3.1–3.7. As the uses to which running covenants are put change, as concepts of public policy evolve, so too will the doctrines by which courts control servitude arrangements in the name of the public welfare. In this regard, the Restatement (Third)'s approach to controlling the substance of covenant arrangements is similar to the "balancing" strand of the traditional touch and concern requirement. But the Restatement (Third) drops the confusing "touch and concern" rhetoric and more clearly surfaces and separates the appropriate policy concerns.

Q105: Would the Restatement (Third) invalidate the covenant involved

    a.   in Q89?

        A: No. Under the Restatement (Third) running covenants are not invalid on substantive grounds unless they violate widely accepted public policy. This question involves an anti-competitive covenant. Although anti-competitive covenants might violate the policy against imposing unreasonable restraints on trade, it is doubtful that the retail drug trade is so small that barring A's lot from that use will pose much of a problem for consumers. Also, the proscription is not perpetual; it is limited in time. Without special facts, under Restatement (Third) § 3.6, which focuses on anti-competitive covenants, the covenant in this Question is valid.

    b.   in Q90?

        A: Probably. This question involves a tying arrangement by which the landowner is bound to use O as a general contractor. Tying arrangements are subject to invalidity under the Restatement (Third) if they unreasonably restrain trade, indirectly restrain the alienation of property, are unconscionable, or arbitrary. Compelling a landowner to use a particular general contractor in the construction of her home could well violate several of these public policy concerns. The lower purchase price may well justify enforcing the covenant against A, who agreed to it, has the advantage of the lower price, and has some personal dealing with O. Remote purchasers from A, however, do not take any advantage from O's price reduction and have not established any working relationship with O. It seems justified to conclude that the covenant is valid between the original parties, but invalid, because they unreasonably burdensome, against remote parties.

    c.   in Q91(a) and (b)?

        A: Yes, for the covenant in Q91(a); no, for the covenant in Q91(b).

        The covenant in Q91(a) is capricious: it has no justification other than gratifying the O's vanity. Restatement (Third) § 3.1 authorizes courts to void capricious covenants because negatively affect land utilization, marketability and value without sufficient public benefit. See id. at com. (i).

        In contrast, the covenant involved in Q91(b) is not capricious. By preserving an historic name, the covenant benefits the public, not just O's vanity.

    d.   in Q103 (a) and (b)?

        A: Yes. As stated in the answer to Q103 (a) and (b), many jurisdictions would not allow the covenant's benefit to run because they do not permit third-party beneficiary contracts to run between landowners. Many jurisdiction also would not allow the covenant burden to run because they do not burden land unless other land if benefited. The Restatement (Third)'s decision to allow covenants to run unless they violate clear public policy overcomes these limits. Under the Restatement (Third), there is no impediment to allowing third parties to benefit from running covenants.

Similarly, there is no requirement that prevents running burdens when the covenant benefit is in gross. Of course, since the Restatement (Third) would uphold the third-party beneficiary covenant in favor of B's and C's lot, it is true that the covenant benefit is not entirely in gross. The point is, however, that O could also sue any successor to A, even though O's benefit clearly is in gross. Thus, under the Restatement (Third), the covenant will be enforced as written. The Restatement (Third) will not invalidate any aspect of it on public policy grounds.

Q106: Discuss the following fact patterns under the traditional touch and concern doctrine and under the Restatement (Third).

a.   Shady Grove is a 600 acre condominium with extensive common areas and 400 single-family homes, each situated on an acre of land. Shady Grove's declaration limits occupancy of each home to "one of more people, related by blood, marriage or adoption, living as a single housekeeping unit, exclusive of household servants." A, who purchased her home from the developer, resells her unit to B, who is a widow. After living alone for several years, B allows her male significant other to move into the house, but they do not marry. Does the burden of Shady Grove's limitation on occupancy run against A?

A: Under traditional analysis, probably yes; under the Restatement (Third), probably no.

Under tradition touch and concern doctrine, the discussion of Shady Grove's occupancy limitation is confusing. The covenant does affect the physical use of the land by restricting who can live there. Yet a distinction can be drawn because the covenant affects the social characteristic of land-use rather than its physical characteristics. The same number of people, even the same people, may live in each home, provided they are related or married. Common sense tells us that the covenant is directed at the social characteristic of the occupants, not their physical use of the land, which remains the same. Under a balancing analysis, it is clear that the importance of the covenant must be weighed against its intrusion into the owner's intimate relations. By analogy: under traditional doctrine, analysis of Shady Grove's occupancy limit is analogous to the analysis of anti-competitive covenants. Some courts say anti-competitive covenants do not touch and concern the land because they affect the business use, not the physical use, of the land.

Under the Restatement (Third), courts would directly address the covenant's intrusion into intimate relations. Restatement (Third) § 3.1 invalidates covenants that "unreasonably burden fundamental constitutional rights." This covenant burdens A's privacy and associational rights. Whether a court would declare the covenant unconstitutional if enacted as part of a municipal zoning ordinance is a factor, but not determinative of whether it is a valid running covenant. The Restatement (Third)'s requirement is not that the covenant be unconstitutional, but only that it "unreasonably burdens" a fundamental right. See Restatement (Third) § 3.1 illus. 16 (analyzing a similar covenant and concluding that it is invalid).

b.   O develops a 30-story condominium. Among the covenants in the declaration is Covenant 35. Covenant 35 provides that after 50% of the units are sold, but before 85% are sold, O may veto any decision of the Board of Directors unless all the unit owners ratify the Board's decision. Is Covenant 35 a valid running covenant?

A: Probably not, under both the traditional and the Restatement (Third) analysis.

Even though the answer is the same for this question, there is an important difference in the appropriate analysis. Condominium developers have an understandable interest in maintaining control of their projects after half the units are sold, at which point the developer has less than half the votes. Yet maintaining developer control too long is unduly oppressive to the purchasers. At some point, past 50%, but probably short of 85%, continued developer control becomes overreaching.

Traditional touch and concern doctrine does not directly address this issue. The physical effects, which considers whether land-use is physically affected, and the common sense test, which asks whether the parties entered into the covenant as landowners, cannot directly distinguish between a covenant based on point at which the developer cedes control of the project. These tests cannot directly distinguish between a covenant that maintains developer control until 55% of the units are sold and one that maintains developer control until 99% of the units are sold. Of course, the balancing test, which is similar to the Restatement (Third) approach, could make this distinction. But most courts do not admit that they use a balancing approach. If they do, they balance sub silentio, using the language of the physical effects or common sense approach in a confusing manner.

In contrast, Restatement (Third) § 3.7 invalidates running covenants that are "unconscionable." Thus the Restatement (Third) directly considers whether Covenant 35 represented overreaching by the developer, whether the purchasers were fully informed, and whether the covenant operated in an unduly harsh manner. Although, the precise point at which an understandable covenant becomes overreaching is hard to determine, the Restatement (Third) addresses it candidly.

[4] Miscellaneous topics

Three topics associated with the touch and concern requirement should be considered along with it: (a) a connection between horizontal privity and the touch and concern requirement; (b) a connection between the apportionment of covenant benefits and burdens and the touch and concern requirement; and (c) the circumvention of the touch and concern requirement by providing that a covenant is enforceable by a lien.

[a] A connection between horizontal privity and the touch and concern requirement

When horizontal privity is necessary, the covenant must touch and concern the land providing the privity. The burden of the covenant need not touch and concern the land conveyed, but, if not, its benefit must. The reason for this is that unless the covenant touches and concerns the land that supplies the privity, the parties do not have, with regard to that covenant, the relationship required to allow it to run.

To illustrate: Suppose O conveys a lot to A, and in the deed there is a covenant restricting to residential use other land that A owns. The covenant runs in equity where there is no horizontal privity requirement; but it cannot run at law in those jurisdictions that require horizontal privity for a real covenant to run. A corollary of this rule is that when horizontal privity is required, a covenant cannot run with the retained land of the grantor unless it runs with the land of the grantee, for it is the land conveyed to the grantee that supplies the horizontal privity required for a real covenant to run. (This undoubtedly is difficult to grasp. See 2 ALP § 9.13; Restatement (First) § 534 com. (d).)

Q107: O owns two parcels of riverfront land that are separated by 10 miles. The riverbanks of both lots are protected by levees. O sells one of the parcels to A. The deed contains a covenant that A will maintain the levee on O's retained land. In jurisdictions requiring horizontal privity for a covenant benefit to run, does this covenant's benefit run?

    A: The covenant's benefit does not run at law; it does run in equity. The covenant's benefit clearly touches and concerns O's retained land: it calls for acts to be performed upon the land that are physically beneficial to it. However, the covenant's burden does not touch and concern A's land because it is so far removed from O's land that it will not be benefited by performance of the covenant. See Q93, above.

Therefore, the land that was transferred, i.e., the land that provides the privity, is not touched and concerned by this covenant. Consequently, O and A are not in horizontal privity with regard to this covenant. In jurisdictions that require horizontal privity for a covenant benefit (or burden) to run at law, this covenant benefit will not run. Since no jurisdiction requires horizontal privity for a covenant benefit (or burden) to run in equity, the covenant will run in equity. In practical effect, A may be compelled to perform the covenant, and held in contempt of court if she fails to perform it; but she will not be held liable for damages for nonperformance. See § 3.05, underline.

[b]   A connection between the apportionment of covenant benefits and burdens and the touch and concern requirement

Consider the following: A has a parcel of land that is part of a subdivision. A's parcel fronts on two roads. One of the roads is a public way. The other is a private way running through the subdivision; it is maintained by the homeowner's association; and A is, under the subdivision's declaration of covenants, assessed by the homeowner's association for the maintenance of the road. A subdivides her parcel into two lots. Only one lot fronts on the private road. The other lot fronts on the public road. Will the assessment be apportioned between the two lots or will the entire assessment be imposed on the lot still fronting on the private road?

Every court that has dealt with a fact pattern like this has ruled that the part of the land no longer served by the private road is not subject to the burden of the covenant to pay for the private road's maintenance. The part of the land that is no longer served by the road, the courts observe, is no longer touched or concerned by the covenant. But the courts are unclear whether their ruling is based on a rule of law that only the part of the land that is touched and concerned may continue to be subject to a covenant; or whether their ruling is based on the presumed intent of the parties for allocating covenant burdens after subdivision of the burdened land.

Q108: O and A own adjacent parcels of land. O has a drainage ditch easement over A's land; the easement agreement requires A to maintain the ditch. A subdivides her parcel into 5 lots, and sells them all. The subdivision is designed so that the ditch runs across only lot 3.

ditch→			O's	
lots→ 1	2	3	4	5

a.   Are the owners of lots 1, 2, 4, and 5 liable for any damages to O's land that occur due to the ditch being clogged.

A: No. Now that the land has been subdivided, performance of the covenant no longer requires physical acts upon lots 1, 2, 4 and 5. These lots are no longer touched and concerned by the covenant. Whether the basis for this ruling is that the parties did not intend for the lots to be subject to the covenant after subdivision, or that the lots cannot be subject to the covenant after subdivision is not clear. Compare this analysis with the analysis of Problem 30, § 2.05[C], above, where the ditch ran across all the lots.

b.   Rediscuss part (a) on the assumption that until A subdivided her land the ditch was open and O was required to maintain it; and that to facilitate lot sales, A agreed to maintain the ditch as consideration for O's permission to tile and cover it.

A: Maybe. The argument is that lots 1, 2, 4 and 5 still benefit in their physical use and enjoyment from this covenant. Covering the ditch might well substantially improve the physical environment of the lots. If so, then all the lots are touched and concerned by A's agreement to maintain the ditch because it is part of an agreement which redounds to their physical benefit. See Restatement (First) § 537. The notion that a covenant might touch and concern burdened land because its performance redounds to the actual benefit of the burdened land is not limited to covenants requiring monetary payments.

[c] The circumvention of the touch and concern requirement by providing that a covenant is enforceable by a lien

As an equitable property interest, a lien directly affects a landowner as owner of the land. Providing that a covenant whose burden does not otherwise touch and concern land is enforceable as a lien makes it touch and concern the land subject to the lien. The only limitation on the use of liens to make covenant burdens satisfy the touch and concern requirement is the limitation on the kinds of obligations that can be enforced through a lien. But, as stated in § 2.05[B][5][c], above, all covenants requiring the payment of liquidated sums, indeed, all covenants whose value is ascertainable and nonspeculative, may be enforced through liens.

Q109: O, owning a parcel of land, conveys it to A. The deed contains a covenant by which A agrees to pay a debt that O owes to B. The covenant provides that A's promise is secured by a lien upon the land. The purchase price of A's lot is reduced by the amount of the debt. Does the covenant's burden run with A's land?

    A: By itself, the covenant to pay O's debt to B does not touch and concern A's land. It does not run with A's land. See Q96, above. But the lien is a separate property interest that attaches to the land and remains attached to it in the hands of any subsequent taker with notice. Thus the answer is yes, in the sense that the land is subject to the lien's foreclosure even after the land is transferred to subsequent parties; and no, in the sense that the subsequent taker is not personally liable for the promise. (Depending on the size of the debt this difference would be of no practical importance.)

For further reading on the Touch and Concern requirement, see 9 Powell §§ 60.04[2][a], 60.06; 2 ALP §§ 9.13, 9.14, 9.16, 9.28, 9.36; CSW §§ 8.15, 8.24; Restatement (Third) §§ 3.1–3.7.

[C] Review Problems

PROBLEM 32

Ann Able is the area wholesaler of GoMo gasoline and oil products. She operates several automobile filling stations and supplies others. A few years ago, Ann sold one of the stations she owned and operated to Ben Baker. The deed conveying the station to Ben contained covenants by which Ben agreed a) for the next 15 years to conduct, or cause to be conducted, an automobile filling and service station business on the property; and b) to use and sell only GoMo gasoline and oil products as long as the property was used as an automobile filling and service station and Ann was GoMo's area wholesaler. The deed said the covenants ran with the land conveyed to Ben. This year, Ben sold the station to Charlene Castern. Charlene contracted with the area distributor of PowerTrain products for supplies of gasoline and oil.

Ann learned of Charlene's agreement with PowerTrain's distributor when Charlene stopped ordering products from Ann. Ann immediately sued for damages and for an injunction prohibiting Charlene from using PowerTrain's gasoline and oil products.

a. Does the burden of the covenant to use and sell only GoMo gasoline and oil products touch and concern Ben's land?

b. Does the burden of the covenant to conduct an automobile filling and service station touch and concern Ben's land?

c. Assuming that the burden of the covenants discussed in parts (a) and (b) touch and concern Ben's land, do they run with it?

ANALYSIS

    a.   In many jurisdictions the covenant would touch and concern the land. These jurisdictions say that the covenant compels an activity, the vending of GoMo gasoline and oil products, that a landowner normally has the privilege of not engaging in upon her land. It affects the mode of enjoying the property. Therefore, it touches and concerns the land.

Other jurisdictions, however, observe that this covenant affects the mode of enjoying the land only indirectly and collaterally. The covenant directly relates to the conduct of a business on the land, rather than the land itself. As one court said "[a]s far as the land. . . is concerned, it makes little difference whose gasoline products are sold. The name on the gasoline pump is not essential to the land, certainly not in the sense that. . . a fence or landscaping may be." Bill Wolf Pet. Corp v. Chock Full of Power Gas. Corp., 333 N.Y.S.2d 472, 478 (Sup. Ct. 1972), rev'd 344 N.Y.S.2d 30 (App. Div. 1973). In these jurisdictions, the covenant does not touch and concern the land.

In other words, the analysis of this covenant parallels the analysis of covenants not to compete, discussed in Q89, above. Indeed, this covenant seems one step further removed from touching and concerning the land than covenants not to compete. Covenants not to compete restrict the conduct of an entire business or line of business on the land. The covenant to sell a particular brand of gasoline or oil relates to but one aspect, albeit a central aspect, of a business. Assuming any distinction between the conduct of a business and use of the land is viable, this covenant more clearly relates to the conduct of a business than a covenant not to compete.

Nonetheless, economically attuned commentators probably would say that the covenant to sell a particular brand of gasoline and oil products touches and concerns the land more clearly than a covenant not to compete. These commentators reason that so holding promotes decentralization of the automobile service station business. Allowing the national refiners to "tie" service stations encourages national refiners not to distribute their products through wholly owned service stations. Thus the monopoly concern that should underlie the conclusion that a covenant not to compete does not touch and concern the land does not apply to this covenant.

In contrast to the traditional approach, the Restatement (Third) does not ask whether the covenant's burden touches or concerns the land. Instead, the Restatement (Third) asks whether the covenant violates any widely accepted public policy. The Restatement (Third) directly addresses whether this covenant is anti-competitive or whether it is unconscionable. The result of the analysis probably would not change, but it considers the relevant issues more articulately.

   b.   The analysis of this covenant is similar to the analysis undertaken in part (a). It is an open question whether this covenant is made in respect of the land or the business and whether that distinction matters. To the extent that the distinction between covenants respecting the land or the business should be drawn, there is this difference between the covenants in parts (a) and (b): the covenant in part (b) requires that the land be used as part of an entire line of business, not just for the sale of a product as part of that business. Looked at this way, the covenant controls the use of the land less completely than a covenant that, for example, insists upon residential or commercial use, but more completely than a covenant controlling only the type of product sold in the business. Courts would be more likely to conclude that this covenant touches and concerns the land than the covenant in part (a).

   The remarks made in part (a) concerning the Restatement (Third) carry over, with even more force, to this part. The Restatement (Third) suggest courts consider whether a covenant violates public policy. Covenants that unreasonably restrain trade or are unconscionable violate widely accepted public policy.

   c.   Whether or not the covenant runs depends upon whether or not the jurisdiction has a twofold touch and concern requirement. Clearly, the benefit of the covenant is in gross. If the benefit of a covenant must be appurtenant for the burden to run, then the burden of this covenant does not run. The Restatement (Third)'s analysis, in contrast, would not be affected because the Restatement (Third) does not impose a twofold requirement.

PROBLEM 33

Denise Developer owned two adjacent parcels of land. On one parcel, she developed a sports club. On the other parcel, she developed a twenty story, 200 unit residential condominium building. The condominium's declaration of covenants includes within it the following provisions:

15.1 Club Facilities. The Developer intends to form or has already formed a sports club to be located on land immediately adjacent to this Condominium. The club will be owned by the Developer and operated for profit by the Developer. The intended facilities of such Club may include a lounge, food and beverage service, a swimming pool, tennis and racquetball courts, a running track, and weight room. The nature of any such intended facilities, improvement or development of such Club and the authority to determine whether any facility or service of such Club shall be continued, altered, changed or terminated are hereby in all respects fully reserved to the title holder, owner and operator of such Club.

15.2 Membership in Club. Each Owner of any Unit in the Condominium shall, upon acquisition of title, by such Owner become a member of the Club, without any membership or initiation fee therefore. Said Owner of any Unit in the Condominium shall pay the annual membership fee and such other fees occasioned solely by the use of the facilities of the Club by such Unit member. The said membership fee and other fees may be set from time to time by the Owner of said Club in such amounts that are deemed reasonable by said Owner, which fees are to be the same fees applicable, generally, to the entire membership of the Club for any particular facility or service.

15.3 Termination of Membership or Privileges. Clauses 15.1 through 15.4 inclusive are to remain in full force and effect unless terminated by a vote of three-quarters of the Unit Owners at a special election called for that purpose; or, with the agreement of the Developer, by a vote of a majority of Unit Owners at a special election called for that purpose.

15.4 Clauses 15.1 through 15.3 inclusive are to run with the land, and be enforceable by and against the grantees, successors, heirs and assigns of the Developer.

Shortly after completing the Club facility, Denise sold it to SportsWorld, Inc.

A year after Denise sold the last unit in the condominium, Inez Inactive purchased a unit in a resale. She immediately began spearheading a drive to make membership in the club voluntary. At a special election called under clause 15.3, Inez's motion to terminate mandatory club membership failed because only 60% of the unit owners voted in its favor.

Inez then adopted other tactics: she stopped paying her annual membership dues, which SportsWorld had set at $50 per month, and urged other unit owners to do the same. SportsWorld responded by suing to enforce its claim for Inez's unpaid dues.

a. Does the burden of the covenant requiring unit owners to pay the annual membership dues touch and concern Inez's unit?

b. On the assumption that the covenant touches and concerns Inez's unit, does its burden run with Inez's unit?

c. Reconsider parts (a) and (b) on the assumption that there was a provision 15.2(a) that said "Liens. All unpaid charges shall be a lien against said Unit, subject, however, to the rights of any mortgages on said Unit."

ANALYSIS

a.   Maybe. This is a close case. The covenant is a covenant to pay money. As with all covenants requiring monetary payments, it need not be performed on the land and the current landowner is not uniquely situated to perform it. This covenant touches and concerns the land only if it redounds to the physical use and quiet enjoyment of the burdened land.

Covenants compelling monetary payments to support sports facilities may meet this test. Consider a sports club that was located on, and was part of, the common facilities of the condominium. Its maintenance would redound to the physical use and quiet enjoyment of the burdened land as much as maintenance of any other common facility, such as the landscaping and walking paths. Sports facilities may be as much a part of the ambience of a condominium as a footpath and landscaping. Whether a covenant to pay for sports facilities runs with the land "depends not so much on whether it is to be performed on the land itself as whether it tends directly or necessarily to enhance [the land's] value or render it more beneficial or convenient to those by whom it is owned or occupied." Chesapeake Ranch Club, Inc. v. C.R.C. United Members, Inc., 483 A.2d 1334, 1337 (Md. App. 1984).

Certainly some "sports facilities" covenants do sufficiently enhance the use and enjoyment of condominium units to touch and concern them. Whether this one does is a matter of fact. Most courts would phrase the ultimate issue as whether, on the one hand, this condominium project is identified with and distinguished by the provision of sports facilities so that there is a cognizable or possible benefit to the units' use or value, or, on the other hand, whether the condominium's benefit from the sports facilities is no different from the general community's. Probably the courts actually are thinking of the ultimate issue as, on the one hand, whether the sports facilities are as much part of the ambience of the condominium as its footpaths and landscaping, or, on the other hand, whether the condominium's tie-in to the sports facilities is an extraneous imposition that simply exploits the unit owners for the benefit of the developer/sports club owner.

That the sports club in this Problem is immediately adjacent to the condominium is a factor that helps support the conclusion that it sufficiently affects the condominium units. Certainly, if the sports club were located in the condominium building there would be a closer relationship. If the sports club were located blocks away there would be less of a relationship.

That the sports club is open to the public is a factor that detracts from the conclusion that it sufficiently affects the condominium units. However, this factor, by itself, should not be determinative because a rule to that effect would make condominiums fairly hesitant to open their facilities to the public.

That the sports club is separately owned is a factor that detracts from the conclusion that it is sufficiently a part of the condominium's units ambience to touch and concern them. But this factor, too, should not be determinative. The physical effect of sports facilities upon the use and enjoyment of the condominium units is not affected by who owns it. Still, the common sense and balancing approaches to the touch and concern test should be vitally sensitive to this consideration. They help define whether the sports club's assessment redounds to the benefit, or to the exploitation, of the condominium owners.

Finally, there is one additional factor that should be considered. It may be a surprising one, but it may vitally affect one's ultimate conclusion about the relation between the sports club and the units. That factor is that the unit owners have the power, under clause 15.3, to terminate the tie-in by an extraordinary majority vote. The clause means that if a sufficient majority of unit owners feel exploited by the arrangement, they can end it.

In sum, it is left to you to discuss the ultimate outcome under the physical effects, common sense, and balancing approaches. As stated at the outset, this is a close case. Reading a number of cases that address this issue will give you a feel for the factors that push the outcome in one direction or another. See Chesapeake Ranch Club, Inc., above (assessment does not touch and concern); Ebbe v. Senior Estates Golf and Country Club, 657 P.2d 696 (Or. App. 1982) (same); Raintree Corp v. Rowe, 248 S.E.2d 904 (N.C..App. 1978) (same); Streams Sports Club, Ltd, v. Richmond, 457 N.E.2d 1226 (Ill. 1983) (assessment does touch and concern); Four Seasons Homeowners' Ass'n v. Sellers, 302 S.E.2d 848 (N.C. App. 1983) (same); Bessemer v. Gersten, 381 So.2d 1344 (Fla. 1980) (same).

In a departure from traditional analysis, the Restatement (Third) does not ask whether the covenant burden touches or concerns Inez's unit. Instead, the Restatement (Third) inquires directly into the public policy of upholding this covenant. This covenant involves a "tying" arrangement, whereby condominium purchasers are compelled to buy another "product" along with their condominium. Tying arrangements raise restraint-of-trade and unconscionability concerns. The Restatement (Third) directly considers whether, in this particular condominium, the tying arrangement is unreasonable or overreaching. The factors discussed above detail what the discussion under the Restatement (Third) would involve.

b. Maybe. Even if the covenant's burden touches and concerns Inez's unit it may not run with it. It is possible that the covenant's benefit does not touch and concern the land upon which the sports complex is built. The covenant may be held to benefit the business currently established upon that land. This financial benefit may not be the type of benefit that satisfies the touch and concern requirement, at least in a suit at law. Of course, it may be argued that financial benefit to businesses currently established on land are sufficient to touch and concern the land. Cases involving anti-competitive covenants may be cited for this proposition.

But on the assumption that the covenant's benefit does not touch and concern any land, we have a covenant with a benefit in gross. In jurisdictions with a twofold touch and concern requirement, the fact that the covenant's benefit is in gross would prevent the covenant's burden from running with the land that it touches and concerns. In these jurisdictions public policy mandates that covenant burdens be in gross when covenant benefits are in gross. Of course, in jurisdictions that do not have a twofold touch and concern requirement, that the benefit is in gross would not ipso facto prevent the covenant burden from running.

The Restatement (Third)'s analysis would not be affected by whether the covenant benefit was in gross. The Restatement (Third) allows burdens to run even if no land is benefited.

c. Now Inez's unit is unquestionably subject to the sports club's assessment covenant. It is certain that a lien may be imposed to secure payments of charges that are to be assessed in the future. Valid liens are equitable property interests encumbering land. Providing that unpaid assessments are liens obviates any need to discuss the touch and concern requirement. The lien, in effect, makes the covenant run in equity.

PROBLEM 34

A clause in the declaration of covenants of the 64 Bison Street Condominium provides that whenever a unit owner contracts to sell her unit the condominium board has 30 days to exercise a right of first refusal. Olivia Owner knew of this provision because when she bought her unit, in a resale from the previous owner, she went through the process by which the board screens potential owners. Yet, she is now suing to have the covenant providing for the right of first refusal declared inapplicable to her.

The problem is that the board exercised its right of first refusal when Olivia decided to move and contracted to sell her apartment—at slightly less than market value—to a close friend. The board's reason for exercising its preemptive right is unclear. Perhaps it was because they believed rumors about Olivia's friend and thought that made her an undesirable neighbor; perhaps they thought they could make a profit by reselling the unit at the market price (and use the profits to temporarily decrease assessments); perhaps they thought they would like to resell the unit to a friend of the board's president.

In any event, Olivia and the board are now in court. Olivia is not attacking the reasons for the board's exercise of the right of first refusal. Her claim is that the board may not enforce the covenant against her on any grounds because it does not run with the land.

a. What are the arguments for and against holding that the burden of the right of first refusal touches and concerns Olivia's unit?

b. What are the arguments for and against holding that the benefit of the right of first refusal touches and concerns the other units in the condominium?

ANALYSIS

a. The argument for holding that the burden of the right of first refusal touches and concerns Olivia's unit is that the right restricts one of the privileges a landowner normally has over her title: the freedom to select her successor. This freedom is one of the most prized incidents of ownership. By affecting it, the right of first refusal burdens one of the legal rights associated with the owner's estate. Moreover, it can affect the landowner only so long as her ownership continues. No one, except the current owner, is in a position to perform the covenant.

The argument against would focus on the insubstantiality of the burden on the landowner's rights. The right of first refusal does not compel a transfer of title when the burdened landowner does not want to transfer it. It does not affect the price that the burdened landowner will receive because the right must be exercised at the price negotiated with the third party. Thus the current landowner is not affected in the timing or value of her sale. She is affected only in the identity of her successor, something she is not interested in as current landowner, since she no longer owns the land after she sells it. In sum, a right of first refusal does not affect a landowner as landowner, and in any event, its effect is de minimis.

The Restatement (Third)'s policy-oriented approach to the validity of running covenants shifts the analysis away from the categorical approach employed by the traditional analysis. Under the traditional approach, the touch and concern inquiry seeks to determine whether rights of first refusal as a generic type of covenant should be allowed to run. The Restatement (Third) considers rights of first refusal to be a form of direct restraint on alienation. Direct restraints on alienation prevent owners from transferring their property whenever, to whomever, and under whatever terms they choose. Traditional public policy voids direct restraints on alienation when they are unreasonable. Restatement (Third) § 3.4 applies real property law's policy against unreasonable direct restraints to running covenants. The result is that some rights of first refusal would be upheld and others voided. The outcome turns on such factors as the price and procedures for exercising the right. See Restatement (Third) § 3.4 com. (f).

The Restatement (Third) § 3.1 also requires that covenants not be arbitrary or capricious. There are hints in this Problem that the Board may be exercising the right for arbitrary reasons—to make a quick profit or to resell to a friend of the Board's president. There also are hints that the Board may be exercising the right for a legitimate reason—that Olivia's friend will be an undesirable neighbor. The Restatement (Third) finds these factors relevant to determining the validity of the Board's action. The Restatement (Third) inquires into the particular exercise of the right, and not only whether rights of first refusal are valid in the abstract.

b. The argument for holding that benefit of the right of first refusal touches and concerns the other units in the condominium is that it is the central device by which condominium owners control the selection of their neighbors. Such control may be abusively exercised in particular cases. But in general the neighbors' control is important in terms of public policy; and it significantly affects the quiet enjoyment of the neighbors' units. Neighbors are interested in the ability of unit owners to pay assessments and not harm the atmosphere of their cooperative residence. The potential for abusive exercise of preemptive rights may be met by other legal responses than a blanket prohibition on enforcing them by and against remote parties.

The argument against is that the right of first refusal does not benefit the physical use or enjoyment of the neighbors' units. The identity of residents, which is what preemptive rights control, is a social characteristic. It is also subject to abuse and should not be supported by public policy.

Moreover, think of the analogy between a right of first refusal and covenants compelling a particular product to be sold on the premises, discussed in Problem 32, above. Rights of first refusal, like "tie-in" covenants, do not restrain the overall use of the property; they affect the particular "product" that uses or is used on the property.

The Restatement (Third) does not discuss the validity of the benefit of a covenant separately from the validity of the burden. As discussed in part (a), the Restatement (Third) investigates whether the covenant at bar, and its exercise, violates any widely accepted public policy. The comments made in part (a) apply to part (b) also.

PROBLEM 35

Elkhorn Lager Beer Co. is a small, old-time, independent beer company. Elkhorn has a history of good labor relations based primarily upon the higher than average wages and benefits provided for in its collective bargaining agreements.

Local 522 of the Brewery Workers of America is the collective bargaining agent for the employees in Elkhorn's single brewery. The local is aware that over the past two decades the beer industry has been consolidating. National brands have been buying out small, independent labels. Local 522 is concerned that should this happen to Elkhorn, the workers will end up with a less favorable employment contract.

One consolidation technique that Local 522 is particularly concerned about, because of its frequency and anti-union potential, is for a national to buy the independent's assets but not its business. When this occurs, the national company acquires the independent's functioning brewery but not its labor contracts.

Accordingly, when Elkhorn's and Local 522's contract was renegotiated, the local insisted upon inclusion of a clause that the new contract ran with the land upon which Elkhorn's brewery was located. The life of the agreement was limited to five years.

One year into the contract, a national company purchased Elkhorn's assets and announced that it was not honoring Elkhorn's collective bargaining agreement. The national company said it would employ workers according to the terms of the collective bargaining agreement it had with its unions. When the national company began activities at the former Elkhorn facility, Local 522 sued to enjoin it.

a. Does Local 522's collective bargaining agreement touch and concern the land the brewery is located upon?

b. On the assumption that the collective bargaining agreement touches and concerns the land the brewery is located upon, and that federal labor law statutes do not preempt the issue, does the collective bargaining agreement run with the land the brewery is located upon?

ANALYSIS

a. Analytically, it is difficult to think of how to distinguish this covenant from a covenant to sell only a particular brand of gasoline and oil products that was discussed in Problem 32, above. Both covenants affect aspects of the conduct of a particular business. In terms of doctrine, therefore, a jurisdiction that holds that a covenant to sell a particular brand of gasoline and oil touches and concerns the land should hold that a collective bargaining agreement touches and concerns the land.

Nonetheless, from a common sense point of view, i.e., the layman's understanding, collective bargaining agreements directly affect the conduct of businesses, and only indirectly affect the "value" of land or the "mode of enjoying" it. It would be difficult to overcome this initial, common sense presumption. Moreover, many courts which say that a covenant to sell only particular gasoline and oil products touches and concerns land indicate that an important factor is that the land would not have been sold to the independent filling station operator without the covenant. The covenant was a crucially important part of the consideration for the conveyance of the land. This cannot be said about the land upon which the Elkhorn brewery stands: the covenant at bar was not involved in the land's sale to Elkhorn.

Departing from the traditional approach, the Restatement (Third) does not ask whether the collective bargaining agreement touches or concerns the land. Rather, the Restatement (Third) allows all covenants to run that do not violate public policy. Examples of covenants that violate public policy are covenants that are arbitrary, covenants that unreasonably restrain trade, and covenants without rational justification that indirectly restrain the alienation of property. It seems evident that Elkhorn's collective bargaining agreement transgresses none of these policies. Under the Restatement (Third), the collective bargaining agreement would be allowed to run.

It may well be that the running covenant at issue in this Problem has nothing to do with the land other than the parties' desire (i.e., intent) to subject the land to it. But underlying the Restatement (Third)'s approach is the judgment that landowners should "enjoy the freedom to construct servitudes as they wish as long as they do not exceed limits set by . . . public policy." Restatement (Third) § 3.1, com. (a). Under the Restatement (Third), landowner intent governs unless it threatens cognizable social harm. Running covenant arrangements are valid if they have rational justification and do not violate widely accepted public policy.

b. Some jurisdictions have a twofold touch and concern requirement. In these jurisdictions a covenant burden does not run unless the covenant benefit is appurtenant to some land. In this Problem, the covenant benefit is in gross. Consequently, in jurisdictions with a twofold touch and concern requirement, the covenant burden does not run. Nonetheless, in jurisdictions that do not have a twofold touch and concern requirement, the covenant burden would run.

[D]   Recapitulation

1. Touch and concern is the relationship required between a covenant affecting land-use and a parcel of land for the covenant to run with the land. Touch and concern is a public policy limitation that overrides the parties' intent to create a running covenant; it is a public policy limitation on the type of obligation that may become a running covenant. Through the touch and concern requirement, courts address and directly control landowner discretion to impose running covenants.

2. The touch and concern requirement has no settled definition that can be applied in all cases. In general, there are three approaches to the concept—

    a. The physical effects test: Under this approach, covenants touch and concern land when they affect the physical use or enjoyment of the land, or title to the land.

    b. The common sense test: Under this approach, covenants touch and concern land when laymen would regard the covenant as aiding the promisee, or hampering the promisor, as landowners.

    c. The balancing test: Under this approach, covenants touch and concern land unless they are "too inconvenient" to the parties or society.

3. In application, these tests mean that covenants compelling some act to be done or not done on certain land generally touch and concern the land; that covenants which may be performed either on or off the land generally do not touch and concern the land; that covenants to pay money touch and concern the land only if the covenant is spent on services that redound to the physical enjoyment or use of the benefited land.

4. Some commentators urge the abolition of the touch and concern requirement. They argue that the parties' intent should determine whether covenants run. The touch and concern concept should be used only as an aid in construing the parties' intent regarding running when their intent is ambiguous. However, no court has adopted this position.

5. In all jurisdictions, a covenant burden cannot run unless it survives the touch and concern test. The same is true for a covenant benefit. Also in all jurisdictions, a covenant benefit that touches and concerns land may run even if the covenant burden is in gross. However, the courts are evenly divided on whether a covenant burden that touches and concerns land may run when the covenant benefit is in gross. Slightly more than half the jurisdictions impose a "twofold" touch and concern requirement for a covenant burden to run. For public policy reasons, these jurisdictions do not allow a covenant's burden to run unless the covenant's benefit is appurtenant.

6. The Restatement (Third) abrogates the touch and concern requirement in favor of an approach that directly asks whether the running covenant arrangement violated widely accepted public policy.

a. Among the policies the Restatement (Third) discusses as frequently implicated by running covenant arrangements are the policies against unreasonably burdening fundamental constitutional rights, unreasonably restraining trade, imposing unreasonable direct restraints on the alienation of property, imposing irrational indirect restraints on the alienation of property, and imposing burdens that are arbitrary, capricious, spiteful, or unconscionable.

b. The policies discussed by the Restatement (Third) are not exhaustive of the policies that running covenants may infringe. They are particular applications of a broad principle that invalidates running covenants that harm social welfare.

c. The Restatement (Third) mentions two policies that should not be used to invalidate running covenants: the Rule Against Perpetuities and the rule that a covenant's burden may run only when the covenant's benefit is appurtenant.

7. When horizontal privity is necessary, the covenant cannot run unless it touches and concerns the land providing the privity.

8. When land is subdivided, a running covenant no longer runs with any part of the land it no longer touches and concerns.

9. The touch and concern requirement is circumventable by providing that the running covenant is enforceable by a lien. Liens may secure a running covenant whenever the covenant calls for the payment of money, and whenever the covenant has a calculable, nonspeculative value.

§ 2.07 TERMINATION

[A] Definitions

TERMINATION: A running covenant terminates when the covenant's beneficiary may no longer compel its performance. Because real covenants are enforceable in law and equity, they terminate when their enforceability in law and equity ends. Because equitable servitudes are enforceable only in equity, they terminate when their enforceability in equity ends.

ABANDONMENT: Abandonment occurs when the covenant beneficiary's conduct manifests an intention to give up her rights under the covenant.

ACQUIESCENCE: Acquiescence occurs when the covenant beneficiary permits the covenant's violation.

UNCLEAN HANDS: Unclean hands arises when the covenant beneficiary breaches the covenant she seeks to enforce.

[B] Discussion and Questions

There are almost as many ways to terminate running covenants as there are ways to terminate easements. They are grouped and listed below. A good number of termination doctrines need not be discussed here because their concept should be readily understandable (albeit there always are debatable applications), or because they are discussed elsewhere in the typical property course. They will not be discussed further. We will focus on the remaining termination doctrines, those marked with an *.

Discussion of the termination rules is complicated by differences in the consequences that follow from the various doctrines' application. Many of the doctrines terminate running covenants in both law and equity. But several of the doctrines bar only equitable enforcement of a running covenant; actions at law survive their application. Practically, this means that all the doctrines listed below terminate equitable servitudes and bar injunctive relief for the violation of real covenants. But actions for damages caused by violations of real covenants survive some of the doctrines. In addition, the real covenant remains as an encumbrance on the burdened land's title. The difficulty this causes the area of running covenant termination is complicated further by the fact that courts differ on whether one of the doctrines—the doctrine of changed conditions—bars only equitable, or both legal and equitable, relief for covenant violations.

The doctrines that preclude both legal and equitable remedies are marked with one + in the listing below. The doctrines that bar only equitable enforcement are marked with two ++'s. The doctrine about which the courts differ is marked with three +++'s.

I.   Termination by express limitation

   +1.   End of time period specified by the terms of the interest's creation

   +2.   Breach of condition to which the interest was subject

II. Termination based upon subsequent events

   1.   Acts of covenantee

      +a.   Release

     +*b.   Abandonment

    ++*c.   Acquiescence

    ++*d.   Unclean hands

     ++e.   Laches

     +f.   Running of statute of limitations

   2.   Acts of covenantor

      +a.   Transfer to a bona fide purchaser

   3.   Acts of covenantor and covenantee

      +a.   Merger

      +b.   Estoppel

   4.   Not based solely upon the intent or subsequent acts of the covenantor and the covenantee or their successors

    ++*a.   Relative hardship

   +++*b.   Changed conditions

      +c.   Eminent Domain

      +d.   Tax Sales

      +e.   Statutory enactment

[1] Abandonment

As was discussed in § 1.06[B][3], <u>above</u>, abandonment is defined as the giving up of possession accompanied by the intent to give up title. Because of the Statute of Frauds, an abandonment of a running covenant cannot be predicated upon mere words. To give mere words legal effect would allow an informal release to be as effective as a formal release, thereby undercutting the statute. Rather, conduct is required—conduct by the covenantee that unequivocally manifests an intention to give up the benefit of the covenant.

Abandonment may be found in the way the covenant's beneficiary deals with the benefited land. For example, should the beneficiary of a covenant restricting neighboring land to residential use build a factory on the benefited land, a court would probably find an abandonment of the covenant. The court's rationale for finding abandonment is that the covenantee's own actions prevent her from realizing any true benefit from the covenant's enforcement. Presumably, a covenantee does such a thing only when she no longer intends to enjoy the rights given by the covenant. (Of course, the court's finding should be different if the evidence shows that the purpose of the residential use restriction was to eliminate competition for the commercial development of the benefited land. Then the beneficiary of the covenant's actions would not be barred from realizing the benefits of the covenant.)

Abandonment may also be found in the way the beneficiary of a covenant allows the burdened party to deal with the burdened land. Should the beneficiary of a covenant restricting neighboring land to residential use allow most of the burdened lot owners to build factories, a court would probably find an abandonment of the covenant. Again, the rationale would be that the beneficiary's own actions (or, in this case, inaction) prevent her from realizing any true benefit from the covenant's enforcement.

Abandonment terminates both the legal and equitable enforcement of running covenants. A few courts and commentators discuss abandonment as if it precludes only equitable enforcement. But this is a misconception caused by the fact that in many of the cases in which abandonment is litigated all that is in issue is the covenant's equitable enforcement. Abandonment, after all, terminates the legal as well as the equitable enforcement of easements. Abandonment is a legal as well as an equitable doctrine.

[2] Acquiescence

On occasion, the beneficiary of a running covenant permits violations of the covenant, but the violations are insufficient in either number or degree to ground a finding that the covenant has been abandoned. In this situation, a court might refuse to enforce the covenant on the grounds of acquiescence.

Acquiescence arises when the beneficiary of a running covenant, after permitting some violation of the covenant, attempts to enforce the covenant against a new violation. Suffering just any violation of a covenant does not amount to an acquiescence. The permitted violations must sufficiently damage the beneficiary's interests. In most situations this means that the violations must be more than de minimis; and if they are sufficiently significant, they must not be geographically distant from the beneficiary's parcel.

The rationale of the doctrine of acquiescence is not that the covenant is of no value to its beneficiary—that rationale is the rationale of the doctrine of abandonment. Rather, the rationale is that the burdened parties have been mislead into believing that the benefited party would not insist on her rights. Acquiescence, understood this way, is akin to—or a variant of—estoppel.

The estoppel basis of acquiescence is important for understanding other distinctions between abandonment and acquiescence:

(a) Abandonment terminates running covenants in both law and equity; acquiescence bars only their equitable enforcement. Actions at law for damages survive a finding of acquiescence.

(b) Abandonment ends any right based upon the covenant; acquiescence leaves those rights that are not substantially similar to those violated. For example, acquiescence to the violation of a single-family residential use restriction by permitting the construction of semi-detached structures would not permit the construction of multi-unit apartments and commercial structures.

Obviously, there is much overlap between the doctrines of abandonment and acquiescence. As a result, courts continually shift between the two doctrines in a confusing manner. The Restatement (First) § 558 com. (c) suggests confining the notion of abandonment to situations that arise from the way the beneficiary of the covenant has dealt with the benefited land. Acquiescence, therefore, covers situations that arise from the way the beneficiary of the covenant has allowed the burdened parties to deal with the burdened land. The Restatement (First)'s suggested usage is a substantial aid to clarity. Nonetheless, few courts follow it.

Q110: O, owning a 100 acre parcel, subdivided it into 50 lots and recorded a declaration of covenants restricting the land to single-family residential development. O sold the first 10 lots to A who warehoused the land because she thought the time not ripe for single-family development. O sold the next 25 lots to B, who built multi-unit residences in violation of the covenant. O sold the last 15 lots to C, who built single-family residences.

Now A wishes to build a shopping center on her land. C objects and brings suit to enjoin A's plans.

   a.   A defends on the ground of abandonment. Does A state a good defense?

   A: Yes. Running covenants are abandoned when they are violated to such a degree that a) it seems that no one is taking the covenant seriously; and b) it seems that the benefits for which the restrictions were imposed cannot be realized. B's disregard of the single-family covenant on 25 of the 50 lots—and A's and O's disregard of B's actions—is a sufficiently large violation to amount to an abandonment.

C purchased after B violated the covenant on 25 of the 50 lots. C took subject to the legal import of B's violations. Accordingly, when C purchased, the single-family use restriction was no longer in effect. C did not acquire the benefit of any covenant restricting A's land.

b. A defends on the ground of acquiescence. Does A state a good defense?

    A: No. Acquiescence applies only when the prior permitted violations and the proposed violations are substantially similar in kind or degree.

c. Rediscuss part (b) on the assumption that A plans to build multi-unit residences.

    A: Probably still no, despite the fact that now B's permitted violation and A's proposed violation are identical. Acquiescence is the proper defense when the permitted violations are insufficient in number or degree to amount to an abandonment. The objection to saying that acquiescence is a proper defense is that B's violations were so massive that the inaction of C's predecessor in interest goes beyond acquiescence to abandonment.

    Note that the objection to saying that C acquiesced is not that C did not own the land at the time of B's violation. C purchased land from O, and as her successor, is bound by O's actions or inaction. If O acquiesced, then we may properly say that C has.

    Some courts might mix their doctrines by saying that C's predecessor abandoned the covenant by acquiescing to its violation. It is suggested that this is dangerous because it leaves unclear whether C might be able to sue A for damages from her violations. Acquiescence bars only equitable relief; abandonment would bar legal relief as well.

Q111: A, B and C own contiguous lots in a 100 lot subdivision that is subject to a residential use restriction. B's lot is between A and C's. For the past 3 years, C has used her home to provide day-care for up to 6 children. Nonetheless, when A began to use his home to provide day care for up to 4 children, B brought suit.

a. A defends on the ground of abandonment. Does A state a good defense?

    A: No. Abandonment requires that the violation of a covenant is so pervasive that the covenant's purpose is no longer accomplishable. C's violation of the covenant apparently is the only violation in a subdivision that covers 100 lots. C's violation probably has a localized effect. Enforcement of the covenant is still of substantial value to the subdivision.

b. A defends on the ground of acquiescence. Does A state a good defense?

    A: Yes. When a lot owner permits a violation of a covenant that materially affects her interests, she will be held to have acquiesced to other violations that are similar in kind and degree.

c. Rediscuss part (b) on the assumption that C's lot is not adjacent to A's and B's, but is 5 blocks away from them.

    A: No. A day-care facility for 6 children located 5 blocks from B's lot would not have any material impact on her interests. The doctrine of acquiescence does not require a lot owner to meticulously police the restricted area for violations. It requires only that she act when the violations are apparent to her and materially affect her interests.

d. Rediscuss part (b) on the assumption that A intends to provide day-care for 25 children.

    A: No. Acquiescence applies only to violations that are similar in nature or degree. Suffering a minor violation does not prevent objecting a violation with more severe consequences. Providing day-care for 25 children is far more intrusive on neighbors than providing day-care for 6 children. Consequently, B has not acquiesced to A's new use of her lot.

[3] Unclean hands

The unclean hands doctrine arises when the beneficiary of a running covenant is in violation of the covenant. The beneficiary's violation must be more than de minimis. Moreover, the beneficiary must be in violation of the same covenant that she is seeking to enforce. Violation of a different restriction does not ground a finding of unclean hands. This is because the unclean hands doctrine is akin to the concept of dependent promises in contract law. (Indeed, the Restatement (First) denominates this doctrine "breach of corresponding promise.") Only the breach of a dependent promise, not the breach of an independent promise, justifies the suspension of the innocent party's performance.

However, the relation of the defense of unclean hands and the contract concept of dependent promises is not exact in that the unclean hands defense bars only equitable enforcement. Actions at law for damages survive.

Q112: A and B own adjacent lots in a 100 acre subdivision that is subject to a declaration of covenants containing set-back restrictions and a ban on signs. The relevant part of the set-back covenant states that "no part of any residence, other than the front steps, may be within 20 feet of the front lot line." A's home has a porch that is 15 feet from the front lot line, violating the set-back restriction. Nonetheless A sues for an injunction when B places a sign reading "Put God Back Into The Schools" on her front lawn. B defends on the ground of unclean hands.

    a.   Does B state a good defense?

        A: No. The doctrine of unclean hands requires that the dominant landowner violate either the same covenant as the servient landowner, or a covenant that is, in the words of Restatement (First) § 560, "corresponding" to the covenant that the servient landowner has violated. The set-back covenant and the sign ban are independent covenants; observance of one is not dependent upon observance of the other. The doctrine of unclean hands does not apply.

    b.   Rediscuss part (a) on the assumption that the declaration of covenants contains no sign ban, but the relevant part of the set-back covenant states that "except for the front steps of any residence and landscaping, the lot must remain free and open space within 20 feet of the front lot line."

        A: Yes. With the change in wording, A is in violation of the same covenant that B is violating. A has not violated it in the same manner. But if anything, A has violated in a far more major way. Her hands certainly are not clean. A court of equity would not allow her to maintain that others should obey the set-back provision when she does not.

    c.   Rediscuss part (a) on the assumption that the declaration of covenants contains no set-back provision; but it does contain a sign ban, and nonetheless, every year A has placed an election campaign sign on her front lawn during the month prior to election day.

        A: Possibly yes. A annually violates the same covenant that B is violating. Moreover, it is the same type of violation—a political sign. Thus it would seem that A has unclean hands.

          However, A's violation is narrower than B's. A's sign remains for one month, and the timing of the sign's placement—the election season—makes it clear that it is temporary. B's sign, though political in nature, concerns an issue that has some permanency. The context thus broadens the precedent set by A's violation in that it addresses a political issue that will not be resolved immediately. B's sign threatens to be permanent.

          In sum, whether A has unclean hands in part (c) is a closer case than in part (b).

[4] Relative hardship

Relative hardship arises when enforcing a running covenant substantially harms the covenantor without materially benefiting the covenantee. Although Restatement (First) § 563 and Restatement (Third) § 8.3 com. (f) take the position that all the doctrine requires is sufficiently large disproportion between the harm to the covenantor and the benefit to the covenantee, only a minority of courts so hold.

Most courts require some additional factor, such as facts that implicate but do not by themselves support a finding of another termination doctrine (i.e., abandonment, acquiescence, laches), or that the covenantee's right under the covenant is ambiguous. Without these additional factors, courts feel that the covenantor is only being compelled to abide by her bargain. Moreover, it is said that unless the relative hardship defense requires these additional factors, the doctrine inevitably would tend to favor large landowners to the detriment of small landowners.

The gravamen of the relative hardship doctrine, then, is a "balancing of equities." In their balancing, courts divide on whether the equities must involve more than mere disproportion in financial impact on the covenantor and covenantee.

Despite their differences on this point, courts agree that relative hardship bars equitable relief only. Indeed, in this respect, relative hardship is a traditional aspect of equitable remedial jurisprudence. Relief at law through a suit for damages cannot be barred due to relative hardship. Relative hardship terminates equitable servitudes and bars injunctive relief for the violation of real covenants. Real covenants survive as does an action at law for their violation.

Q113: A purchased a lot in a subdivision subject to a declaration of covenants prohibiting mobile homes. Nonetheless, A purchased a mobile home. When A moved it on to her land, B, her neighbor sued for a mandatory injunction to compel its removal. The uncontroverted evidence is that A's mobile home is not significantly different in appearance than standard construction. Although having a mobile home in the vicinity bothers the neighbors, the actual damages caused to their land value is no more than $1,000. The uncontroverted evidence also is that A's loss in removing the mobile home, selling it, and building a standard home would be $25,000. A defends upon the ground of relative hardship.

   a.   Does A state a good defense?

       A: Probably not. In most all jurisdictions relative hardship is not made out simply by comparing the financial burden and benefit to the parties, no matter how disparate it is. Financial loss, by itself, is not considered a sufficient hardship. Relative hardship requires comparison of the parties' equities, that is, the financial impact of the covenant's enforcement and other factors.

       The first and third Restatements and a minority of jurisdictions do allow sufficiently disparate financial impact alone to bar equitable relief. Mere disparity is insufficient. The disproportion in benefit and loss must be "gross" or "one of considerable magnitude." The difference here probably meets that standard.

   b.   Rediscuss part (a) on the assumption that the declaration's banning of mobile homes was ambiguous, requiring judicial interpretation to be established, and the reading adverse to A's interest was established in the suit against her.

       A: Probably yes. The new fact presents another factor that is an additional equity in A's favor. The covenant banning mobile homes was ambiguous. A, in other words, was not clearly aware that she was violating the covenant. In many jurisdictions the gross disproportion in gain and loss and the additional equity would support the defense of relative hardship.

       Anyone who purchased subsequent to the law suit would probably be on notice that the covenant has been construed to ban mobile homes. Thus the equity arising from the covenant's lack of clarity would no longer be available.

[5] Changed conditions

On occasion land-use in the vicinity of the restricted land changes so unexpectedly and substantially that there is no benefit remaining to the covenant's enforcement. Just as courts will terminate easements when their purpose can no longer be accomplished, see § 1.06[B][1], courts will terminate running covenants when conditions since the covenant's creation have so changed as to make it impossible to secure the benefits sought to be realized. Indeed, in light of the similarity, Restatement (Third) § 7.10 com. (a) specifically extends the changed conditions doctrine to easements.

There are three major controversies regarding the changed conditions doctrine. The first concerns whether the doctrine requires that there be no benefit remaining to the covenant's enforcement or only that the benefits cannot be substantially realized. Most courts and the Restatement (Third) invoke this doctrine only when the covenant no longer is of any value to the benefited land. A few courts invoke the doctrine when there is some remaining value in its enforcement to the benefited land if, due to the change in neighborhood conditions, that value is sufficiently small compared to the substantial hardship compliance with the covenant imposes on the burdened land. These courts, in effect, treat changed conditions as an additional factor in the application of the relative hardship doctrine that was discussed above.

The second controversy concerns the doctrine's application to the lots on the border of a restricted tract. Most courts refuse to invoke the changed conditions doctrine when the neighborhood changes are entirely external to the restricted tract. These courts argue that releasing border lots from compliance with the restrictive covenants inevitably creates a "domino effect" that threatens to engulf the entire tract. Thus, they say, when there has been no significant departure from the restrictions within the restricted tract, there is always some value to the interior lots remaining in the covenant's enforcement against border lots. The border lots' hardship results from their buffering the internal lots. This is an occurrence of which the border lots purchasers were cognizant when they purchased and which should have been reflected in the price they paid.

In other words, in the majority of jurisdictions the doctrine of changed conditions requires either a) that when the changes in land-use are entirely external to the restricted tract, the changes be sufficient to render the covenant valueless to all the restricted lots—the internal as well as the border lots; or b) that there be sufficient internal departures from the covenants, along with the external changes, to implicate (but not independently to support a finding of) abandonment, acquiescence or some other ground that makes the covenant's enforcement inequitable.

A minority of courts and Restatement (Third) § 7.10 do not adopt this position. These courts and the Restatement (Third) are less sympathetic to the domino argument. They think that there are occasions when releasing border lots will not affect the internal lots. Some of the courts acknowledge that they are willing to release the border lots despite covenants having minor residual value to the internal lots. The minority position is that the balance of the convenience to the internal lots and the hardship to the border lots renders enforcement against the border lots unconscionable. Moreover, enforcement of the covenant in such situations impedes land utilization.

The third controversy concerns whether the doctrine of changed conditions terminates running covenants or only bars their equitable enforcement. Until recently, most courts held that changed conditions was a defense in equity only. Consequently, changed conditions terminated equitable servitudes and barred the equitable enforcement of real covenants. Changed conditions did not affect actions at law. Thus, despite a sufficient change in conditions to bar equitable relief, a real covenant continued to be enforceable through a damage suit. And the real covenant survived as an encumbrance on title.

It is not clear whether this limitation on the effect of the doctrine of changed conditions continues as the majority rule. The trend is towards applying the doctrine at law as well as in equity. However, some of the states that apply the doctrine at law do so only upon payment of damages by the servient landowner. Most of the states that apply the doctrine at law do so without requiring the burdened party to pay damages caused by the covenant's termination. The Restatement (Third) adopts a flexible solution to this issue. On the one hand, Restatement (Third) § 7.10 counsels courts to apply the changed conditions doctrine in both law and equity. On the other hand, Restatement (Third) § 7.10 com. (a) urges courts to allow themselves discretion to award compensation in appropriate cases.

Q114: Thirty years ago, O, owning one-quarter of the block bounded by North, South, First and Second Avenues, subdivided it into lots. O sold the lots subject to a common scheme of covenants requiring that the lots be used for single-family residential use only. At that time most land-use in the area was single-family residential.

Over time North and Second Avenues became major thoroughfares, with a traffic count in excess of 26,000 vehicles a day at their intersection. Land-use in the vicinity of A's subdivision shifted to commercial and high-rise residential development.

The single-family residences in O's subdivision have become run-down. Some are vacant; a few have been remodeled into residences for two families; most rent for little money.

Now A, who owns two adjacent lots in O's subdivision wishes to develop a highrise on her parcel. Many of the other lot owners do not object. Some do, and they sue to enjoin A's development.

A defends based upon changed conditions. Does she state a good defense?

> **A:** Yes. The defense of changed conditions requires that the vicinity of the lot seeking release from its restrictions change so completely that it is impossible to secure the benefits that the covenants were created to secure. O imposed the covenants to protect the single-family residential characteristic of the community. The single-family character of the area is gone. Evidently, O's subdivision is small enough so that all the lots suffer from the changes in the area. The fact that the houses are run-down, rent for little money, and have, to some extent, been converted to multi-family use evidences this. There is no residual benefit from enforcement of the single-family restrictions.

Q115: Fifty years ago, Shady Acres was subdivided into 100 lots and subjected to single-family residential use restrictions. At present, most of Shady Acres is developed with expensive single-family homes. None of the 100 lots have at any time been used in violation of the restrictions.

Main Avenue is the eastern border of Shady Acres. When Shady Acres was subdivided, Main Avenue was bordered by farms and a few single-family residences. Over time, Main Avenue became a busy commercial street. For over thirty years, no residence has been built on Main Street in the vicinity of Shady Acres.

Ten of Shady Acres' lots front on Main Street. Residential use was attempted on some of these lots, but has been abandoned. Residential use was never attempted on others. All 10 are vacant at present.

Last year Denise Developer purchased 3 of the lots fronting on Main Avenue. Contemplating a commercial use of the lots, she secured releases from all the lots immediately adjacent to them. The immediately adjacent lot owners realized that their lots were already depreciated by the proximity of commercial uses and would not be further depreciated by Denise's development. Indeed, they thought their lots would be benefited by the commercial development of the unkempt vacant parcels, especially since Denise's design would buffer them from Main Street. Nonetheless, when the owners of lots deeper within Shady Acres learned of Denise's plans, they brought suit to enjoin her plans.

a. Denise defends on the ground of changed conditions. Does she have a good defense?

> **A:** In most jurisdictions, no. In most jurisdictions, the defense of changed conditions requires that the purpose of the covenant be impossible to accomplish, i.e., that enforcement of the covenant is no longer of any benefit to the dominant parcels. That certainly seems to be the situation under the facts presented. Indeed, releasing Denise's lot from the covenant would seem to offer some gain by allowing a vacant, unkempt lot to be utilized as a buffer to the noise from Main Avenue. Nonetheless, most jurisdictions apply the requirement of the doctrine rather severely to border lots due to their concern that releasing a border lot may become the opening wedge in a string of suits by lot owners wishing to convert to more profitable commercial uses. Although Denise's lots cannot be used for residential purposes, the character of the subdivision is still residential. Fearing a domino effect from releasing Denise's parcel, most courts would rule that the covenant is still of benefit to the dominant lots.
>
> In effect, these jurisdictions have a rule that so long as the there is no deviation from the restrictions within the restricted area, border lots may not be released from restrictions due to changes that are external to the subdivision. Covenants may be terminated due to changes

that are external to the restricted area only when the external changes directly affect all the lots, entirely ending the covenant's benefit.

A minority of jurisdictions, and the Restatement (Third) would rule differently, i.e., that even when the changes are entirely external to a restricted area the restrictions may be terminated as to border lots when, due to the changes in external conditions, the border lots' continued restriction is of no benefit to the dominant parcels.

At bottom, these courts and the Restatement (Third) are not convinced that releasing border lots creates an inevitable domino effect. Consequently, these jurisdictions believe that the domino effect argument cannot provide the basis for ruling that the covenant is still of value to the dominant parcels.

Except for the domino effect argument, the facts in this Question clearly establish that restricting Denise's lots is of no benefit to the dominant parcels.

b.   Rediscuss part (a) on the assumption that there are violations of the restrictions that are internal to the restricted area, to wit: approximately 15 of the subdivision lots are developed with two and three family structures; 1 lot is developed with a three story, 20-unit structure; and that 5 years ago, the lot owners released two of the border lots near Denise's property from the covenant in order to permit the construction of a church.

A: In the majority of jurisdictions that would have ruled against Denise in part (a), Denise still does not have a good defense. The essential question these courts ask is whether, due to changed conditions, the character of the restricted area is so altered that enforcing the restrictions no longer benefits the community. That the restrictions have been violated is important evidence of whether the character of the community has fundamentally changed. Internal changes are given greater weight than external changes in answering the ultimate question of whether the restrictions are of continued benefit. But not all covenant violations are significant enough to have the required effect of making the purpose of the covenants impossible to be accomplished.

In particular, courts are hesitant to uphold a changed conditions defense. As Restatement (Third) § 7.10 com. (c) says, "[t]he test is a stringent one and few cases that have reached the appellate level have resulted in the termination of servitudes." On the assumption that the violations are spread around the subdivision and not concentrated in the vicinity of Denise's parcel, these changes would be found to be relatively minor, not substantially affecting the single-family residential character of the community. On the assumption that the changes are concentrated around Denise's parcel, a court would still find that the changes were insufficient to release her property entirely from the covenant. Rather, the court would apply the doctrine of acquiescence and allow Denise to construct on her parcel a 2 or 3 family residential structure, or a church, or 20-unit residential structure at most.

c.   Rediscuss (a) and (b) on the assumption that Denise defends on the ground of relative hardship.

A: The disparity between the harm to Denise and the benefit to the dominant lots is grossly disproportionate. Thus, in part (a), Denise is in effect arguing the doctrine of relative hardship, with external changed conditions as the additional equity weighing in her favor. In part (b), Denise is in effect arguing the doctrine of relative hardship, with the external and internal changes as the additional equity weighing in her favor. Accordingly, the courts' response, described in the answer to part (a) is in effect the courts' response to the relative hardship argument.

Changed conditions may be thought of as a special case of the relative hardship doctrine. The key to seeing the unity of the two doctrines is that to make out a changed condition defense every court requires that the covenant's residual benefit to the dominant parcel be negligible while the covenant's present harm to the servient parcel be large. Courts may differ on whether cases predicated on external changes ever can involve negligible residual benefits to the dominant parcels, due to a fear of the domino effect. Thus, the courts may differ on what facts present a case of gross disproportion in harms and benefits, but they still require it.

If anything, the changed conditions defense is more generous than the relative hardship defense. When due to changed conditions the benefit to the dominant parcels is negligible, the servient parcel will be released from the covenant even if the harm flowing from its restriction is not that great. No case that loses under changed conditions should be won under relative hardship where changed conditions is the additional equity.

[6]   The Restatement (Third) and the termination of running covenants

The Restatement (Third)'s approach to the termination of servitudes generally employs traditional principles. It recognizes and employs all of the termination doctrines discussed above, usually in a manner that reflects the courts' consensus. Particulars of the Restatement (Third)'s treatment of the relative hardship and changed conditions doctrines have been discussed in § 2.07[B][4] & [5] above.

However, in an important reform, the Restatement (Third) urges courts to be flexible when selecting remedies to enforce or terminate running covenants. There are two aspects to the Restatement (Third)'s remedial flexibility.

The first aspect is Restatement (Third) § 8.2's principle that servitudes may be enforced by any remedy or combination of remedies. Depending on the balance of equities, under the Restatement (Third) approach, courts may elect to enforce running covenants by such diverse remedies as damages (compensatory or punitive), injunction, restitution, liens, to name a few. Courts should not be limited, for example, to enforcing equitable servitudes with injunctions. Nor should courts be limited to all or nothing decisions in deciding to enforce or terminate running covenants. Termination with compensation should always be among the panoply of remedial options.

The second aspect is the Restatement (Third)'s approval of judicially imposed covenant modification. Specifically, Restatement (Third) § 7.10 authorizes courts to modify servitudes, rather than extinguish them, due to changed conditions, if modification will allow the servitudes to continue to accomplish their purpose. Similarly, Restatement (Third) § 7.11 authorizes courts to modify covenants to pay money for services to the property if changes in economic conditions make the agreed upon sum unfair to either of the parties. The Restatement (Third)'s approach is akin to the cy pres doctrine in trust law. Cy pres allows courts to change the stipulated terms of a trust, rather than terminate it or enforce it as written, when a change would best accomplish the settlor's general purpose. Of course, cy pres in trust law functions where the settlor is deceased and unable to make changes herself. In the running covenant context, the parties always may consent to a change. When courts modify running covenants, they are imposing change on an unconsenting party.

Perhaps the Restatement (Third)'s remedial flexibility accounts for some of the rules its adopts regarding changed conditions. As discussed, Restatement (Third) adopts the severe rule that changed conditions terminate a running covenant only when there is no residual benefit to the covenant beneficiary. But Restatement (Third) § 7.10 com. (b) indicates that the harsh outcomes possible under this rule may be taken into account and ameliorated through flexible remedial decisions. Covenants which are not terminated may still be enforced with appropriate modification or by an award of nominal damages rather than an injunction.

Q116: Discuss the following facts under traditional changed condition doctrine and under the Restatement (Third)'s approach:

Fifteen years ago, O developed a subdivision of summer homes. On one parcel, O dug a well that supplied the homes with water. In each deed of sale, O inserted covenants obligating O to supply water from the well from April to October and obligating the grantee to pay $35 a month for the water. The deeds specifically said the covenants were to run with the land.

Now, half the homes in the subdivision have been renovated into year-round homes. In addition, the local water utility has extended its service area to include O's subdivision. The utility will charge the homes $10 a month for water. May the owners of the renovated houses, who use their homes year-round, terminate their agreement with O based on changed conditions?

A: No, under traditional termination doctrine; maybe, under the Restatement (Third). Most courts, and the Restatement (Third), refuse to terminate covenants based on changed conditions when there is still some benefit remaining to the covenantee from the covenant's enforcement. Clearly, O has some benefit from selling water to the subdivision residents. For the minority of courts that might apply changed conditions even when there is some benefit from the covenant's enforcement, the hardship to the year-round subdivision residents of paying for more expensive water from April to October does not seem that substantial.

However, the Restatement (Third) urges courts to approach covenant enforcement issues with remedial flexibility. Under the Restatement (Third), the remedial options are not limited to complete enforcement or complete termination. The Restatement (Third) reminds courts that in appropriate cases covenants could be terminated but compensation paid in recompense for the residual benefits to the covenantee. Particularly for covenants to pay money for services to property, Restatement (Third) § 7.11 provides for modification if over time the charge becomes excessive in relation to the cost of providing service or the value received. Depending on cost to O for providing water service, and whether O has already amortized her original investment, the year-round residents may well have good grounds for seeking a modification of their covenant, if not complete termination. With the extension of the water utility's lines to their area, even the summer residents may have a claim for covenant modification.

[7] A note on terminology

There is obvious overlap among the doctrines that terminate running covenants, and courts frequently shift between the separate doctrines without regard to differences in their meaning. In particular, the courts use the term "waiver" to cover any termination doctrine that involves volitional activity by the owner of the benefited land. Waiver, therefore, has no meaning independent of the specific grounds of abandonment, acquiescence, and unclean hands (which we discussed) and release, laches, running of statute of limitations, and estoppel (which we have not discussed). Because waiver is a general catch-all concept with no independent meaning, we have not discussed waiver. In reading judicial opinions that employ the term waiver, you should be curious about the specific grounds upon which the waiver is predicated.

Judicial opinions use the term "abandonment" as something of a catch-all also. Judicial opinions are rife with such phrases as "the owner of the dominant land has abandoned the covenant through acquiescence" (or laches, unclean hands, and changed conditions). Courts may even say that there has been an abandonment through waiver!

Misuse of the term abandonment is more difficult to remedy than misuse of the term waiver. Misuse of the term waiver may be remedied by simply not using the term because it has no independent meaning. Abandonment, however, does have independent meaning. Consequently, it must be retained, but confined to its proper sphere, i.e., a description of conduct that manifests an intent to give up entirely the benefit of a running covenant.

Moreover, misuse of the term abandonment is more dangerous than misuse of the term waiver. Abandonment, as discussed above, terminates both real covenants and equitable servitudes in both law and equity. Some of the concepts for which abandonment is improperly used, i.e., acquiescence, laches, unclean hands, and changed conditions (in many jurisdictions), bar only equitable relief.

In sum, in reading judicial opinions, be extra cautious when the term abandonment is used and determine whether abandonment or some other termination doctrine is involved.

Q117: A owns a lot on the border of a 10 lot subdivision that is subject to a residential use restriction. Twenty years ago, A built a 2,000 square foot structure on her lot that she has used as a "mom and pop" grocery store. Over the past twenty years, the avenue on which A's lot fronts was redeveloped from a 2 to a 4 lane highway, and it now is a major commercial street. Three other lots within the subdivision have been devoted to other commercial uses. The potential for A's business has grown so much that she seeks to build a 20,000 square foot structure for use as a supermarket.

a. Does it matter whether the court finds that A's right to maintain a grocery store is predicated upon the doctrine of abandonment or acquiescence?

A: Yes. If the court finds an abandonment, the covenant is terminated in both law and equity. A would then own unrestricted land and she could redevelop it as she wished.

Predicating A's rights on acquiescence allows for two different consequences. One is that acquiescence bars equitable relief only. Actions at law would survive. A would be liable for any damages caused by her altered use, and, the covenant would survive as a cloud on title. Subsequent purchasers might be wary of purchasing property subject to the covenant.

The other consequence is that if A's rights are predicated upon acquiescence A might not be able to alter substantially either the nature or size of her commercial use. Acquiescence may be thought of as a partial abandonment. By acquiescing to a 2,000 square foot "mom and pop" grocery, A's neighbors may not have lost their right to object to a 20,000 square foot supermarket, which is a far more intense violation of the residential use covenant. Thus, A might not be able to increase the size of her store as she wishes.

b. Does it matter whether the court finds that A's right to maintain a grocery store is predicated upon the doctrine of abandonment or changed conditions?

A: Maybe. Predicating A's rights on changed conditions may or may not have different consequences for A. In some jurisdictions, and under the Restatement (Third), changed conditions has the same effect as abandonment: the doctrine terminates running covenants at law as well as in equity. A would then own unrestricted land and she could redevelop it as she wished.

But in other jurisdictions changed conditions terminate real covenants only after the owner of the burdened land pays damages to the owners of the benefited land that is losing the right to enforce the covenant. The Restatement (Third) urges courts to be flexible and award compensation in appropriate cases. In addition, in still other jurisdictions, changed conditions cannot terminate real covenants. In these jurisdictions, equitable enforcement of real covenants may be barred by the doctrine of changed conditions, but legal enforcement—through actions for damages—survive. In addition, the real covenant remains as a cloud on title.

For further reading on the Termination of running covenants, see 9 Powell § 60.10; 2 ALP §§ 9.22–9.23, 9.37–9.940; CSW §§ 8.20, 8.30; Restatement (Third) §§ 7.1–7.12.

[C] Review Problems

PROBLEM 36

The declaration of covenants to a 100 lot subdivision bans signs of any kind. Nonetheless, over the years no one has complained that various residents—no more than 10 at any one time—have placed political signs on their front lawns during election campaigns. Similarly, no one has complained that various residents—no more than 5 at any one time —have placed "for sale" signs on their lawns when their homes were for sale. Now, one of the residents is contemplating placing a sign on her lawn advertising that she provides astrology services in her home. May she do so, based on the doctrine of

a. abandonment;

b. acquiescence;

c. unclean hands (assuming that the complaining neighbors have placed either election or "for sale" signs on their lots).

d. Rediscuss part parts (b) and (c) on the assumption that the contemplated sign says "Bring God Back Into the Schools."

ANALYSIS

a. No. Abandonment requires that prior violations of the covenant have made it impossible to realize any of the covenant's intended benefit. It is unlikely that the occasional erection of election or for sale signs has had that substantial an effect.

b. Probably not. The doctrine of acquiescence probably does not apply because this violation is different and more significant than the violations that have been permitted prior to this time. The prior signs were temporary in nature. In addition, they were political signs or signs that all homeowners have an interest in erecting. They were not signs that detracted from the residential nature of the community by advertising commercial services.

Moreover, with more facts an additional ground for nonapplication of the acquiescence doctrine might be made out. We do not know if the homeowners immediately surrounding the homeowner who is contemplating erecting the astrology sign are the homeowners who previously have displayed election or "for sale" signs. On the assumption that they are not, the neighboring homeowners will not be held to have acquiesced to the display of signs that were distant violations not having a significant impact on them. The doctrine of acquiescence does not require one to police an entire subdivision, just one's immediate environs.

c. Probably not. The rationale for nonapplication of the clean hands doctrine is similar to the rationale for the acquiescence doctrine in the answer to part (b). The homeowners who have erected election or "for sale" signs have violated the same provision. But they have not violated it as significantly in that they have not erected permanent signs. The erection of their signs would not tend to induce another into thinking she could erect a permanent sign advertising a commercial service.

d. Probably not. The new fact means that the contemplated sign is political in nature. The homeowner who wishes to erect it may argue that it is like the election signs. However, election signs are temporary in nature. The political dispute that the contemplated sign is part of is one that will not be resolved in a short period of time. It will tend to be permanent in nature and thus represent a more significant violation. Perhaps the answer would be different if there was a particular school board vote coming up and this sign was relevant to an issue that would be decided at that meeting. Then it would be more like the election signs and probably come within the doctrines of acquiescence and unclean hands.

PROBLEM 37

This year, Dr. Judi Johnson purchased a home in a 20 lot subdivision that is subject to residential use restrictions. When Judi purchased her lot, she knew that 5 of the homeowners had remodeled their homes into combined residences and offices. Three of the homeowners who did so conducted active medical practices out of their offices. Nonetheless, when Judi's neighbors learned that she was remodelling her structure into an office, not a combined residence-office structure, they sued to enjoin her violation of the residence only restriction.

a. Judi defends on the ground of abandonment. Is that a good defense?

b. Judi defends on the ground of acquiescence. Is that a good defense?

c. Rediscuss part (a) on the assumption that Judi remodeled her structure into a combined residence and medical office, but that she did not reside there herself. Rather, Judi located her medical practice in the office portion of the structure, and rented out the residence portion.

ANALYSIS

a. Probably not. If the covenant has been abandoned, the subdivision is unrestricted. Courts hesitate before reaching such a conclusion. To support an abandonment, covenant violations must be both pervasive and severe.

In this Problem it may seem that the covenant has been generally ignored. Nonetheless, courts would not conclude that the violations are severe enough to rule that the covenant is no longer of any benefit to the subdivision. Combined office-residence use is a violation of a residential use restriction. But courts do not regard it as particularly severe. Combined office-residence use must be fairly widespread before permitting it amounts to an abandonment of a residential use restriction. The extent of violation in this Problem— 25% of the lots—may not be sufficiently widespread given the court's attitude about the innocuousness of it and the dire consequences of finding an abandonment.

b. Probably not. Acquiescence applies when the proposed use is similar to violations already permitted. Judi's use seems similar to those already permitted; but it is not. Courts sharply distinguish between combined office-residential use and office use. They regard office use as far more objectionable than combined office-residence use. Whether Judi would be allowed to rebut this presumption by showing that her practice would be no more active than those already allowed is problematic.

c. Probably not. Just as courts distinguish between office use and combined office-residence use, the only court that has been presented with the issue has distinguished between combined office-residence use when the office user is the resident and when he is not the resident. See Chevy Chase Village v. Jaggers, 275 A.2d 167 (Md. App. 1971) (For 20 years a doctor combined office and residence use in violation of a residential use restriction. He moved his residence, rented the residential part of the structure and continued his practice in the office part. When neighbors brought suit to enjoin his new arrangement, the court ruled against the doctor's defense of acquiescence.).

PROBLEM 38

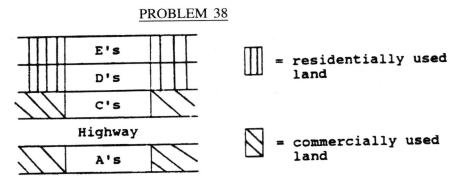

Twenty years ago, Sammie Subdivider, owning a rectangular parcel of land that was oriented in a north-south direction, subdivided it into five contiguous lots. She recorded a declaration of covenants restricting the property to residential use. Andy Adams, Bob Burton, Carrie Cummings, Darlene Drew, and Ephraim Epson purchased one lot each. Andy's lot was the most southern. Bob's lot bordered Andy's on the north. Carrie's lot was the next one north of Bob's. Darlene's lot was the next lot north of Carrie's. And Ephraim's lot was the most northern.

Ten years ago, the State Highway Commission condemned Bob's lot and built a new major thoroughfare through it. Over time, the land adjacent to the new road was put to commercial use, but typically to a depth of only one lot. The land surrounding Sammie's subdivision was part of this trend. Thus, at present, the unrestricted land adjacent to Andy's and Carrie's lots are devoted to commercial use. The unrestricted land adjacent to Darlene's and Ephraim's lots are still residential in character.

Before the development of the new road, Andy's and Carrie's lots were worth $60,000. Due to the new road, and its attendant commercial development, Andy's and Carrie's lots are worth $40,000. If they were unrestricted, they would be worth $120,000. Consequently, Andy and Carrie have sued for a declaratory judgment that their lots are no longer bound by the residential use restrictions. Darlene and Ephraim object.

a. Will Andy receive his requested declaration?

b. Will Carrie receive her requested declaration?

c. Rediscuss part (a) and (b) on the assumption that Andy's and Carrie's lots are worth only $5,000 as restricted.

ANALYSIS

a. Yes. There is a preliminary issue of whether the jurisdiction will terminate running covenants based upon changed conditions, or only bar their equitable enforcement. Assuming that the jurisdiction will terminate the covenant (or assuming that Andy and Carrie are interested only in preventing the commercial use of their lots from being enjoined), Andy has a good claim.

All courts will bar equitable enforcement of running covenants, and some will terminate them as the Restatement (Third) urges, when due to changed conditions internal to the restricted land continued enforcement of the covenant is of no benefit to the dominant land. Andy's parcel is now physically separate from the dominant lots owned by Darlene and Ephraim. (It is across the new road.) It is unlikely that commercial development of Andy's parcel will have any impact on Darlene's and Ephraim's parcels. The purpose of enforcing the covenant against Andy's parcel, protection of the other lots, can no longer be accomplished.

b. No. Carrie's parcel is situated differently than Andy's. Carrie's parcel is adjacent to Darlene's, and buffers it from the new road. Darlene's and Ephraim's lots are still generally bordered by residential uses. It is likely that releasing Carrie's parcel from the restrictions will affect Darlene's and Ephraim's lots. Most courts, therefore, would not find a sufficient change in conditions—even though the changes are internal to the restricted area—because there is still some benefit to the dominant parcels from enforcing the covenant.

In addition, Carrie probably would not prevail in those jurisdictions that terminate running covenants due to changed conditions even when there is some residual benefit remaining to the dominant parcels. These jurisdictions are actually applying the doctrine of relative hardship, with changed conditions supplying the additional factor other than disparate impact on the servient and dominant land. The impact on Darlene's and Ephraim's parcel is unknown. But the facts indicate that Carrie is not faced with too great a hardship. Her land did not depreciate that much. The gravamen of her complaint is that she could make a nice profit were she released from the restriction. Thus, even courts that balance the equities in this situation would not be too sympathetic to Carrie's claim.

c. There would be no change in part (a) because Andy would prevail without the additional facts. There may well be a change in part (b) because with the additional facts Carrie may well have a claim based upon relative hardship. The construction of the highway is a changed condition, an additional equity that may support a relative hardship defense. Of course, the extent to which releasing Carrie's lot would harm Darlene and Ephraim would have to be determined before the relative hardship defense could be decided. Under the Restatement (Third) approach, with its remedial flexibility, it is possible that this would be an appropriate case for terminating the covenant with compensation paid to Darlene and Ephraim.

PROBLEM 39

Eighty years ago, Oceanside was founded as a church related summer resort community. The original development consisted of 200 acres which were subdivided subject to covenants prohibiting commercial development and the sale of intoxicating liquors.

Over the years, Oceanside has grown in size and popularity. The original 200 acres is now the hub of a town of 1,000 acres (1 and 3/4 square miles) that is the core of a residential-resort area of some 50 square miles. The area's permanent population is 300. In summer over 10,000 people live in the town, and some 48,000 more live within the 50 square mile Oceanside area.

Many years ago, the community lost its church affiliation. None of the area outside the original 200 acres is subject to anti-commercial or liquor covenants. Nonetheless, despite its development, the Oceanside area is still a quiet, family oriented resort.

Commercial development, of course, has come to this area. Despite the anti-commercial covenants, from about two decades after Oceanside's founding, the original 200 acres have been the hub of the area's commercial services. Most of the banks, shops, restaurants, doctors' offices, small hotels—all the conveniences a thriving family resort community requires— are located there.

Intoxicating liquor, however, is sold in none of the commercial establishments located within the 200 restricted acres. Liquor is sold in the parts of the town and surrounding community that is not subject to the restrictive covenants. "Brown-bagging," which technically is not a violation of the anti-liquor covenant, is encouraged in many restaurants and permitted in many hotels in the restricted area.

Now Ann Andrews has announced plans to open a beer, wine and liquor store on a lot she owns within the 200 acre restricted area. Neighbors have brought suit to enjoin her plans.

a. Ann defends on the ground of changed conditions. Does she state a good defense?

b. Rediscuss part (a) on the assumption that although Oceanside's original 200 acres are the hub of the area's commercial development, only 30 commercial establishments are located there, and only 5 more are located in the rest of the town. Two of the 5 commercial establishments within the town, but outside the restricted 200 acres, are liquor stores.

ANALYSIS

a.   This is a close case. As a preliminary point, it is clear that the anti-commercial covenant has been abandoned. But that is not the issue. The issue is whether the anti-liquor covenant, which has always been respected—after a fashion—is still enforceable. Abandonment of the anti-commercial covenant is relevant to arguing the changed conditions defense's application to the anti-liquor covenant. But it is not determinative.

In most jurisdictions the changed conditions defense arises when due to changes in land-use, enforcing the covenant is of no benefit to the benefited land, i.e., the goal of the covenant is no longer accomplishable. In some jurisdictions, it is enough for the defense to apply that due to changes there is a great disparity between the benefit to the dominant land and the harm to the servient land. The difference between jurisdictions, however, does not matter in this Problem. In both the majority and minority jurisdictions it is a matter of fact and judgment whether the anti-liquor covenant continues to have any, or more than <u>de minimis</u>, benefit for the dominant land.

The central factual investigation in this Problem concerns whether the availability of liquor in the surrounding town, the general commercial development of the restricted area and the toleration of brown-bagging within it, means that the tone and character of the restricted 200 acres will be unaffected by terminating the anti-liquor covenant.

In favor of maintaining the anti-liquor covenant is the fact that two hundred acres is a large enough area to maintain its separate integrity and tone despite undesirable development of the surrounding territory. Yet, the establishments that sell liquor, if allowed into the restricted area can substantially alter that area's separate character.

Nonetheless, the anti-liquor covenant may be viewed as part of a total vision of the community imposed by a religious mission that was been abandoned long ago. Moreover, the anti-liquor covenant may be seen as a mere appendage to the anti-commercial covenants. Since the one has been abandoned, the other no longer can serve its purpose.

Ultimately, the case might turn upon a concrete appreciation of the tone of the restricted area and whether the anti-liquor covenant is at all important to its maintenance.

b. The additional facts indicate that the covenant should not be terminated due to changed conditions. Thirty of the town's 35 commercial establishments may be located in the 200 restricted areas. That may make the restricted area the "hub" of the town and surrounding county's commercial activity. Nonetheless, 30 commercial establishments in an area of 200 acres may not set the overall tone of that area. Two hundred acres is a little less than 1/3 of a square mile. It is reasonable to assume that the 30 commercial establishments occupy relatively little of the 200 restricted acres. (This claim is based on the assumption that none of commercial establishments is a large shopping center requiring land not only for stores but also for parking.) In short, the restricted area may well still be fairly residential. In that case, the intrusion of liquor stores would be viewed by a court as more than de minimis.

Upon this view of the facts, it is surprising to note that the court that adjudicated the facts upon which this Problem is based decided, over dissent, to terminate the covenant. El Di, Inc., v. Town of Bethany Beach, 477 A.2d 1066 (Del. 1984). This decision applies the changed conditions doctrine in an unusually liberal manner.

PROBLEM 40

Shady Acres is a rural-suburban residential development built 30 years ago. The development includes private roads, bridle paths, an artificial lake and dam and sporting facilities. Maintenance and improvement of the common property is the responsibility of a homeowners' association. Funds for maintenance and improvement of the common property are provided by the lot owners through a scheme of covenants. One covenant, however, provides that although lot owners may be assessed for upkeep and improvement of the common property, "no assessment for any one year shall exceed the sum of 55 cents per front foot."

Recently, the homeowners' board of directors determined that due to inflation a maximum charge of 55 cents per front foot is simply too little to maintain, let alone improve, the common property. Because the covenant setting a maximum assessment is not subject to the declaration's amendment procedure, the board asked the homeowners to release it. A majority of the homeowners have complied; but a minority have refused.

Accordingly, the board has petitioned for a declaratory judgment terminating the covenant setting the yearly assessment's maximum charge at 55 cents per front foot. The board grounds its argument in the doctrine of changed conditions.

a. Does the doctrine of changed conditions apply to inflation—the type of change involved in this Problem?

b. Assuming that the doctrine applies to this type of change, will the board's petition be granted?

ANALYSIS

a. Yes. The usual change involved in changed conditions cases is in the physical characteristics of the surrounding locale. However, the gravamen of the doctrine of changed conditions is that the covenant's purpose is no longer accomplishable. Changes in the physical characteristics of the neighboring land is only one type of change that may render a covenant's purpose impossible to accomplish. See, e.g., Dreher Tp. Bd. v. Solitron Development Corp., 481 A.2d 1207 (Pa. Super 1984) (involving the bankruptcy of the developer who was to install a sewer system to which all landowners were to be tied). Restatement (Third) § 7.11 authorizes the application of the changed conditions doctrine to covenants to pay money for services to the property.

b. Probably not. In most jurisdictions, the doctrine of changed conditions requires that the covenant being terminated have no residual benefit to any objecting beneficiary. It is said that all covenants to pay money or to receive money necessarily have benefit to the recipient. Likewise, with covenants that limit the amount of money to be paid. Thus the covenant still benefits the objecting homeowners by protecting them from assessments larger than 55 cents per front foot.

To this there are two responses. One is that from another perspective, the value of the covenant is gone. This covenant is embedded in a scheme of covenants, the purpose of which is to provide

(Matthew Bender & Co., Inc.)

some limit to assessments while maintaining the common property. This purpose can no longer be effectuated. Thus, the issue is whether the assessment limitation covenant should be read in isolation or in context.

The other response is that the court should balance the hardships. Admitting that the covenant is of value to the objecting minority, the court might join the minority of jurisdictions that invokes the changed conditions doctrine if there is slight remaining value when compared to the hardship to the other parties from the covenant's enforcement. Depending upon what the ultimate charge might be, the additional burden to the objecting minority might be minimal compared to the harm to the majority from a decline in maintenance of the common property.

Even if the changed conditions are sufficient to warrant application of the doctrine, there is an additional hurdle to issuing the ruling the board requests. That hurdle is whether the doctrine of changed conditions applies at law as well as in equity. This covenant, a covenant to pay money, is enforced through damage actions. Thus, this case requires that the doctrine of changed conditions terminate a real covenant, not just bar equitable relief.

Many jurisdictions do not allow the doctrine of changed conditions to terminate covenants at law. But among those that do, there are a few jurisdictions that allow the doctrine to terminate covenants at law only upon payment of damages. In these jurisdictions, the board's victory may well prove fairly hollow.

Whether it would prove hollow or not would depend upon how the damages would be measured. Perhaps the board could argue that if the covenant is not terminated, the common property will not be maintained adequately. This would lower the value of the development, including the objecting homeowners' property. Thus terminating the covenant will protect the objecting homeowners' property. This benefit from terminating the covenant should be set-off against any cost to objecting homeowners due to terminating covenant, i.e., the amount of assessments they will have to pay.

The Restatement (Third), however, gives courts the ability to give the board of directors some relief while still protecting the homeowners. Restatement (Third) § 7.11 provides for judicially supervised covenant modification, rather than termination, when economic circumstances make covenanted agreements unfair to the parties. Under the Restatement (Third), a court has the option of increasing the allowable assessment to a new limit. This would allow the subdivision to meet its obligations while leaving the homeowners with the protection of appropriate limits.

PROBLEM 41

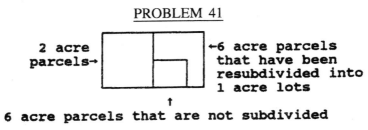

2 acre parcels→   ←6 acre parcels that have been resubdivided into 1 acre lots

6 acre parcels that are not subdivided

Ten years ago, Shady Acres was subdivided into 20 parcels. Twelve parcels, located in the eastern part of Shady Acres, were 2 acres each. Eight parcels, located in the western part of Shady Acres, were six acres each. The entire subdivision was subject to a covenant prohibiting re-subdividing any parcel. Nonetheless, over the years, 4 of the 6 acre parcels were subdivided into 1 acre lots.

a. If an owner of one of the remaining 6 acre parcels wants to subdivide her land into 1 acre lots what termination doctrines, if any, might she rely on?

b. If an owner of one of the 2 acre parcels wants to subdivide her land into 1 acre lots what termination doctrines, if any, might she rely on?

ANALYSIS

a. The lot owner might rely on acquiescence because the same violations have been permitted to other lot owners. The lot owner might rely on changed conditions because there have been sufficient changes internal to the development to make it likely that continued enforcement of the covenant is not of any benefit to the benefited land. The lot owner might rely on unclean hands against those lot owners who own lots that were subdivided in violation of the covenant.

Many courts might say that the lot owner could rely on the doctrine of abandonment. Most courts that would say this would actually be saying that due to the lot owners' acquiescence, changed conditions, or unclean hands, the lot owners have abandoned the covenant. To the extent that the term abandonment is used this way, the courts are draining abandonment of any independent meaning and engaging in confusing analysis. Similarly, courts might say that the lot owners have waived their rights. Waiver is another term that is used without any consideration of whether it has independent meaning in this area.

If abandonment has occurred, it has occurred because the violation of the covenant against resubdivision has been so general that the lot owner's inaction indicates an intention to give up their rights. You might feel that has occurred here. However, abandonment implies that there is a total loss of rights under the covenant. Consideration of part (b) will show that such a declaration might not be desirable. To the extent that the outcome of these facts should be a partial loss of rights, acquiescence is the proper doctrinal cache.

Of course, the Restatement (First) would say that abandonment has not occurred here for lot owners who do not own resubdivided land. The reason is that these neighbors have not used their dominant land in a way that indicates the intent to give up all rights under the covenant. As for the lot owners who own resubdivided lots, they may have abandoned their rights because they have used their dominant land in a way that indicates the intent to give up all rights under the covenant. Abandonment is an important finding, since acquiescence and the clean hands doctrine bar equitable relief only, while abandonment terminates rights at law also.

b. Only the unclean hands doctrine may be raised successfully; and even that defense may be raised only against lot owners who own lots that were subdivided in violation of the covenant.

Acquiescence and changed conditions most likely could not be relied upon. There is no acquiescence because it is likely that allowing the resubdivision of the 6 acre parcels, all of which are located in the western part of Shady Acres, would not immediately and substantially impact on the 2 acre lots, which are located in the eastern part of Shady Acres. Courts do not use the acquiescence doctrine to require that lot owners police all development that does not conform to the restrictions. The acquiescence doctrine is used only to require the lot owners to police nonconforming development that actually affects their interests. Neither is there changed conditions because there is still value in the covenant against resubdivision in the eastern portion. All the changes have been localized in the western part.

[D]   Recapitulation

A running covenant terminates when the covenant's beneficiary may no longer compel its performance. Because real covenants are enforceable in law and equity, they terminate when their enforceability in law and equity ends. Because equitable servitudes are enforceable only in equity, they terminate when their enforceability in equity ends.

Running covenants are subject to a large number of termination doctrines. Some of the doctrines terminate running covenants in both law and equity. Other doctrines, however, terminate running covenants only in equity. The courts disagree on whether one doctrine, the doctrine of changed conditions, terminates running covenants in both law and equity, or in equity only.

The doctrines that terminate running covenants in both law and equity completely terminate both real covenants and equitable servitudes. The doctrines that terminate running covenants only in equity completely terminate equitable servitudes, and partially terminate real covenants. Partial termination of a real covenant means that a suit at law for damages survives application of the doctrine. In addition, the real covenant survives as a cloud on title.

The termination doctrines discussed in this <u>Student Guide</u> are:

1. <u>Abandonment</u>: Abandonment requires conduct that manifests an intent to give up entirely the benefit of a running covenant. Abandonment typically occurs when the covenant beneficiary develops her land in a manner that precludes her from benefiting from enforcement of the covenant. Abandonment also occurs when the covenant beneficiary allows the servient landowners to develop their land in a manner that significantly departs from the covenant restrictions. Abandonment terminates running covenants in both law and equity.

2. <u>Acquiescence</u>: Acquiescence occurs when the beneficiary of a running covenant permits violation of the covenant, but the violations are insufficient in either number or degree to ground a finding of abandonment. Acquiescence does not arise when covenant violations have only a <u>de minimis</u> effect on the benefited land. Covenant beneficiaries need not police all covenant violations, but only those having a noticeable impact on their interests.

   Acquiescence differs from abandonment in that a) abandonment ends any rights based upon the covenant; acquiescence leaves those rights that are not substantially similar to the rights violated; and b) abandonment terminates running covenants in both law and equity; acquiescence bars only their equitable enforcement.

3. <u>Unclean hands</u>: The unclean hands doctrine arises when the beneficiary of a running covenant is in violation of the covenant. The beneficiary's violation must be more than <u>de minimis</u>. Moreover, the beneficiary must be in violation of the same covenant that she is seeking to enforce. Unclean hands bars only the equitable enforcement of a running covenant.

4. <u>Relative hardship</u>: Relative hardship arises when enforcing a running covenant substantially harms the covenantor without materially benefiting the covenantee. The first and third <u>Restatements</u> and a minority of courts hold that all the doctrine requires is a sufficiently large disproportion between the harm to the covenantor and the benefit to the covenantee. Most courts require some additional factor, such as facts that implicate, but do not by themselves support, a finding of another termination doctrine. The relative hardship doctrine bars only the equitable enforcement of a running covenant.

5. <u>Changed Conditions</u>: The changed conditions doctrine arises when land-use in the vicinity of the restricted land changes so substantially that the purpose of the covenant is no longer accomplishable. There are three controversies surrounding the doctrine:

   a. Most courts, and the <u>Restatement (Third)</u>, do not apply the changed conditions doctrine unless there is no benefit remaining from the covenant's enforcement. Other courts apply the doctrine when the covenant's benefit cannot be substantially realized.

   b. Most courts refuse to apply the changed conditions doctrine to subdivision border lots when the neighborhood changes are entirely external to the restricted land. These courts fear that releasing border lots will create a "domino effect," threatening to engulf the entire tract. Other courts, and the <u>Restatement (Third)</u>, apply the doctrine to subdivision border lots when the neighborhood changes are entirely external to the restricted land, if releasing the border lots will not affect the internal lots.

   c. Many courts allow the changed conditions doctrine to bar a running covenant's equitable enforcement only. Many other courts, and the <u>Restatement (Third)</u>, allow the doctrine to terminate running covenants in both law and equity. A few jurisdictions allowing the doctrine this enlarged effect do so only if the servient landowner pays damages to the dominant landowners. The <u>Restatement (Third)</u>, which provides for remedial flexibility in all covenant enforcement disputes, allows for, but does not require, this result.

d. The <u>Restatement (Third)</u>'s remedial flexibility in covenant enforcement disputes allows courts to enforce covenants with a panoply of remedies, including damages, injunction, restitution, or compensated termination. Under the <u>Restatement (Third)</u>, remedial flexibility also includes judicial modification of covenants if, due to changed conditions, modification will allow the covenants to continue to accomplish their purpose.

6. Courts frequently use the term "waiver" confusingly to cover any termination doctrine that involves volitional activity by the owner of the benefited land. Waiver has no meaning independent of the doctrine for which it is substituting. Courts also use the term "abandonment" as a catch-all. In reading judicial opinions in which the terms waiver or abandonment are used, you should be careful to determine which termination doctrine actually is involved.

THREE

DISTINGUISHING EASEMENTS, REAL COVENANTS AND EQUITABLE SERVITUDES & THE <u>RESTATEMENT (THIRD)</u>'S UNIFICATION OF SERVITUDE LAW

§ 3.01 INTRODUCTION

One of the most frustrating aspects of the study of servitudes is the obvious overlap among them. The rules concerning easements, real covenants, and equitable servitudes are difficult enough. But the difficulty in learning the various servitudes' diverse rules is compounded by the obvious similarity among the different interests. Moreover, students struggle both with the interests' overlap and with a vague notion that nothing all that much—besides analytic purity—turns on distinguishing them.

The goal of this concluding Chapter, therefore, is to give some notion of the differences between easements, real covenants and equitable servitudes—both in terms of the nature of the interest and the outcomes that turn upon it. You may well find it useful to study this Chapter at any point during your study of the law of servitudes, especially when you feel a need to understand the various servitudes' differences. You may well feel that one of the major arguments for the <u>Restatement (Third)</u>'s reform of servitude law is that—as this chapter will explain—it almost entirely obviates the need to differentiate among servitudes.

§ 3.02 DISTINGUISHING BETWEEN EASEMENTS AND RUNNING COVENANTS

Some servitudes are easements, others are running covenants. Whether or not distinguishing between easements and running covenants has contemporary validity, it is a part of modern law that is more a product of history than rational design. A review of the history of easements and running covenants is a useful preliminary—if not a necessity—to discussing their contemporary differentiation.

Real covenants and equitable servitudes developed in the late-eighteenth and early nineteenth century so that the common law of servitudes could escape the narrow confines and limitations of the law of easements. There was no necessity of this. One supposes that the common law judges could have developed a less confining law of easements. It is a comment on the jurisprudence of common law judges that they did not do so, and that they felt more comfortable developing other doctrines. For our purposes, what is important is not why they did, but simply that they did develop other doctrines to circumvent the limitations of easement law.

What were the limitations of easement law that real covenants and equitable servitudes were developed to overcome?

First, easements generally were limited to servitudes that required only passive duties of the fee owner. There were exceptions. English law developed a catalogue of "spurious" easements in which the servient owner had affirmative duties to perform—such as building or maintaining a party wall or fence. But spurious easements were few in number. By and large, easements only restrained the fee owner from interfering with the rights of the easement owner.

Perhaps this limitation in the concept of easements grew out of a fundamental distinction between the concepts of property and contract. When an easement owner has the right to make a specific use of land, or restrain the fee owner from making a specific use of it, that right is good against all the world. Courts most frequently state that the easement holder's right is good against the fee owner because the fee owner is the person most likely to interfere with it. But, in actual fact, all the world is under a duty not to interfere with the easement owner's rights.

But should an easement owner have the right to compel the fee owner to do something affirmative on her land, that right is good only against the fee owner, not all the world. Rights that are good against only a particular individual, and not the whole world, typically are understood as contract rights. Since easements are property rights, and not contract rights, they can include the former but not the latter.

Of course there is a sense in which affirmative obligations are good against all the world and are a property right. They are good against all the world who become owners of the servient land. Subjection to affirmative running covenants is not based upon the individual consent of the remote servient fee owner. (This is the link that has allowed running covenants to become conceptualized as property interests in many jurisdictions.)

Second, under traditional easement law easements generally were limited to affirmative easements, affirmative in the sense that the easement holder had the right to do something on the servient land. As usual, there were exceptions. English judges recognized a catalogue of negative easements, negative in the sense that the easement owner only could prevent the servient owner from using her land in a particular manner. But negative easements in English law were strictly limited to five types: easements of light, air, lateral or subjacent support, and the flow of an artificial stream.

The origin of this limitation is said to be in the absence of a recording system in England which gave notice to all the world of property rights. Affirmative easements tend to leave physical marks on the property, and thus be observable and give notice to prospective purchasers of the land. Negative easements leave no such indicia and are more likely to unfairly surprise subsequent purchasers of land (unless there is a recording system which gives them documentary notice as a substitute for the physical notice).

From this history, 4 overall distinctions between easements and running covenants emerge:

(1) Servitudes that authorize the benefited party to make an affirmative use of the servient land generally are easements, not running covenants

The traditional easement concept most frequently involved arrangements that authorized someone to make affirmative use of land that she neither owned nor possessed. With the coming of the industrial revolution, jurists needed no new legal doctrine within which to conceptualize those arrangements. All particular arrangements authorizing affirmative nonpossessory uses of land—even new ones spawned by the industrial revolution—could be and were easily cabined within the easement concept. In short, the law of running covenants was not developed to deal with disputes over arrangements authorizing affirmative nonpossessory uses of land.

Due to this history, servitudes that authorize the benefited party to make affirmative use of the servient land tend to be conceptualized as easements, and not as running covenants. There is nothing in the concept of running covenants mandating that such servitudes not be running covenants. It is a product of tradition and common usage.

(2) Servitudes that impose affirmative obligations on servient landowners generally are running covenants, not easements

That a servitude imposes an affirmative burden on the servient landowner is not an infallible test of whether the servitude is a running covenant rather than an easement. Before the industrial revolution there were a few arrangements imposing affirmative obligations on servient landowners, such as party wall and fence maintenance agreements, that arose with some frequency. These arrangements, known as "spurious easements," were treated as easements by the traditional common law, well before the development of the doctrine of running covenants. They continue to be treated as easements.

But by and large, easements impose only passive obligations on servient landowners. Except for a historically based residue, agreements that impose affirmative obligations on servient landowners are running covenants.

(3)   Servitudes that restrain servient landowners from making a use of their land generally are running covenants, not easements

That a servitude allows the benefited party no affirmative use of the servient land, but only restrains the servient landowner from making a particular use of her land is not a foolproof indicium that the servitude is a running covenant rather than an easement. The traditional common law recognized five negative easements: easements of light, air, lateral and subjacent support, and the flow of an artificial stream. This list is short and easily memorizable. Unfortunately, it does not encompass the entire list of negative easements recognized by the modern common law.

The modern common law recognizes a few other negative easements. Restatement (First) § 450(e) and com. (k)–(m) states a notoriously vague standard for determining whether other servitudes that only restrain the activity of the servient landowner may be easements rather than running covenants. The central concept is tradition. That is why land conservation, building preservation, scenic, and even solar access easements have been recognized recently. These servitudes may be conceptualized as a slight extension of the traditional negative easements of light and air.

But by and large, servitudes that only restrain the servient landowner, and do not empower the servitude owner to make a use of the servient land, are running covenants. That is why laymen know the phrase "restrictive covenant" and not "restrictive easement." A restrictive covenant is a covenant that merely restrains the use a servient landowner may make of her land. Restrictive covenants are far more frequent than "restrictive" easements. Hence laymen are far more familiar with the former that with the latter.

(4)   Servitudes that do not have a servient estate are running covenants and cannot be easements

This test is foolproof. However, it is not frequently useful because there are very few servitudes the burden of which is in gross. The most frequent are covenants not to compete and promises by utilities to provide service to particular land without specifying the land from which the service is to be provided. Infrequently, there are other examples, such as the promise of a railroad to provide free service to a particular parcel of land; or of a contractor to build at a reduced rate on a particular parcel of land.

Q118: Are the following agreements typically construed as easements or running covenants? The agreements are between the owners of Blackacre and Whiteacre, and provide that:

a.   the owner of Blackacre has a right of way over Whiteacre.

    A: An easement. The servitude allows the dominant owner to make an affirmative use of the servient land and requires the servient owner merely to permit that use.

b.   the owner of Whiteacre will maintain a right of way that the owner of Blackacre has over Whiteacre.

    A: A running covenant. The servitude requires the servient owner to undertake affirmative acts for the benefit of the dominant owner.

c.   the owner of Blackacre may provide her land with water from a well on Whiteacre.

    A: An easement. The reason is the same as expressed in the answer to part (a). The traditional common law denominated this servitude as a profit.

d.   the owner of Whiteacre will provide water from a well on her land to Blackacre.

A: A running covenant. The reason is the same as expressed in the answer to part (b).

e.   the owner of Whiteacre will allow the owner of Blackacre to mine 5,000 tons of gravel annually from Whiteacre.

A: An easement. The reason is the same as expressed in the answer to part (a). As with the agreement in part (c), the traditional common law denominated this servitude as a profit.

f.   the owner of Whiteacre will provide the owner of Blackacre with 5,000 tons of gravel annually from Whiteacre.

A: A running covenant. The reason is the same as expressed in the answer to part (b).

g.   the owner of Whiteacre will use her land for single-family residential purposes only.

A: A running covenant. The servitude does not permit the dominant owner to make an affirmative use of the servient land. It requires only that the servient owner not make a particular use of her land. It authorizes no affirmative use of the servient land by the dominant owner but imposes a negative obligation on the servient owner only. Yet it is not one of the few negative easements recognized by the traditional common law.

h.   the owner of Whiteacre will not sell her land without first offering it to the owner of Blackacre.

A: A running covenant. The reason is the same as expressed in the answer to part (g).

i.   the owner of Whiteacre will preserve her land in its natural state.

A: An easement. Although the reason expressed in the answer to part (g) seems to apply to this servitude, courts have found this servitude sufficiently analogous to the traditional negative easement of light and air to consider it an easement. It is called a "conservation" easement.

j.   the owner of Whiteacre will not build on her land so as to materially diminish the owner of Blackacre's view of Main Street.

A: A running covenant. This easement would seem to be analogous to the traditional easement of light and air to be considered an easement. Yet, one famous part of traditional easement law was that a view could not be the subject of an easement. Easements of light and air, mostly in the form of easements protecting light falling on windows, were far more circumscribed, and imposed less of a burden, on servient landowners than alleged easements of view. At the same time, access to light for a window was far more important in the centuries preceding the invention of electric lights. Accordingly, the traditional common law proscribed easements of view. Since a servitude of view cannot be an easement, it must be a running covenant.

k.   the owner of Whiteacre will not build on her land so as to materially diminish sunlight falling on Blackacre's solar energy cells.

A: An easement, for the same reason expressed in the answer to part (g). It is called a "solar" access easement and is thought to be as circumscribed and important as the ancient easement of light.

§ 3.03   THE OUTCOMES THAT TURN UPON WHETHER A SERVITUDE IS AN EASEMENT OR A RUNNING COVENANT

A variety of outcomes depend upon whether a servitude is an easement or a running covenant. The most important are:

(1)   If a servitude is an easement, it is enforceable by and against remote parties without need to apply the criteria of running covenants

Another way of making this point is to say that if a servitude is an easement it necessarily meets the elements of running covenants. Easements create their own privity of estate because their grant involves the transfer of a traditional property interest; easements always touch and concern the land because they involve the physical use of the servient land.

(2) **The rules regarding the implication of servitudes are significantly different for easements and running covenants**

All jurisdictions are willing to imply servitudes that are easements. Some jurisdictions find that, except for the traditional doctrine of estoppel, the Statute of Frauds bars the implication of servitudes that are running covenants. In addition, only servitudes that are easements may be implied by necessity and from prior use. Conversely, only running covenants are implied from the existence of a common plan.

(3) **Servitudes that are easements may be enforced at law regardless of whether the parties are in horizontal or vertical privity**

The practical import of this point is that damages may be obtained for the breach of an easement regardless of privity. Obtaining damages for the breach of a servitude that is a running covenant requires privity. This is a consequence of the fact, discussed below, that real covenants are the only running covenant that give rise to damages for their breach. And real covenants require privity to be enforced by or against remote parties.

(4) **Some of the doctrines that terminate easements are different from those that terminate running covenants**

The most significant difference is that easements are not subject to the doctrine of changed conditions. There is an argument that this does not matter because easements are terminated by an analogous doctrine: easements terminate when their purpose is accomplished or is no longer accomplishable. See Berger, Integration of the Law of Easements, Real Covenants and Equitable Servitudes, 43 Wash. & Lee L. Rev. 337, 366–67 (1986). However, these termination doctrines are not totally analogous in those jurisdictions which apply changed conditions even though there is some remaining benefit to the dominant land. (Those are the jurisdictions that have turned the doctrine into a relative hardship defense. See § 2.06[B][5], above.)

(5) **When a servient estate is condemned by eminent domain, compensation is always due to the servitude owner if the servitude is an easement; but compensation is not due to the servitude owner, in some jurisdictions, if the servitude is a running covenant**

The Constitution requires just compensation to be paid only for the condemnation of property, not for the condemnation's incidental effect on contract rights. Easements are considered property rights in all jurisdictions. Running covenants, in contrast, are considered contract rights in some jurisdictions. Consequently, only in those jurisdictions that consider running covenants property interests is compensation due to the covenant beneficiary when the servient estate is condemned.

Q119: A and B, who are adjacent landowners, reach an agreement providing water for A's land from a well on B's land. A then leases her land for 10 years to C. B then leases her land for 10 years to D.

    a.   The agreement is that A, her heirs and assigns can provide her land with water from the well on B's land. If D interferes with C's access to the well can C enjoin D's interference? Can C sue D for damages caused by the interference?

        A: C may both sue D for an injunction and for damages. The servitude is an easement. Whoever has the possessory interest in the land is the beneficiary of the easement and may sue in law or equity for protection. Whoever is on the land is subject to the servitude.

    b.   The agreement is that B, her heirs and assigns will provide water from the well on her land to A's land. If D fails to provide the water, can C obtain a mandatory injunction compelling D to provide the water? Can C sue D for damages caused by the failure to provide water.

        A: C may sue D for an injunction; but C may not sue D for damages. The servitude is a running covenant. It has the requisite elements for an equitable servitude. Accordingly, the owner of the possessory interest in the benefited land may sue whoever is in possession of the burdened land in equity for an injunction. However, D is not in vertical privity with the original covenantor. Thus, one of the elements for enforcing a burden of a real covenant is absent. Accordingly, C may not sue D at law for damages.

Q120: Twenty years ago, O, owning a 200 acre tract conveyed 10 acres in the middle of it, together with an easement of access, to the Metropolitan Sanitary District (MSD). As the land MSD purchased was to be used as a garbage dump, in part of the conveyance O released any right she may have to sue in law or equity for injury to her retained land arising from MSD's nonnegligent operation of the dump. Then O subdivided and sold her retained 190 acres.

Over the past 20 years, both O's retained 190 acres and the surrounding land have become a residential area. The value for residential use of the lots on the 190 acres formerly owned by O is drastically depressed due to the operation of MSD's dump. Accordingly, the lot owners who purchased from her bring a declaratory judgment action to declare the release in O's deed terminated due to changed conditions.

MSD responds to the suit with a motion to dismiss claiming its rights are not subject to termination due to changed conditions. O's grantees, however, argue that MSD's rights are subject to a changed conditions defense.

a.   Is MSD's contention correct if MSD's rights are an easement?

A: If MSD's rights are an easement, MSD's contentions are correct. Easements are not subject to termination due to changed conditions.

b.   Is MSD's contention correct if MSD's rights are a running covenant?

A: If MSD's rights are a running covenant, the contentions of O's grantees are correct. Running covenants are subject to termination due to changed conditions.

c.   Whose contentions are correct?

A: MSD's contentions are correct. In releasing her right to sue for nonnegligent injuries resulting from MSD's operation of its dump, O implicitly gave MSD the right to affect air quality over O's retained land. That agreement is sufficiently analogous to the traditional easement of air, one of the few traditional negative easements, to be considered an easement. As an easement, it is not subject to the changed conditions defense.

§ 3.04 DISTINGUISHING BETWEEN REAL COVENANTS AND EQUITABLE SERVITUDES

The primary distinctions between real covenants and equitable servitudes were discussed briefly in § 2.01, above. This section and the following section extend those remarks.

Like the distinction between easements and running covenants, the distinction between real covenants and equitable servitudes is more a product of history and tradition than rational design. A review of the history of real covenants and equitable servitudes is a necessary preliminary to learning to differentiate between these two servitudes.

When English judges first felt that the law of easements was too confining, their initial response was to develop the law of real covenants. Real covenants had an ancient lineage in the law governing property arrangements between feudal landowners and, consequently, in the law governing arrangements between landlords and tenants. Real covenants were a logical area for the judges to turn to because relations between feudal landowners, and landlords and tenants, are characterized by a high degree of interdependence, far more than typically existed between fee owners prior to the urban-industrial revolution. Real covenants were the legal doctrine that governed the feudal landowners' and landlords and tenants' private arrangements accommodating their interdependence. For a long time real covenants had countenanced what easement law proscribed: the imposition of affirmative obligations, and a greater catalogue of negative obligations, on servient estates. By turning to the law of real covenants, the English judiciary found a ready made model for a more expansive law of servitudes.

Unfortunately, in the late-eighteenth century and early nineteenth centuries, when English judges first began developing the law of real covenants into a body of doctrine governing private arrangements accommodating the increasing interdependence among fee owners, they still approached servitudes cautiously and suspiciously. Servitudes, after all, burden fee simple estates. Unencumbering, not encumbering, fee simple estates had always been the common law's preferred policy. Consequently, the English judiciary, concerned about the liberality of real covenant doctrine, engrafted limitations on to it. Chief among them were that a) real covenants required privity of estate, b) real covenants had to touch and concern the land, and c) the burden of a real covenant could not run.

In short order, these limitations on the enforcement of real covenants by and against remote parties proved too confining. The Court of Equity, as so frequently has happened in the history of English property law, came to the rescue. In 1848, in Tulk v. Moxhay, 41 E.R. 1143 (Ch. 1848), the Court of Equity began developing the concept of equitable servitudes as an expansion of the real covenant concept.

Equitable servitudes were developed by Equity as the most liberal servitude. Nonetheless, limitations were placed on the equitable servitude concept. As with all equitable property interests, the Chancellors made equitable servitudes subject to being cut-off in favor of subsequent purchasers who paid value and took the property without notice of the pre-existing claim. As with real covenants, the Chancellors required that equitable servitudes touch and concern the land they burdened or benefited. As with easements, the Chancellors required that they could not impose affirmative obligations, or have benefits that were personal to the covenantee (i.e., England does not recognize easements in gross).

In America, certain of the English judiciary's limitations on real covenants and equitable servitudes never were adopted. American courts never had any trouble allowing the burden of real covenants to run. Almost all American courts never had any trouble allowing equitable servitudes to enforce affirmative obligations. Most American courts had no trouble enforcing equitable servitudes whose benefits were in gross. In addition, American recording acts generally make the requirement of notice as applicable to real covenants as equitable servitudes.

From this history, 3 means of distinguishing real covenants and equitable servitudes emerge:

(1)   If the horizontal privity requirement is not satisfied, a running covenant cannot be a real covenant; it can only be an equitable servitude

Satisfying the jurisdiction's horizontal privity requirement is a necessary part of creating a real covenant. Equitable servitudes do not require horizontal privity for their establishment. A servitude that does not satisfy the jurisdiction's horizontal privity requirement cannot be a real covenant. If it is a running covenant, it must be an equitable servitude.

(2)   Running covenants that are more effectively enforced through damages generally are thought of as real covenants; running covenants that are more effectively enforced through injunctions generally are thought of as equitable servitudes

Traditionally, the remedy available in the law courts of England was damages and in the equity courts an injunction. The beneficiaries of running covenants that were more effectively enforced by damages, such as covenants to pay money for services, typically sought relief at law; the beneficiaries of running covenants that were more effectively enforced by injunction, such as building restrictions, sought relief in equity. Due to this, and due to the fact that the law courts developed the concept of real covenants and the equity courts developed the concept of equitable servitudes, the custom developed of referring to the former as real covenants and the latter as equitable servitudes.

Part of what is important about this ground of distinction is that it means that many servitudes that are described as real covenants can be enforced in equity as equitable servitudes; and many servitudes that are described as equitable servitudes can be enforced in law as real covenants. Many servitudes, in short, are both real covenants and equitable servitudes. Tradition, custom and usage—usage that usually follows from the most frequent means of enforcement—leads us to think and talk of them as one or the other. But a particular servitude might possess the requisite elements of a real covenant (i.e., intent, privity, and touch and concern), and the requisite elements of an equitable servitude (intent, notice, and touch and concern). If it does, it actually is both a real covenant and an equitable servitude. A building restriction, for example, most frequently is described as an equitable servitude. But if the building restriction meets the criteria for a real covenant, the remedy for its breach includes damages as well as an injunction. The damages are awarded because it is a real covenant, the injunction because it is an equitable servitude. Similarly, a covenant not to compete most frequently is described as a real covenant (for reasons to be discussed below). But if a covenant not to compete was created without the requisite privity, it still can meet the criteria of an equitable servitude and be enforced as such.

Admittedly, this is confusing. But think of it this way. Equity has always specifically enforced real property contracts. Injunctions, therefore, are obtainable to enforce real covenants. It would be conceptually neater if any running covenant that met the criteria of a real covenant were denominated as such whether or not its enforcement typically was sought in law or equity. Then we would not have servitudes that are both real covenants and equitable servitudes.

Unfortunately, as explained above, analytic purity has given way to custom and usage. Running covenants that meet the criteria for real covenants are described as equitable servitudes if they typically are enforced in equity. We do not say, with regard to these covenants, that they are real covenants whose beneficiaries typically seek specific enforcement, rather than damages, for their breach.

There is some logic to this tradition. The requirements for equitable servitudes are more liberal than the requirements for real covenants. There is, in America, no running covenant that meets the criteria of a real covenant that does not also meet the criteria of an equitable servitude. Consequently, when equitable relief alone is sought, why bother to determine if the agreement at bar would also be enforceable at law as a real covenant. Call it an equitable servitude and be done with it.

Yet this logic means that the distinction between real covenants and equitable servitudes is unlike other distinctions in property law. In every other area of property law, a property interest is either one interest or another. For example, a fee interest is either a fee simple absolute, fee simple determinable, fee simple subject to a condition subsequent, or a fee simple subject to an executory limitation. But in servitude law, a servitude may be both a real covenant and an equitable servitude. Analytic purity could insist that real covenants and equitable servitudes are distinct interests. For example, that some running covenants are real covenants, which are enforceable in both law and equity; and other running covenants are equitable servitudes, which are enforceable in equity only. Convenience, however, has prevailed.

It might help to think of running covenants as acts that amount to crimes. Due to the separation of state and federal jurisdiction (something analogous to the traditional separation of law and equity), some acts are state crimes, some are federal crimes, and some are both. When an act is both a state and a federal crime, how we categorize it usually depends on whether the state or federal government typically takes the lead in prosecuting it.

(3)   Affirmative running covenants generally are thought of as real covenants; negative running covenants generally are thought of as equitable servitudes

Distinguishing real covenants from equitable servitudes on the basis of whether the covenant is affirmative or negative is, in part, a corollary of the comments just made. Affirmative running covenants typically are enforced through damages; negative running covenants typically are enforced by injunctions. But there is another source of the customary means of classifying affirmative and negative running covenants. Affirmative running covenants could not be easements because they impose affirmative obligations on the servient landowner. Negative running covenants could be easements because they may be analogized to negative easements that impose only passive duties on the servient landowner. Equitable servitudes tend to be thought of as an equitable analogue of the easement concept. Hence, running covenants that are closely analogous to traditional easements tend to be thought of as equitable easements, i.e., equitable servitudes.

Accordingly, covenants to pay money are thought of as real covenants even when their enforcement is sought through a lien foreclosure in equity. Similarly, covenants to provide services are thought of as real covenants even when their enforcement is sought through a mandatory injunction. But covenants that restrain a landowner from using her property in certain ways (e.g., a prohibition against building over 35 feet from ground level) are thought of as equitable servitudes even when damages are sought for their violation.

This ground of distinction merely accounts for the way that conventional usage describes running covenants. An affirmative covenant that meets the requirements of both a real covenant and an equitable servitude is both a real covenant and an equitable servitude. A negative covenant that meets the requirements of both a real covenant and an equitable servitude is both a real covenant and an equitable servitude. The only exception to this are covenants to pay money that have not created liens for their enforcement. Such affirmative covenants, even if they meet the requisites for an equitable servitude, cannot be an equitable servitude. The reason for this is that an injunction requiring the payment of money is regarded as indistinguishable from an award of damages. Equity, of course, generally does not grant damages. Consequently, equity generally will not issue an injunction compelling the payment of money.

But aside from this one exception, meeting the elements of the two types of running covenants—not conventional usage—is what is ultimately important.

(4) Running covenants in which there is no servient land are generally described as real covenants

Easements must always have servient land. Running covenants, however, need not have servient land. Covenants to provide utility services that do not specify particular land from which the service is to be provided, and covenants not to compete in which an individual agrees not to engage in a particular trade near land she has just sold, are examples of running covenants in which the burden is in gross. There is no servient land. Due to the absence of servient land, these running covenants are not closely analogous to traditional easements. For this reason they tend to be denominated real covenants, not equitable servitudes.

But once again, conventional usage is misleading. A running covenant whose burden is in gross may be both a real covenant and an equitable servitude. If such a covenant meets the requirements of a real covenant, it is a real covenant. If such a covenant meets the requirements of an equitable servitude, it is an equitable servitude also. Thus, for example, if a running covenant whose burden is in gross lacks sufficient privity to be enforced as a real covenant, it may still be enforced as an equitable servitude if the intent, notice and touch and concern elements are met.

Q121: Are the following agreements typically described as real covenants or equitable servitudes? Assume that all the elements of a real covenant and an equitable servitude are present. The agreements are between the owners of Blackacre and Whiteacre, and say that:

    a.   the owner of Whiteacre will use her land for single-family residential purposes only.

        A: An equitable servitude. This servitude is typically enforced by an injunction. Not only is an injunction an effective remedy, damages are frequently only speculative.

    b.   the owner of Blackacre will maintain a sea wall on her land.

        A: A real covenant. It is an affirmative obligation. In addition, either damages or an injunction is an effective and useful remedy, depending upon the consequences that flow from a breach of the servitude.

    c.   the owner of Whiteacre will pay an annual assessment of $500 to the owner of Blackacre for the maintenance of a sea wall on Blackacre.

        A: A real covenant. This is an affirmative obligation. Moreover, it involves the payment of money. Damages for breach of the servitude are readily ascertainable.

    d.   the owner of Whiteacre will maintain a right of way that the owner of Blackacre has over Whiteacre.

    A: A real covenant. The reason is the same as expressed in the answer to part (b).

    e.   the owner of Whiteacre will provide water for Blackacre from a well on her land.

    A: A real covenant. The reason is the same as expressed in the answer to part (b).

    f.   the owner of Whiteacre will provide the owner of Blackacre with 5,000 tons of gravel annually from Whiteacre.

    A: A real covenant. The reason is the same as expressed in the answer to part (b).

    g.   the owner of Whiteacre will not build on her land so as to materially diminish the owner of Blackacre's view of Main Street.

    A: An equitable servitude. The reason is the same as expressed in the answer to part (a).

    h.   the owner of Whiteacre will not sell her land without first offering it to the owner of Blackacre.

    A: A real covenant. This servitude would seem to be an equitable servitude for the reason expressed in the answer to part (a): it is frequently and effectively enforced by injunction; damages are frequently an inadequate and speculative remedy. Nonetheless, the agreement here—a right of first refusal—is familiar as a matter of personal contract. Thus, when it became possible to allow it to run between landowners, courts were already used to thinking of it as a matter of contract, not property law. Hence it is described as a real covenant, not an equitable servitude.

Q122: Assume that all the agreements in Q121, parts (a)-(h), <u>above</u>, meet the requirements of real covenants and the requirements of equitable servitudes. Regardless of how they are typically described, are they real covenants, equitable servitudes, or both?

    A: All of the servitudes, except the servitude in part (c), are both real covenants and equitable servitudes. These servitudes are not easements, and the Question states that they meet all the elements of a real covenant (intent, privity, and touch and concern) and an equitable servitude (intent, notice, and touch and concern). Thus they are both types of running covenants. The servitude in part (c) is a covenant to pay money, the injunctive enforcement of which is said to be too similar to a damage award to be ordered by equity. Of course, if the agreement in part (c) provided for a lien to secure payment of the money, it could be enforced by equity, by foreclosure action, for that reason.

§ 3.05 THE OUTCOMES THAT TURN UPON WHETHER A RUNNING COVENANT IS A REAL COVENANT OR AN EQUITABLE SERVITUDE

A variety of outcomes turn upon whether a running covenant is a real covenant or an equitable servitude. They are:

  (1)   Many real covenants are enforceable in both law and equity; equitable servitudes are enforceable only in equity

Real covenants originated in the English law courts and are enforceable at law. Because English equity courts enforce real property contracts, real covenants also are enforceable in equity. Equitable servitudes originated in the English equity courts and are enforceable only in equity.

The functional importance of this is that real covenants may be enforced by both damages (a legal remedy) and injunction (an equitable remedy); equitable servitudes may be enforced by injunction only. Therefore, if a running covenant lacks some element that permits it to be a real covenant, but has all the elements that permits it to be an equitable servitude, damages are unobtainable for its breach.

There are exceptions to these observations. Real covenants that infringe some general principle of equitable jurisprudence will not be enforced by injunction. For example, real covenants to pay money (e.g., a condominium assessment) will not receive equitable enforcement (absent a provision providing for a lien for unpaid assessments) because equity will not compel monetary payments. See § 3.04(3), <u>above</u>.

(English equity courts refuse, as a matter of general principle, to issue mandatory injunctions. Consequently, affirmative real covenants are not enforceable in equity in England. Upon the same principle, England does not recognize affirmative equitable servitudes. Few American courts have qualms about issuing mandatory injunctions, enforcing affirmative real covenants, or recognizing affirmative equitable servitudes.)

It is true that frequently equity courts grant damages for breach of running covenants that are described as equitable servitudes. Most frequently, this occurs because someone has applied to equity for damages and an injunction for breach of a servitude that meets all the requirements of a real covenant and an equitable servitude. Probably, no one has bothered to label or analyze the running covenant at bar correctly because no part of the dispute turns on it. In these cases the equity court actually is granting damages for breach of the real covenant as part of its "clean up" jurisdiction. "Clean up" jurisdiction allows the equity court to dispose of an entire controversy, both the equitable and legal matters, so that a separate action at law is unnecessary.

On rare occasion, equity courts grant damages for breach of a running covenant that clearly cannot be a real covenant. This occurs on the infrequent occasion when a petitioner has demonstrated her right to equitable relief, but due to unique circumstances an injunction cannot be issued. (For example, the defendant may have sold the servient land during the pendency of the action to a third party who had no notice of either the restriction or the action.) Equity's general power to fashion a remedy to afford complete relief allows it to grant damages when an injunction would be fruitless.

(2) Equitable servitudes are subject to the changed conditions defense in all jurisdictions; real covenants are not subject to the changed conditions defense in all jurisdictions

All jurisdictions recognize changed conditions as a defense in equity. Many jurisdictions, however, do not recognize that doctrine as a defense in law. Accordingly, in all jurisdictions the changed conditions defense completely terminates equitable servitudes. But in many jurisdictions, the changed conditions defense terminates only the equitable enforcement of real covenants; legal enforcement survives.

Thus, in many jurisdictions, if a running covenant is a real covenant, damages are obtainable for its breach even when the defense of changed conditions is made out. In addition, the real covenant, but not the equitable servitude, remains as a cloud on title.

(3) Equitable servitudes are subject to the termination doctrines of acquiescence, unclean hands, laches and relative hardship; only equitable enforcement of real covenants are subject to these defenses

The termination doctrines of acquiescence, unclean hands, laches, and relative hardship are equitable, not legal, defenses. These doctrines bar equitable relief only. Legal relief for the breach of a real covenant is unaffected. Consequently, these doctrines terminate equitable servitudes; they terminate only equitable enforcement of real covenants. If a running covenant is a real covenant, damages for its breach are obtainable even when these doctrines apply and bar injunctive relief.

It should be noted at this point that the controversy over the effect of changed conditions may be thought of as a controversy over whether that doctrine is both a legal and equitable defense, or only an equitable defense.

(4) It frequently is said that courts apply a more relaxed criteria of touch and concern to equitable servitudes than they do to real covenants

This claim is hard to document. There is no case in which the touch and concern requirement allowed the same covenant to run in equity but not at law. There is, however, little doubt that the development of equitable servitudes has generally broadened the scope of the touch and concern requirement. Equitable servitudes are enforced that bear less of a relation to the land than real covenants typically do. But should a case arise that requires it, most probably courts would apply to real covenants the broadened touch and concern standard that was developed in the equitable servitude context. Nevertheless, the issue should be noted.

Q123: A and B are adjacent landowners. B's land fronts on a lake, and A's view of that lake is over part of B's land. A and B reach an agreement, intended to run with their respective property, that B will not build on her land in such a way as to block A's view of the lake. A and B also formalize the agreement in a transaction that meets the jurisdiction's horizontal privity requirement. A conveys her land to C, and B conveys her land to D. D announces plans to build in violation of the agreement.

    a.   May C enjoin D's plans.

        A: Yes. C may enjoin D's plans because C's land has an appurtenant equitable servitude burdening D's land. The servitude prohibits any building on D's land from interfering with C's prospect.

    b.   If D builds in violation of the agreement, may C sue for damages the loss of prospect causes her land?

        A: Yes. C may sue D for damages, if any, because the agreement at bar meets all the requisites of a real covenant.

    c.   Rediscuss parts (a) and (b) on the assumption that the agreement was written and signed by A and B, but not formalized as part of a transaction that met the jurisdiction's horizontal privity requirement.

        A: C may enjoin D's plans, but cannot sue for damages. The agreement possesses all the requirements for an equitable servitude. An injunction is obtainable for its breach. But now its creation failed to meet the horizontal privity requirement. Accordingly, it cannot be a real covenant. Thus damages are not obtainable for its breach.

    d.   Rediscuss parts (a) and (b) on the assumption that A leased her land to B for ten years, and C leased her land to D for ten years.

        A: C may enjoin D's plans, but cannot sue D for damages. Since the agreement meets all the requirements for an equitable servitude, C, the owner of the present possessory interest in the dominant land, may sue D, the owner of the present possessory interest in the servient land, in equity for an injunction. But since D is not in vertical privity with the original covenantor, D may not be sued at law for damages for breach of the covenant.

§ 3.06 THE <u>RESTATEMENT (THIRD)</u> AND THE NEED TO DISTINGUISH AMONG SERVITUDES: THE UNIFICATION OF SERVITUDE LAW

Relying on the modern unification of law and equity, the <u>Restatement (Third)</u> abolishes all differences between real covenants and equitable servitudes, ending the need to distinguish between them. Specifically, by abrogating the horizontal privity requirement, see § 2.05[B][2] <u>above</u>, by making vertical privity turn on whether the covenant is affirmative or negative, see § 2.05[B][5] <u>above</u>, and by subjecting all servitudes to the same termination doctrines, see § 2.07[B][6] <u>above</u>, the <u>Restatement (Third)</u> removes any need to differentiate between running covenants enforceable in law and in equity. The result is the complete unification of real covenant and equitable servitude law. Indeed, the <u>Restatement (Third)</u> never uses the terms "real covenant" and "equitable servitude" except to describe the evolution of servitudes law.

The <u>Restatement (Third)</u>'s unification of running covenants and easements is almost as complete. <u>Restatement (Third)</u> §§ 2.1–2.18 ascertains the express and implied creation of easements and running covenants by the same doctrines. <u>Restatement (Third)</u> §§ 3.1–3.7 subjects easements and running covenants to the same public policy limitations. <u>Restatement (Third)</u> §§ 7.1–7.15 subjects them to the same termination doctrines.

However, <u>Restatement (Third)</u> § 4.8 allows the owner of a servient estate some power to relocate an easement but specifies that this power "does not apply to . . . affirmative obligations imposed by covenant."

Id. at com. (f). See § 1.04[B], above (discussing location of undefined easements). More importantly, Restatement (Third) § 5.3 imposes a modified vertical privity requirement on affirmative running covenants but not on negative running covenants or on easements. See § 2.05[B][5] above. Due to § 5.3, lessees of land benefited or burdened by easements may always sue or be sued in law and equity in disputes involving easements. Yet, for example, a lessee of land benefited by an affirmative running covenant may enforce the covenant in law or equity only when doing so neither diminishes the covenant's value to the lessor nor increases the burden on the party subject to the covenant. A lessee of land burdened by an affirmative running covenant may be sued in law or equity only when she is in a better position to perform the covenant than her lessor.

Although the Restatement (Third) sometimes does require us to distinguish between easements and running covenants, the distinction is easy to make due to the way the Restatement (Third) defines those terms. Restatement (Third) § 1.2 defines easements as "nonpossessory rights to enter and use land in the possession of another." All other servitudes are running covenants.

By this definition, all servitudes that restrain servient landowners from making use of their land are running covenants, not easements. The Restatement (Third)'s definition excludes from the term "easement" the short list of negative easements recognized by the traditional common law—easements of light, air, lateral or subjacent support, and the flow of an artificial stream. In the Restatement (Third)'s view, traditional negative easements are completely indistinguishable from restrictive covenants and should be denominated as such. Under the Restatement (Third), party wall agreements, for example, create running covenants, not easements.

Also, by this definition, all servitudes that impose affirmative obligations on servient landowners are running covenants. On the one hand, the Restatement (Third)'s definition of easement totally subsumes the historically based notion of profits a prendre, see § 1.04[A] above, into the easement concept. On the other hand, it totally excludes the historically based residue of "spurious easements" from the Restatement (Third)'s concept of an easement.

In other words, according to the Restatement (Third), a servitude is an easement if and only if it allows the benefited party to make an affirmative use of some servient land. This straightforward definition eliminates the historical residue that clouds the easement-running covenant distinction. To the very minor extent the Restatement (Third) does not totally integrate the law of servitudes, it provides clarity about which servitudes are to be treated as easements, and which as running covenants.

Q124: Determine whether the follow servitudes are easements or running covenants under the traditional common law and under the Restatement (Third). A servitude

    a.   allowing A to cross B's land.

        A: An easement under both the traditional common law and under the Restatement (Third). Under common law tradition, and under the Restatement (Third), a servitude that gives someone the right to make a specific use of land possessed by another is an easement.

    b.   restraining A from using her land for nonresidential purposes.

        A: A running covenant under both the traditional common law and under the Restatement (Third). Under traditional common law, most servitudes that restrain landowners from using their land in specified ways are running covenants. Under the Restatement (Third) all servitudes that restrain landowners from using their land in specified ways are running covenants.

    c.   restraining A from blocking sunlight from reaching solar collectors on B's land.

        A: An easement under traditional common law; a running covenant under the Restatement (Third). Servitude arrangements concerning access to sunlight are among the small group of negative easement recognized by the traditional common law. Under the Restatement (Third), the concept of negative easement is abrogated and integrated into the concept of running covenants.

d.   requiring A to keep her store, located in B's shopping center, open from 10 A.M. to 8 P.M., seven days a week.

> **A:** A running covenant under both traditional common law and the Restatement (Third). Under traditional common law, most servitudes requiring a landowner to do a specified affirmative act are running covenants. Under the Restatement (Third) all servitudes requiring a landowner to do a specified affirmative act are running covenants.

e.   requiring A to maintain a party wall that is located on the property line separating her property from B's property.

> **A:** An easement under traditional common law; a running covenant under the Restatement (Third). Servitude arrangements concerning party walls are among the small group of spurious easements recognized by the traditional common law. Under the Restatement (Third), the concept of spurious easement is abrogated and fully integrated into the concept of running covenants.

For further reading on the unification of servitude law, see Restatement (Third) xix–xxvii (T.D. No. 1, 1989); Berger, Integration of the Law of Easements, Real Covenants and Equitable Servitudes, 43 Wash. & Lee L. Rev. 337 (1986); Symposium, 55 S. Cal. L. Rev. 1177 (1982); Newman & Losey, Covenants Running With the Land and Equitable Servitudes: Two Concepts or One?, 21 Hastings L.J. 1319 (1970).

INDEX

[References are to sections.]

A

ABANDONMENT

Acquiescence, compared to . . . 2.07[B][2]
Covenants (See COVENANTS)
Easements
    Generally . . . 1.06[B][3]
    Defined . . . 1.06[A]

ACQUIESCENCE

Generally . . . 2.07[D]
Abandonment, compared to . . . 2.07[B][2]
Defined . . . 2.07[A],[B][2]
Review problems . . . 2.07[C]

AFFIRMATIVE COVENANTS

Running covenants and . . . 2.01
Touch and concern and . . . 2.06[B][1]
Vertical privity, affirmative running covenants and . . . 2.05[B][5]

AFFIRMATIVE EASEMENTS

Defined . . . 1.01

C

CHANGED CONDITIONS DOCTRINE

Generally . . . 2.07[D]
Application of . . . 2.07[B][5]
Review problems . . . 2.07[C]

CONSERVATION EASEMENTS

Review problems . . . 1.05[C]

CONVEYANCE

Deeds
    Generally . . . 1.02[A]
    "Stranger to the deed" . . . 1.02[B][3],[D]
Easements
    Generally . . . 1.02[A]
    "Stranger to the deed" . . . 1.02[B][3],[D]

COVENANTS

Abandonment of
    Generally . . . 2.07[D]
    Acquiescence compared to . . . 2.07[B][2]
    Defined . . . 2.07[A]
    Findings of . . . 2.07[B][1]
    Misuse of term . . . 2.07[B][7],[D]
    Review problems . . . 2.07[C]
Acquiescence (See ACQUIESCENCE)
Affirmative covenants (See AFFIRMATIVE COVENANTS)

[References are to sections.]

D

[References are to sections.]

E

EASEMENTS APPURTENANT

EASEMENTS (GENERALLY)

PRIVITY—Cont.

Assignment of ownership interest, covenantor's liability following . . . 2.05[B][6][a]
Defined . . . 2.05[A]
Horizontal privity (See HORIZONTAL PRIVITY)
Instantaneous privity
    Generally . . . 2.05[B][1],[D]
    Defined . . . 2.05[A]
Liens, privity rules circumvented by . . . 2.05[B][6][c]
Mutual privity
    Generally . . . 2.05[D]
    Defined . . . 2.05[A],[B][1]
Restatements' position regarding (See RESTATEMENT (THIRD))
Review problems . . . 2.05[C]
Subdivision of land, apportionment of burdens following . . . 2.05[B][6][b]
Vertical privity (See VERTICAL PRIVITY)

PROFITS A PRENDRE

Generally . . . 1.05[B],[B][2]
Defined . . . 1.05[A]

Q

QUASI-EASEMENTS

Generally . . . 1.03[A],[B]

R

REAL COVENANTS

Defined . . . 2.01
Equitable servitudes, distinguished from . . . 2.01; 3.04
Running covenants, as . . . 3.05

RELATIVE HARDSHIP DOCTRINE

Application of . . . 2.07[B][4],[D]

RESTATEMENT (FIRST)

Easements in gross, transfer of . . . 1.05[B][2]
Privity, horizontal . . . 2.05[B][2]

RESTATEMENT (THIRD)

Easements
    In gross, transfer of . . . 1.05[B][2]
    Implied . . . 1.03[B],[C]
    Termination of . . . 1.06[B][6]
Privity
    Generally . . . 2.05[D]
    Horizontal . . . 2.05[B][2]
    Review problems . . . 2.05[C]
    Vertical . . . 2.05[B][5]
Review problems . . . 2.07[C]
Running covenants
    Changed condition doctrine and . . . 2.07[B][5],[D]
    Implied running covenants . . . 2.03[B][3]
    Termination of . . . 2.07[B][6]

S

T

[References are to sections.]

U

V

(Pub.674)